P9-EDW-729

Optical Networking
A Wiley Tech Brief

Debra Cameron

Wiley Computer Publishing

John Wiley & Sons, Inc.

NEW YORK · CHICHESTER · WEINHEIM · BRISBANE · SINGAPORE · TORONTO

Publisher: Robert Ipsen
Editor: Margaret Eldridge
Assistant Editor: Adaobi Obi
Managing Editor: Micheline Frederick
Text Design & Composition: D&G Limited, LLC

Designations used by companies to distinguish their products are often claimed as trademarks. In all instances where John Wiley & Sons, Inc., is aware of a claim, the product names appear in initial capital or ALL CAPITAL LETTERS. Readers, however, should contact the appropriate companies for more complete information regarding trademarks and registration.

This book is printed on acid-free paper.

This publication is designed to provide accurate and authoritative information in regard to the subject matter covered. It is sold with the understanding that the publisher is not engaged in professional services. If professional advice or other expert assistance is required, the services of a competent professional person should be sought.

Library of Congress Cataloging-in-Publication Data

Cameron, Debra.
    Optical networking : a Wiley tech brief / Debra Cameron.
      p. cm.— (Wiley tech brief series)
    "Wiley Computer Publishing."
    Includes bibliographical references and index.
    ISBN 0-471-44368-9 (pbk.: alk. paper)
      1. Optical communications. 2. Computer networks. 3. Fiber optics. I. Title. II. Series.

    TK5103.59 C36 2001
    621.382'7—dc21
                                                           2001046755

Printed in the United States of America.

10 9 8 7 6 5 4 3 2 1

Wiley Tech Brief Series

Other books in the series:

Tom Austin, *PKI*. 0471-35380-9

Jon Graff, *Cryptography and E-Commerce*. 0471-40574-4

Traver Gruen-Kennedy, *Application Service Providers*. 0471-39491-2

Steve Mann and Scott Sbihli, *The Wireless Application Protocol (WAP)*. 0471-39992-2

Ray Rishchpater, *Internet Appliances*. 0471-44111-2

Ray Rischpater, *Palm Enterprise Applications*. 0471-39379-7

William Ruh, Francis Maginnis, and William Brown, *Enterprise Application Integration*. 0471-37641-8

Chetan Sharma, *Wireless Internet Enterprise*. 0471-39382-7

Wiley Tech Brief Series

To my hometown, Titusville, Pennsylvania, and visionary communities of all sizes, with the hope that the geography of bandwidth will help their economies to thrive once more.

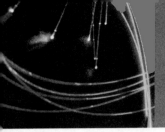

Contents

Acknowledgments

First of all, I would like to thank CANARIE's Bill St. Arnaud for his vast contributions to optical networking research and to this book. His CAnet-3-NEWS mailing list helps spread his vision of customer-empowered networking and provides concrete examples of its implementation. His writings and presentations significantly shaped this book. I also want to thank him for taking the time to meet with me as well as for his prompt and helpful responses to e-mail.

Many people helped me in preparing the case studies for this book, including Bill St. Arnaud, Stan Hanks, Dr. Joel Mambretti, Doug Power, William Ray, Jr., Grant Cheney, Guy Jones, Dr. Jerald Feinstein, Jason Wallin, Tomas Björnerbäck, Bernard Daines, Jon Moore, and Brian Ford. I would also like to thank the people who worked behind the scenes to set up interviews and make the case studies possible: Kim Hunt, Nancy Goodspeed, Sarah Morford, and Todd Smith.

I would also like to thank Thomas Afferton, Kathleen Rankin, and Lee Allentuck as well as Tom Austin, who put me in touch with John Wiley & Sons. Joe St. Sauver provided greatly appreciated feedback on Chapter 2. Special thanks go to my editor, Margaret Eldridge, for working closely with me on a very tight deadline to my production editor, Micheline Frederick, as well as to Adaobi Obi, my assistant editor.

Finally, I would like to acknowledge a tremendous debt of gratitude to my husband, Jim, for his untiring love and willingness to listen as I hashed and rehashed research for the book. I would also like to thank Meg, David, Beth, Kevin, Michele, and my mom for their support.

Introduction

F iber-optic networks have a staggering capacity to carry data of all types. A single fiber thinner than a human hair can carry 100 terabits of data per second. Fibers are typically deployed in a bundle, so multiply that capacity by the number of fibers and the amount of information that could be transmitted becomes increasingly difficult to conceptualize.

Fiber has many other advantages. The carrying capacity of optical networks dwarfs wireless networks (which can be deployed in a complementary fashion). Fiber is now as inexpensive as copper for a LAN, effectively allowing the same technology to be deployed from LAN to WAN and enabling corporate WANs to be managed by those with LAN skills. Fiber is a long-term investment; it won't be obsolete in months as the computer on your desktop will. It can be depreciated over 20 years. As bandwidth needs increase, only the components that light the fiber need to be upgraded. Fiber is secure, unlike wireless or copper, where transmissions can be easily intercepted.

Fiber offers unlimited bandwidth; is as cheaply deployed as copper, particularly for smaller networks; and provides a secure, long-term investment. That's only the beginning of the paradigm shift we're seeing.

Fiber-optic networks also change the way we talk about networks. *Wired* magazine talks about being at the forefront of the digital generation, but it might have to change its name as wire becomes a medium of the past. If *Wired* were to change its name to *Glass* tomorrow, though, there are few who would see the bandwidth revolution behind the change of the magazine's moniker.

Dense wavelength division multiplexing (DWDM) effectively multiplies the capacity of each strand of fiber and allows for more flexible virtual network topologies from the same physical network. Gigabit Ethernet is making fiber cheaper and easier to deploy, because no investment in expensive SONET equipment is needed and the wide base of experience with Ethernet in the LAN can be leveraged. These important technologies are discussed throughout the book.

Overview

Optical networking is a fast-changing field. Because the aim of this book is to discuss real-world applications driving optical networking today, it focuses primarily on where optical networking is being deployed and on the trends driving that deployment.

One critical trend is customer-empowered networking. When most people think of optical networks, they think of these huge yet paradoxically hair-thin bandwidth pipes belonging to major telecommunications carriers, not to the school around the corner, the city hall, the small business down the street, or to their next door neighbors.

Not so long ago, only huge businesses owned computers, too. The fact is that the economics of fiber is radically changing the markets where fiber is deployed. Further, while in the past only carriers and service providers have deployed networks, optical networks are also being deployed in new ways, where customers own the networks and can choose from a variety of service providers.

These trends in optical networking are democratizing bandwidth, making it possible for end users to gain access to virtually unlimited bandwidth that will change the way they work and the economies of communities and corporations that adopt this vision. It is my hope that many people will read this book and choose to implement these new paradigms of optical networking, paradigms that have the promise to transform local economies.

It is important to note that I, as an author, do not have a vested interest in any company or technology; I don't work for an optical networking firm or hold any related investments. I have written this book as an independent author and consultant who has observed the phenomenal evolution of networking technology for more than 15 years with great interest.

How This Book Is Organized

Optical networks are spreading outward, from the backbone networks of telecommunications providers to cities to corporations to homes. This diffusion of optical networking informed the structure of this book.

Before diving into applications, the first two chapters provide needed background. Who is deploying fiber today? Chapter 1 discusses markets for fiber and examines the supply and demand of bandwidth. Ultimately, applications drive bandwidth demand; Chapter 1 explores these applications as well as describing the relative growth of data and voice traffic, how the capacity of optical networks compare to wireless and satellite technologies, and the advantages of optical networking.

How does optical networking work? Chapter 2 describes the technology in simple terms to establish a conceptual framework for the book and to introduce important concepts such as DWDM, regeneration, and amplification. It also describes optical components, types of fiber, network architectures and designs, and protocols. Recognizing that each of these topics is complex enough to warrant a book-length treatment, the resources and references for this chapter provide many avenues for those who are interested in learning more about optical networking technology.

Telecommunications providers are the chief market for optical networking, with long-haul networks that span continents. Chapter 3 describes how telcos are deploying optical networking. It describes the relationships among *incumbent local exchange carriers* (ILECs), *competitive local exchange carriers* (CLECs), and *interexchange carriers* (IXCs) as well as discussing how the Telecommunications Act of 1996 has impacted U.S. markets. Global carriers, international carriers, and emerging carriers (who are becoming increasingly important in terms of the proportion of fiber they deploy) are also described.

Traditional telecommunications network architectures run voice as well as data over SONET. Running data over an architecture optimized for voice traffic is inefficient, however. Chapter 4 describes optical internets, which run IP directly over fiber without intervening layers of ATM and SONET. Optical internets have been deployed both by emerging carriers and on research networks.

Increasingly, cities, schools, and publicly owned utilities are building their own optical networks, often implementing a Gigabit Ethernet architecture that builds on the optical internet model discussed in Chapter 4. Chapter 5 describes municipal deployments of optical networks. While some cities deploy networks purely for their own use, many are creating networks that will also be used by the private sector. These networks represent the essential municipal infrastructure for the future, complementing water pipes, roadways, and traditional utilities. The availability of high-speed networking has an important impact on where businesses choose to locate.

Companies are using optical networking on a number of levels. Optical connections to the Internet are becoming increasingly common. Corporate WANs and corporate locations in a metropolitan area might also be connected using fiber. Campus networks increasingly deploy fiber between buildings because copper cannot typically handle the distances between buildings. Especially for new locations, LANs are increasingly being built using fiber because it is just as cost-effective as deploying copper, particularly considering that far fewer hubs and wiring closets are needed for a fiber-optic LAN. Chapter 6 describes corporate optical networking deployments that fall into all these categories, as well as the importance of fiber for other technologies such as storage area networks and voice-over-IP. The chapter also explores the potential for free-space optics to provide easily deployed high-speed connectivity between corporate buildings.

Demand for broadband to the home has exploded, and in many areas of the United States and the world, availability of such services is at best uneven. Chapter 7 explores the demand for broadband to the home and the alternatives that exist for providing this high-speed connectivity: DSL, cable modems, fixed wireless, satellite, and fiber-to-the-home. It discusses the relative demand for these services and their advantages and drawbacks. Furthermore, it provides case studies of deployments of Ethernet fiber to the home and ATM-based passive optical networks.

What are the issues that users face in deploying optical networks? Chapter 8 examines the various methods of deploying fiber, from trenching to aerial fiber to sewer installations, and discusses dealing with rights-of-way. Chapter 8 also explores important trends in fiber-optic networking, from peering to bandwidth trading to advanced networks where customers own or lease wavelengths rather than entire fibers. It provides some reality checks about optical networking as well, explaining, for example, that the end-to-end performance of the Internet is considerably slower than the optical network connection to that network of networks. Chapter 8 also looks ahead at optical network technology trends, from the proliferation of DWDM to all-optical networking. As important as technology is, government's role is also critical in helping to spur the development of a pervasive optical infrastructure. Chapter 8 closes with a discussion of the potential role of governments in creating this important infrastructure.

Who Should Read This Book?

If you are interested in the business and applications side of optical networking, this book is for you. You don't need any background in optical networking to read it, just an interest in how optical networks are being used today. Real-world case studies round out information in Chapters 4 through 7.

This book is for you if you are:

- A network manager or an IT manager tasked with evaluating the impact of optical networking on your enterprise

- A CEO or CIO seeking information about the applications of optical networking with a view to forming an optical networking strategy

- A sales or marketing professional at an optical networking firm

- A city manager or concerned citizen who wants to consider the economic impact that optical networking could have on your area

- An entrepreneur interested in examining the business case for various optical networking applications, from long-haul networks to corporate networks to fiber-to-the-home deployments

Although the book follows the diffusion of optical networking from larger enterprises, such as backbone providers, all the way down to networks that bring fiber to the home, it need not be read strictly sequentially. Most readers will want to start with the background material in Chapter 1. Readers who need a background in the terminology and technology of optical networking should then read Chapter 2; readers who are experienced in the field can skip that chapter if desired. Beyond Chapter 2, readers can select chapters depending on their areas of interest.

Online Resources

Cameron Consulting's Web site at www.camconsulting.com includes a section on optical networking specifically as it relates to this book. There, you can easily access all the online resources described in Appendix A and learn more about the various applications of optical networking. Links to relevant online periodicals, articles, tutorials, white papers, e-mail newsletters, books, and mailing lists are provided along with links where you can send feedback or questions to the author.

Summary

A single strand of fiber-optic cable can carry an incredible amount of data. Although it isn't commonly used in homes—yet—a single strand of fiber could provide a home with three phone lines, multiple digital video services (including video-on-demand), and high-speed Internet access. Few people realize how quickly the business of optical networking is moving or the opportunities it presents. Most books available on this subject emphasize the physics of the technology rather than its business applications. This book tells you in straight language how fiber is changing the world of networking and what you should do about it today.

Chapter 1 sets the stage with an analysis of the market for optical networking.

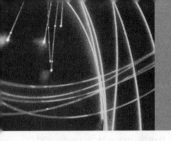

The Optical Networking Revolution

A lthough optical networking is by no means a new technology, optical networks have just recently come into their own. Many data communication links are easily saturated and outgrown, but through scientific advances, our ability to tap the inherent capacity of fiber and create less expensive and more flexible optical networks sets the stage for an ongoing optical networking revolution.

Given what has happened in the last five years, we need optical networks. Personal computers have become increasingly prevalent, the Internet has burgeoned, and carriers have been deregulated in much of the world. Data traffic over the telephone networks has surpassed voice traffic. Technology advances have also helped boost the already rich capabilities of fiber. Improvements have been made in lasers that carry the data, as well as in techniques such as *dense wavelength division multiplexing (DWDM)* that can multiply the capacity of fiber even further.

In this same timeframe, optical networks began to spread outward, moving from *backbone* networks to wide area networks (WANs), metropolitan networks, corporate networks, and, most recently, fiber-to-the-home (FTTH) initiatives. Fiber is spreading from the core of the network to the edge.

Controversies remain, however, about the deployment of fiber. Is it too much? Is there already a glut of fiber? Wouldn't wireless suffice—and be easier to deploy? Can't the capacity of copper be expanded further, obviating the need for a new infrastructure? This chapter explores these issues as well as the market for fiber, its advantages and disadvantages, and important trends in optical networking.

Bandwidth Supply and Demand

Can you get enough bandwidth? Experienced network managers who are satisfied with the performance of their networks know that *enough* is really a matter of the point in time the question is asked. Enough bandwidth for today doesn't mean enough for tomorrow, or for tomorrow's applications. First, let's examine the supply of bandwidth, especially as it applies to fiber optic networks.

The Supply of Bandwidth

Bandwidth capacity is expanding at a phenomenal rate. In 1993 futurist George Gilder predicted, "Total bandwidth will triple every year for at least the next 25 years." This appeared to be an outrageous statement, but as we will see, the availability and capacity of optical networks seem to be upholding Gilder's law. Even if bandwidth only doubles every six months, it's easy to see that it quickly overtakes CPU power, which according to Moore's law doubles every 18 months (see Figure 1.1). Although the network used to be the bottleneck, increasingly the computers at the edge of the network are the chokepoint in networks today.

Only optical networks can provide the bandwidth capacity needed for the long term. Although many other media, such as wireless and copper, are saturated within a few years, the capacity of fiber keeps increasing.

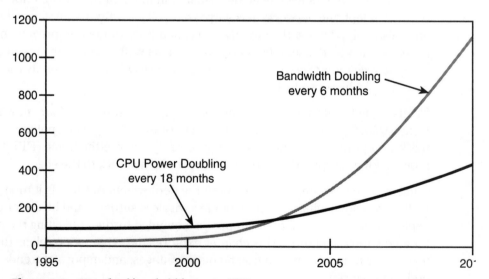

Figure 1.1   Growth of bandwidth versus CPU.

Copyright 1998. Courtesy of CANARIE.

Jeff Hecht, a fiber optic expert, illustrates the capacity of fiber this way: "[P]ut half the people in the world at each end of a fiber optic cable operating at [50 terabits per second], hand everybody a telephone, and it would only take a half-dozen fibers to let everybody talk at once" (Hecht 2000). Hecht was referring to the theoretical capacity reported by Lucent's Bell Labs at that writing. A year later, Lucent's experiments doubled the theoretical fiber capacity to 100 terabits per second, meaning that only three fibers operating at capacity would be needed to accomplish that task. To further conceptualize this throughput, think of sending 20 billion one-page e-mail messages simultaneously.

Lucent's estimate includes the use of fiber-capacity multiplying technology, DWDM, which is discussed in Chapter 2, "Optical Networking Basics." DWDM and other technological advances in expanding fiber capacity are taking existing fiber, even fiber that is 20 years old, and multiplying its bandwidth-carrying potential. According to John Roth, CEO of Nortel Networks, "These advances are doubling the performance of fibre optic networks every nine to 12 months. The cost of bandwidth has dropped 99 percent over the last decade and will drop another 99 percent in the coming decade" (Hughes 2000).

Technological advances mean that organizations with an existing investment in fiber can continue to exploit the capacity of that fiber without laying more cable for the foreseeable future. This ability to increase bandwidth without building new infrastructure particularly benefits telcos, whose existing investment is considerable.

Telcos and others continue to build out and upgrade their core networks, primarily to increase the speed on existing fiber. The speed on backbone networks is increasing from 2.488 *gigabits per second (Gbps)* (also known as OC-48; see Table 1.1) to 10 Gbps (OC-192). Carriers are also planning to deploy 40-Gbps speeds as they become available. And these are raw network speeds, not even considering how the capacity can be multiplied by dividing

Table 1.1   Bandwidth Comparison

T1/DS-1	1.544 Mbps
T3/DS-3	44.736 Mbps
OC-1	51.84 Mbps
OC-3	155.52 Mbps
OC-12	622.08 Mbps
OC-24	1.244 Gbps
OC-48	2.488 Gbps
OC-192	10 Gbps
OC-768	40 Gbps

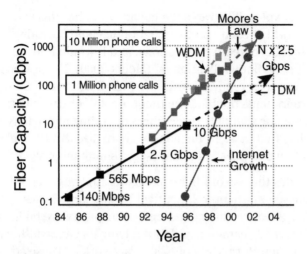

Figure 1.2   Growth in bandwidth capacity.

Copyright 2000. Courtesy of *Compound Semiconductor* magazine (April, p. 36).

the light into wavelengths with DWDM, which allows each frequency or wavelength to carry the same amount of data as the original fiber did. Multiply 40 Gbps by 100 wavelengths to get an aggregate throughput of 400 Gbps over a single fiber.

Despite the seemingly endless capacity of fiber, innovations have been deployed in a just-in-time fashion. As Figure 1.2 shows, the advent of DWDM is the only factor that is increasing the capacity of fiber to keep pace with the runaway growth of Internet traffic. If the only factor increasing backbone capacity was the expansion of traditional time-division multiplexing technologies such as *synchronous optical network (SONET)*, which doubled every 24 months, the growth in Internet traffic would have overwhelmed the backbone networks. Next we address the demand for bandwidth capacity which is driving the need for optical networks.

The Demand for Bandwidth

Demand for bandwidth is coming from several quarters. Voice traffic is increasing, but very slowly by comparison with data traffic. And according to carriers, Internet traffic is growing even faster than data traffic as a whole. Corporations' need for bandwidth is increasing at a rapid pace. Applications continue to require more bandwidth, from conventional applications like e-mail to more advanced applications like video, grid technologies, and peer-to-peer computing services such as Gnutella, Napster, and others.

Data Traffic versus Voice Traffic

Voice traffic growth is slow and steady, with growth rates in the single digits, while data traffic growth is explosive—as mentioned, data traffic has already surpassed voice traffic in terms of bandwidth consumed. The preponderance of data traffic is also borne out by estimates from UK market research firm Ovum. The company estimates that some 90 percent of the traffic on British Telecom's network will be data by 2003 (GiantLoop 2000). AT&T estimates that at the end of 2000, traffic on its networks consisted of 76 percent data.

The Internet and IP Traffic

In the late 1980s and early 1990s, the Internet began to create a demand for fiber optic capacity. The telcos had planned their network expansions for the slow, steady growth of voice traffic. Once Internet traffic really began to expand in the late 1990s and into the next millennium, the telcos were struggling to keep up.

Consider AT&T's installation of TAT-8, the first transatlantic fiber optic cable. In 1988, when this cable was installed, the company believed that it would provide adequate capacity through at least the year 2000. Given that this cable had more capacity than the first seven transatlantic cables put together, this might seem a reasonable assumption. TAT-8 reached its capacity in three years, even before the explosion of Internet traffic that occurred two years later (Cameron 1999).

The Internet's breakaway growth has, in fact, slowed somewhat. Although it could once be said that Internet traffic doubled every quarter, it now doubles about every seven months; more conservative estimates say once every year. Considering that this is still a geometric progression, such a growth rate is not to be dismissed lightly. According to Andrew Odlyzko (2000) head of the Mathematics and Cryptography Research Department at AT&T Labs, "Actual Internet traffic growth rates of 100 percent per year are considerably less than doubling every 3–4 months. But even these rates are still unprecedented and should be provoking new ways of planning." Considering the contrast between a 100 percent growth rate for IP traffic and single digit growth rates for voice traffic, it is clear that data traffic increasingly dominates public networks.

California's power crisis, which caused rolling blackouts in early 2001, was largely blamed on Silicon Valley's power requirements, particularly those of Internet data centers. Silicon Valley's electric usage was up 12 percent compared to 2 to 3 percent for the state as a whole. According to California utility estimates, an Internet data center consumes more power than a manufacturing plant and the industry as a whole shows a 13 to 14 percent growth rate for power consumption compared with a 2 percent growth rate for other industries (Micek 2001).

Corporate Demand for Bandwidth

However, it isn't just Internet companies that are driving the need for bandwidth. According to Forrester Research, 50 percent of corporations expect their bandwidth needs to more than double each year (Aragon 2000). Despite projections of a slowdown in growth, actual corporate demand for bandwidth continues to rise, further driving the need for optical networks and faster connections to the Internet.

Vendors are seeing a demand for bandwidth, too. According to Vivian Hudson, Vice President of High-Capacity Networks for Nortel, "Some of our customers are doubling [transmission capacity] every four months. Not just one, but several of our very large customers" (Hecht 2000).

At the same time, a wave of new services is meeting this demand. Although bandwidth has traditionally been sold in the increments shown in Table 1.1, it is increasingly available in more flexible increments, such as 1 *megabit per second (Mbps)*, through upstart carriers offering *Gigabit Ethernet* services. Such services are further described in Chapter 6, *Optical Networking and the Corporate Network*, which discusses corporate use of optical networking from LANs to WANs to Internet connectivity.

Applications Drive Bandwidth Demand

Behind the scenes, the increased use of networked applications is further fueling bandwidth demand. Existing applications, such as e-mail and instant messaging, are growing (see Figure 1.3), and newer applications are also straining networks with demands for greater bandwidth. Videoconferencing and distance education are both on the rise. Collaborative applications require low-latency, substantial real-time bandwidth availability.

Corporate e-mail usage continues to grow, with a 50 percent growth in the number of e-mail messages expected in 2001 according to Ferris Research. E-mail is a relatively low-bandwidth application, but the volume of the data in question, compounded by large file attachments to e-mail, make it a chief consumer of corporate bandwidth.

Video is expected to grow considerably in proportion to other applications. The bandwidth requirements of video are substantial, particularly to make its transmission smooth and keep down the latency. Video is increasingly used on corporate networks for training and videoconferencing. Canada's National Film Board is using video over that nation's high-speed public networks. It

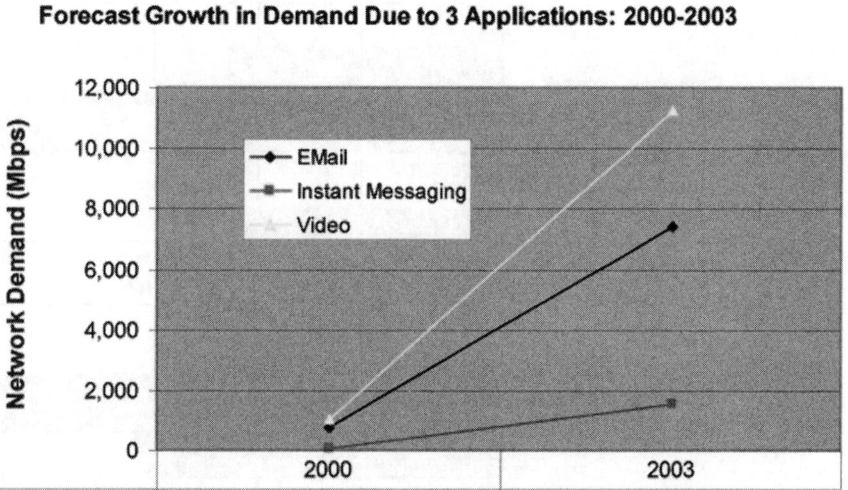

Forecast Growth in Demand Due to 3 Applications: 2000-2003

	2000	2003
—◆— EMail	777	7,424
—■— Instant Messaging	43	1,517
─▲─ Video	1,042	11,250

Figure 1.3   Growth in e-mail, instant messaging, and video.

Copyright 2001. Courtesy of David Prior, PBI Media, and *Cabling Systems* magazine.

offers 700 titles in full-screen format. Over Canada's research network, CA*Net3, any school in Canada can receive whatever titles are in the Film Board's library. Indeed, multiple titles might be requested in different classrooms at once. Each video stream takes 1.5 Mbps of bandwidth. Streaming video and video on demand are becoming popular home uses for broadband; these applications will only increase over time.

In the corporate world, converged networks are also increasing bandwidth demands. Leading companies are converging voice, data, and video on their networks, increasing their bandwidth requirements (see Figure 1.4).

Virtual private networks (VPNs) are another important, bandwidth-hungry application. VPNs are increasingly used to provide remote access to the corporate network as well as to encrypt all data between corporate sites. But encryption increases the bandwidth required for all these tasks. Voice over IP (VoIP) and collaborative applications are also driving bandwidth requirements.

Companies involved in e-commerce and e-business are building sites with increased capabilities that are database intensive. A site's inventory may be linked to its partners' warehouses in real-time. Integrated voice customer service may be offered at the click of a button. All these applications require bandwidth, and a site's performance in part determines its success.

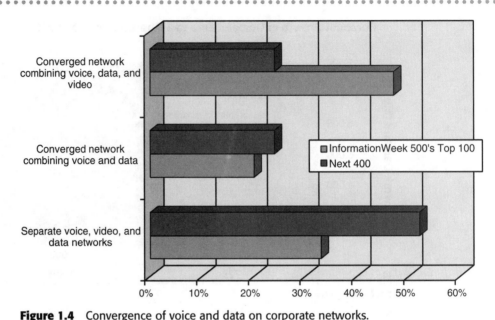

Figure 1.4   Convergence of voice and data on corporate networks.

Copyright 2001. Courtesy of InformationWeek Research's *InformationWeek* 500 Survey of 250 IT Executives.

Peer-to-peer applications are also consuming bandwidth. Napster and other such services (like Aimster) consumed bandwidth at a surprising rate. Network managers at universities watched with alarm as their bandwidth usage climbed overnight as Napster grew in popularity among college students. Although usage of Napster has abated somewhat, the hunger for peer-to-peer services like Napster, where very large files are exchanged, has only increased. In addition, companies like Groove Network are bringing peer-to-peer usage to the corporate world. Bandwidth usage of this application niche will continue to fuel demand in households, educational institutions, and in the workplace. The advent of grid-based computing, where idle processor cycles are used for various causes, is also on the rise. The most well-known example is SETI@home, where PC screensavers are used to help conduct research. Other movements in this area include medical research, such as initiatives to fight AIDS and cancer.

Just as work expands to fill the available time, so applications seem to expand to fill the available bandwidth. Qwest's president and CEO Afshin Mohebbi describes how applications drive the need for increased bandwidth: "When we started building this network, people were laughing. Why do you need so much bandwidth across the country? Who's going to use it? What kind of applications? But people will find a way to use it. You can do videoconferencing, share documents, graphic intensive work, edit film, edit presentations,

Table 1.2   Peer-to-Peer Research Initiatives

INITIATIVE	PURPOSE	WEB ADDRESS
SETI@home	To search for extraterrestrial life forms	setiathome.ssl.berkeley.edu
Folding@home	Research into how genomes fold into proteins	www.stanford.edugroup/ pandegroup/Cosm
Fightaids@home	AIDS research	fightaidsathome.org
Compute Against Cancer	Cancer research	www.acor.org/cac/

have multimedia work, offer customer service on the Web, and be in a remote location. The availability of bandwidth has created this whole ecosystem around the availability of bandwidth and the things you can do with bandwidth" (Wolinsky 2000).

Is There a Glut of Fiber?

Although it is clear that the demand for bandwidth is increasing, there has been speculation that there is in fact a fiber glut. Is there in fact too much fiber already?

There has been a truly frenetic pace of fiber adoption recently, leading to speculation that no more fiber could possibly be needed at this point. And given capacity-multiplying technologies like DWDM, this speculation could have merit. Table 1.3 shows the annual fiber deployment in the U.S. by telcos, including *interexchange carriers (IXCs), incumbent local exchange carriers (ILECs),* and *competitive local exchange carriers (CLECs).*

Certainly, in some areas, building long-haul fiber connections is not cost-effective. Jonah and Ron Yokubaitis, founders of *Internet service provider (ISP)* Texas.net, have found that it's cheaper to buy long-haul capacity from carriers than to own it themselves. According to Jonah Yokubaitis, "In 1997 we bought a fiber IRU between two of our major POPs. We wound up selling the IRU because we found that at least for five years into the future (we are four years from that already) we could buy capacity from the carriers a lot cheaper than we could build it even if the fiber were free. There seems to be a tremendous glut of fiber locally. We have prices being put in front of us that we just

Table 1.3   Annual Fiber Deployment in Thousands of Miles

YEAR	IXC	ILEC	CLEC	TOTAL
1996	923	2085	685	3693
1997	1333	2280	920	4533
1998	2506	2370	1050	5926
1999	5500	2560	1165	9225
2000	9065	5060	1435	15,560
2001e	10,935	6560	1840	19,335
2002e	12,905	7200	2120	22,225
2003e	14,200	7700	2400	24,300
2004e	14,900	8100	2700	25,700

Copyright 2001. Courtesy of *Broadband Week*.

cannot refuse. Given the distance between our four major cities [San Antonio, Austin, Dallas-Fort Worth, and Houston] we haven't seen any indication yet that gigabit Ethernet is really feasible on an inter-city basis" (Cook 2001).

Telecom guru David Isenberg also acknowledges that there is a fiber glut in some metro areas: "Where there is fiber in the metro area, there is perforce way too much fiber. (Everybody buries more fiber than they need—when you can buy a 1000x option on future growth for just a few percent of the cost of construction, you do it.) Once the fiber is deployed, its owners are motivated to turn it into a performing asset. This puts more fiber on the market, which drives prices down further" (Isenberg 2001).

Other voices in the debate dispute that there is a fiber glut at all. Chris Lemmer, director of bandwidth trading and risk management at the Williams Communications Group, states that bandwidth trades are on the rise and that the demand for bandwidth is still there: "We don't see, in our business, an oversupply of bandwidth in the marketplace" (Bryce 2001).

Interestingly, the idea of a glut in the fiber market is not a new idea at all. Richard Mack, Vice President at KMI Corp, points out that in 1989, "People said there was a glut of fiber capacity" (Hecht 1999a). This of course predates the Internet's increased demand for bandwidth.

Like many questions, the answer to this dilemma is more complex than a simple yes or no. In fact, some routes have more fiber capacity than is needed, a fact that will drive down prices on those routes, just as multiple airlines serving the same routes tends to drive down airfares on those routes. However, fiber is a long-term asset, with a useful lifespan of 20 years. It isn't out-of-date within a year or two, like a PC.

Keep in mind that fiber coverage is far from complete, and many routes still need fiber. Worldwide, the market is underserved by broadband connectivity to the home, and there is a pent-up demand for such services rather than a glut of choices. Rural areas are significantly underserved by fiber deployments, both for businesses and consumers. Cities are often fibered in high-rent downtown areas, but the fiber doesn't reach all parts of the city.

In fact, some consultants, including David Prior at PBI Media, argue that there is a bandwidth gap rather than a bandwidth glut. He states that this worldwide shortfall will restrict more than 87 percent of the potential offered load from reaching existing global networks (Prior 2001).

Reaching the end customer is often the issue—the proverbial last mile. If you are located strategically near lit fiber, it's fairly easy and inexpensive to get a high-capacity connection. If you are outside a coverage area, the idea of a fiber glut might seem little more than irony. Tony Thakur at Time Warner Telecom quips, "Is there a glut? I might say that if I hadn't tried to buy capacity lately. They say, 'Okay, we have capacity and here's the price.' But then when they launch the order, they may not have the capacity. There may be local loop issues; we may have to build to get to them. You have to worry about whether they're in the same POP that you're in . . . They may have the wrong address on the building" (Branson 2001).

The so-called fiber glut is certainly selective. As long-time *Internet Engineering Task Force (IETF)* participant Scott Bradner (2001) writes in a recent column, "The view depends on where you stand . . . I doubt there is a fiber glut between Minot, N.D., and Wichita, Kan. And I doubt very much that there is excess fiber into Lima, Peru."

This is ultimately the answer to the fiber glut question. Yes, on some routes, the existing fiber is adequate. However, in many places around the world, including the United States, high-speed connectivity comes with either very long waits for service or an unwillingness to bring fiber to new areas.

Analyst firm Telechoice (2001) recently created a statistical model to see whether indeed there is a glut of capacity in the United States. Telechoice researchers found that rather than a glut, some 63 percent of routes in the United States are at or near their capacity, indicating that more investment in optical networks is needed.

Market forces have to date determined where fiber has been laid. It is not surprising that the most lucrative routes have been fibered while there is little or

Table 1.4 U.S. Public Utilities Offering Telecom Services

SERVICE	NUMBER PROVIDING SERVICE
Broadband resale	32
Cable TV	78
Fiber leasing	97
High-speed data	55
Internet access	91
Local telephone	26

Copyright 2001. Courtesy of *Network World*.

no fiber available in many areas of the country and even in parts of the most fibered cities. It is a case of feast and famine at once. For this reason, companies, municipalities, and institutions may have little choice but to lay their own dark fiber to a *carrier-neutral facility*, where they will have a choice of service providers. We explore alternatives to carrier-owned fiber in greater detail in Chapter 5, "Optical Networking and Urban Planning."

In fact, the reluctance of traditional carriers to serve some areas is drawing alternative providers, such as publicly owned utility companies, into the marketplace. These utilities often have a significant investment in fiber and are becoming suppliers as well. Table 1.4 lists the services provided by utilities in the United States and the number of utilities currently providing such services. Some states had ruled that publicly owned utilities could not provide telecom services, but a recent federal court decision overturned the Virginia statute directed at keeping utility companies out of the marketplace. See Chapter 5 and Chapter 7, "Fiber to the Home," for more information on the role of utilities as possible optical networking providers.

Markets for Fiber

Who is interested in buying fiber? Certainly network backbone providers are. Telcos have traditionally been among the most significant consumers of fiber.

Internet content delivery providers may also be interested in owning their own long-haul fiber infrastructure. Content delivery networks such as Digital Island and Akamai need access to high-speed networks. Some content delivery networks build their own optical networks, including Digital Island, Globix's Earthcache, and others. Optical internets, including Gigabit Ethernet providers, also do their own fiber builds. ISPs may build their own fiber infrastructure or they may buy services from others, in part depending on their size.

Increasingly, however, fiber is moving from large organizations to smaller areas. Cities are building their own optical networks, as are some corporations. Corporations may build out a network infrastructure between buildings on a campus, locations in a metro area, or even between corporate offices in a WAN. However, corporations should make cost comparisons between leasing dark fiber and purchasing services from a carrier for longer distances between corporate offices.

Owners of multi-tenant units may put in fiber as a drawing card for tenants needing high-speed networking. The same applies to developers. If the fiber is connected to a carrier-neutral facility, customers then have a choice of service provider, fostering competition and preventing vendor lock-in.

Hotels have had mixed results with putting in fiber. If they attempt to charge a premium for high-speed access, they, like Hyatt, may find that their take rate is lower than expected. CAIS Internet, which was a provider to many hotels, found that only 5 percent of business travelers were willing to pay $10 more per night for high-speed access, preferring to use their own modems and a phone line to check e-mail. Nevertheless, hotels increasingly see patrons who view high-speed access as an important requirement and they want to make the service available, even if companies like CAIS Internet drop out of the business. If the high-speed access is included in the price of the room, it may be a drawing card for their properties. A bed and breakfast in Grant County, Washington bundles high-speed access with the cost of the room. Their occupancy rates are much higher than other area facilities that do not have high-speed access.

Rather than targeting individual business customers, another approach is to provide fiber in all the meeting rooms, allowing the hotel to provide networks that can handle voice, video, audio, or other media in short order. This is the approach taken by resort hotel Bally's Las Vegas. The meeting facilities are all connected through a fiber optic LAN which can support speeds of 10 to 100 Mbps. This flexibility makes Bally's an attractive destination for conventions needing easily configured network support. It turned out that the price for deploying a fiber LAN was identical to that of a copper LAN. Fiber requires fewer hubs and repeaters, the elimination of which brought the price down to the same level as copper. According to Michael Bendetti, President of Spaghetti Western, the firm that designed Bally's network, "The price of the cable and connectors turned out to be only about 20 percent higher than copper. But when I figured in the savings from eliminating the repeaters, it was a wash. I realized that fiber would provide the assurance of being able to handle all the data, audio, and video needs of the hotel for the foreseeable future" (Silver 2001).

Markets for Fiber and Optical Components

Markets for both fiber and optical components are growing. The market for fiber in particular varies depending on the region of the world in question. Today, North America and Europe are equal in terms of their consumption of fiber. Over the long term, however (by 2010), Europe will consume slightly more fiber than North American markets. By 2010, undersea cable, which comprised some 36 percent of the market in 2000, will have declined to just 4 percent, as adequate capacity will have been deployed by then. Figure 1.5 shows the relative fiber consumption of various areas of the world.

Research from Electronicast (Hailu 2001) shows that fiber optic cable sales worldwide reached $24 billion in 2000 and, with an average annual growth of 10 percent, should reach $39.4 billion in 2005. By 2010, overall consumption is projected to reach $66.1 billion.

According to the Aberdeen Group, the intelligent optical equipment market will experience a compound annual growth rate (CAGR) of 46 percent through 2006. The market for telecommunications equipment as a whole is relatively flat during that period, showing only a 1.6 percent CAGR. Despite the slowed growth of the industry as a whole, intelligent optical equipment from

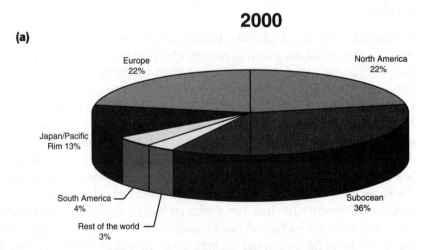

2000

(a)

Europe
22%

North America
22%

Japan/Pacific
Rim 13%

South America
4%

Rest of the world
3%

Subocean
36%

Figure 1.5 a, b, c Global fiber optic consumption by region.

Copyright 2001. Courtesy of Electronicast Corp.

(b)

2005

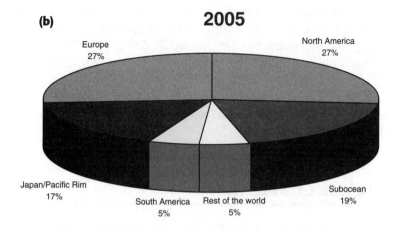

Europe
27%

North America
27%

Japan/Pacific Rim
17%

South America
5%

Rest of the world
5%

Subocean
19%

(c)

2010

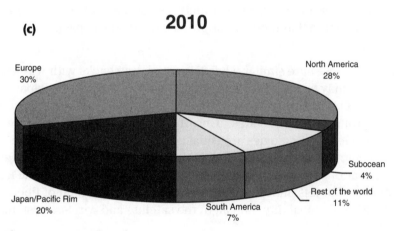

Europe
30%

North America
28%

Subocean
4%

Rest of the world
11%

Japan/Pacific Rim
20%

South America
7%

Figure 1.5   Continued

companies like Ciena, ONI, and Tellium are exceeding expectations, indicating a shift in spending to next generation networks (Aberdeen Group 2001).

Although Gigabit Ethernet is playing an increasingly important role in metro area networks (see Chapter 6 for more information on this), the market for SONET equipment also continues to expand. According to Cahner's In-Stat Group (2000), the SONET market, and its European equivalent, SDH, will expand from $11.89 billion in 1999 to $31.26 billion in 2004.

Although the SONET market is still showing growth, it is beginning to fall off. This is in part because SONET is considered a legacy protocol but also because the SONET market is evolving into something more complex. According to Frost & Sullivan, the market for SONET equipment is changing as DWDM deployment becomes more common. By 2002, SONET/DWDM equipment will outsell plain vanilla SONET equipment for the first time. By 2006, this type of hybrid equipment will completely overshadow sales of SONET-only systems, growing from $9 billion in 2002 to $35 billion by 2006. In the same timeframe, revenue from SONET-only systems will drop to about $7 billion (Jander 2001).

Why not Wireless or Satellite?

One of the objections to optical networking that is frequently put forward is why companies wouldn't use wireless as an alternative to optical networking. Although wireless networks are certainly less problematic than fiber installations, it is also true that they do not provide nearly the capacity of optical networks.

Satellite systems share similar advantages and drawbacks with wireless networks. They may be easier to deploy, but they do not enjoy the capacity that fiber optic networks provide. As Bill St. Arnaud (2001) of Canadian network research group CANARIE states, "One of the great urban myths is that satellite and wireless technologies are equal competitors to fiber. These technologies are complementary but not competitive to fiber. There are many exciting new applications for mobile wireless and short range wireless in the last hundred meters. But it is important to note that one single strand of fiber has more bandwidth capability than all of the satellite and wireless systems combined in Canada."

Fiber has substantial advantages over satellites. Not only does fiber optic cable have more capacity, but it is cheaper to deploy than satellites. According to Karen Bannan (2001), "A single fiber-optic cable can handle a thousand times more capacity than a single satellite. The difference between them is so dramatic that eventually, terrestrial technologies may carry all voice and data traffic. Today, about 80 percent of all voice and data traffic is handled by undersea fiber-optics. A mere ten years ago—before 1988, when the first undersea fiber optic cable was laid, the balance was skewed toward satellites. Fiber optic connections have a shorter lag time (known as 'latency') than today's high-flying geosynchronous satellites, engender fewer transmission errors, and are cheaper to deploy."

Although wireless and satellite systems cannot offer nearly the capacity of optical networks, they are excellent for playing a complementary role with

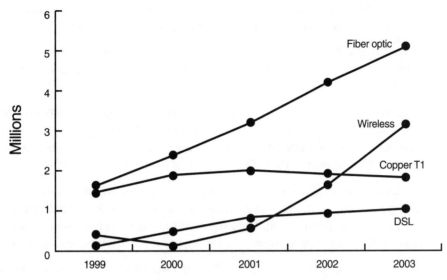

Figure 1.6   U.S. business broadband users by medium, 1999-2003.

Copyright 2000. Courtesy of eMarketer.

such networks. At George Washington University, fiber extends to the classroom where a wireless LAN lets students in the classroom reach the university's network, as they can while roaming in public areas on campus. Satellites
can reach areas too remote for fiber builds. Wireless networks can also provide an excellent last-mile solution for bringing high-speed access from a single point in a neighborhood to surrounding houses.

Further, although wireless LANs are growing in popularity, research firm
eMarketer predicts that optical networks will dominate business broadband
usage, with wireless ranking second. (See Figure 1.6.)

Advantages of Optical Networking

What are some of the advantages optical networking offers?

Astounding capacity. As discussed earlier, a single fiber can carry as much
as 100 *terabits per second (Tbps)* of data, or all the telephone traffic in the
United States during an hour of peak usage.

20-year lifespan. Fiber's useful life surpasses other communications technologies. The fiber itself can be depreciated as an asset over 20 years. It need

not be replaced. To increase the speed on the fiber or take advantage of innovations, the components that light the fiber can be replaced.

Prices are falling. Although fiber was once more expensive than copper, prices are now very nearly equal and in fact are equal if related equipment costs are considered.

Increase speed or change protocols without replacing infrastructure. Fiber is technology- and even speed-agnostic. Different protocols can be deployed over the same fiber. Speeds can be increased by replacing the components that light the fiber. The fiber itself need not be replaced.

Security. Fiber offers a secure medium. Electronic transmissions of data can be tapped and are subject to interference and *crosstalk*, but data transmitted by fiber has no such pitfall. Data transmitted over fiber is secure, which is one reason that banks have invested in fiber optic infrastructures for some time.

Centralized administration. Optical networks are easier to administer than comparable copper infrastructures. Because of their speed, they can be treated as a single large LAN. Rather than having network administrators in each department or on each floor, several corporate locations can be centrally administered, including such functions as backups, as well as adds, moves, and changes.

Optical networks provide substantial advantages wherever they are deployed. Companies interested in optical networking should look carefully at these advantages when making decisions about the direction that their networks will take.

Conclusion

Not only do optical networks provide a host of advantages, but new models of networking make it possible for companies, municipalities, and other institutions to own their own networks more affordably than ever. This trend toward *customer-empowered networking* paves the way for customers, rather than carriers, to own the infrastructure, whether it is a strand of fiber or even a wavelength on a fiber. If the optical network leads to a carrier-neutral facility, companies have more choice of carriers than ever before, fostering true competition. If, on the other hand, carriers build infrastructure to the customer, whether the customer is a city with many locations or a corporation with a single location, the customer is likely to be the captive of that vendor. Since optical networks will ultimately provide a wide range of services and not just high-speed data, keeping such networks competitive is important to prevent powerful long-term monopolies from forming.

Traditionally, in the United States, and in many other parts of the world, the last mile has been owned by the carrier. In the case of the United States, this carrier is the incumbent local exchange carrier or ILEC. Carrier-owned infrastructure has had the effect of limiting or eliminating choice of carriers for customers. It is also extremely difficult for other providers to compete, despite the passage of the Telecommunications Act of 1996, which was supposed to open up local markets in the U.S. to competition. As Dick Martin (2001), Executive Vice President of AT&T, stated five years after the passage of that piece of legislation, "The Bells control 95 percent of the local service market and maintain that stranglehold in part by charging competitors inflated prices for leasing elements of their networks."

Optical networking impacts a wide variety of businesses, from telcos running backbone networks to cities interested in creating a leading-edge infrastructure to stimulate their economies, to corporations that recognize the importance of high-speed access, to home users looking for long-term broadband solutions. In subsequent chapters, we'll examine each of these market segments. But before doing so, Chapter 2 provides an important foundation in technology, discussing how optical networks work. Readers with a background in optical networking technology may instead want to turn to later chapters which discuss real-world applications of optical networking.

Optical Networking Basics

O ptical networking is a complex topic. Because this book focuses more on applications of optical networking than on the technology itself, this chapter provides the briefest of overviews of optical networking technology. In Appendix A, *Recommended Resources*, we suggest supplemental reading for those who want more background on optical networking. What we'll talk about here primarily serves to help define terms used in the remaining chapters of the book.

In the discussion that follows, we'll talk about the equipment used, and how it works together to send data over light waves.

Hardware

What physical equipment is required to construct and operate an optical network? Hundreds of vendors sell fiber, components, and equipment used to install, connect, protect, test, and manage an optical network. In this section we will cover the hardware basics and peripherals for an optical network.

Types of Fiber

Fiber refers to a thin silica glass (or plastic) cable, clad in protective material, that is used to guide lightwaves. There are two basic types of fiber: multimode and single mode.

Multimode is the older variety. It has a comparatively large core (62.5 microns) when compared to a wavelength of light (1.3 microns). As a result, light rays bounce off the walls as they travel through the fiber, a process called modal dispersion or, less formally, smearing. Light waves arrive at their destination a little bit out of synch as a result. Multimode fiber is less expensive than newer single mode fiber and works well for short distances, a few kilometers at speeds of 100 Mbps and a few hundred meters at gigabit speeds. Not only is the fiber cheaper, but the devices at each end (called transceivers) are less expensive as well. An even greater price differentiation is the technology used to light the fiber. Multimode is lit with light emitting diodes (LEDs) while single mode fiber requires lasers.

Single mode fiber has a thinner core at 8 to 9 microns; it admits only a single ray of light. As a result, there is almost no modal dispersion and light travels along the core more smoothly, without bouncing off the walls.

Optical Components

Optical components are hardware elements used in conjunction with fiber to form an optical network. Major vendors of optical components include Corning and Nortel (See Table 2.1). In its most basic form, an optical network consists of a light source, a medium for the light to travel through (fiber), and a receiver for the light.

Additional components are needed because as light travels through fiber, it begins to lose its strength, so the signal has to be periodically amplified. Eventually, though, it must be changed from an optical signal into an electronic signal and back again. The components you would need to build an optical network depend on your physical requirements and the protocols you use. Following are some common optical components, though the list is by no means exhaustive.

Further, newer components may combine the functionality of several individual components into a single unit. For example, a transceiver can both send and transmit optical signals. A transponder performs both of these functions and also multiplexes and demultiplexes optical signals.

Add-drop multiplexer. Add-drop multiplexers (ADMs) are used in SONET networks to add and remove signal components selectively without demultiplexing the entire stream of signals.

Amplifiers. Optical amplifiers are used to amplify signals without electrical conversion. A common type is an *erbium-doped fiber amplifier (EDFA)*,

Table 2.1 Optical Component Vendors

Nortel Networks	www.nortel.com
Corning, Inc	www.corning.com
DigiLens	www.digilens.com
Discovery Semiconductors	www.chipsat.com
Iridian Spectral Technologies	www.iridian.ca
JDS Uniphase	www.jdsuniphase.com
LightLogic	www.lightlogic.com
Optical Solutions Inc.	www.opticalsolutions.com
Vectron International	www.vectron.com
Ciena	www.ciena.com
Corvis	www.corvis.com
Sycamore Networks	www.sycamorenetworks.com
Agilent Technologies	www.agilent.com
Lucent Technologies	www.lucent.com
Marconi	www.marconi.com
3M	www.3m.com
Siemens	www.siemens.com
Broadcom	www.broadcom.com

which uses a laser pump diode in conjunction with the fiber to amplify the signal.

Attenuators. Optical attenuators are used to reduce the intensity of a signal when needed.

Connectors. A connector attaches an optical fiber to another fiber or to an active device like a transmitter. A connector can be disconnected and reconnected, as opposed to a splice, which permanently joins two fibers. Although connectors provide flexibility, they cause attenuation and provide a place where impurities such as grease and fingerprints can be introduced and muddy the signal.

Filters. An optical filter is used to selectively transmit or block a range of wavelengths.

Lasers. A laser produces a single frequency of light that when turned on and off can be used to transmit digital data (ones and zeros). A *tunable laser* is one that can produce and transmit signals at more than one frequency—ideal for use with DWDM since one tunable laser can provide a backup for any frequency; otherwise, backup lasers for each frequency must be kept on hand.

Multiplexers/demultiplexers. A multiplexer is a device that allows two or more signals to be sent over one communications channel. A demultiplexer separates two or more channels previously multiplexed.

Optical switches. Optical switches, also called optical cross-connects (OXCs) move signals between different fibers without conversion to electrical signals. A variety of methods are used to move signals from one fiber to another, including arrays of tiny mirrors and bubbles. See Chapter 8, *The Outlook for Optical Networking*, for more information.

Receivers. A receiver is a device that detects an optical signal, converts it to an electrical signal, and processes it.

Transceivers. A transceiver is a device that both transmits and receives signals.

Transponders. A transponder is a device that transmits, receives, multiplexes and demultiplexes signals.

Additional optical components include mirrors, lenses, couplers, and isolators, among others. For additional information on optical components see *Deploying Optical Networking Components*, by Gil Held (McGraw-Hill, 2001).

Protective Equipment and Materials

There are two parts to the topic of protection. One is protecting the fiber from damage, and the other is protecting workers installing or maintaining optical networks.

Protecting workers means they should wear special goggles (mainly to protect eyes from glass shards). Two other safety issues are proper disposal of the glass shards created by splicing the fiber or accidentally breaking it, and the cleaning chemicals and adhesives used during installation. Fiber waste should be contained, and care taken when handling chemicals.

Fiber optic cables have a high tensile strength, meaning they are very strong— stronger, in fact, than copper wire. The outer jacket material on fiber optic cable is meant to shield it from the environment. Some of the same ducting used for in-building CAT 5 copper installation can be used to house in-building fiber. Where optical fiber is deployed in environments like storm or sanitary sewers, additional housing (typically stainless steel) would be installed to protect the cable.

Installation Equipment

There are a number of methods for installing fiber optic cable (both indoor and outdoor), each requiring different equipment. The pros and cons of various installation methods are discussed in more detail in Chapter 8.

Fiber installation in buildings with ductwork is straightforward and can be done using much of the same equipment used to install copper. New fiber types, such as 3M's Volition, are easier to handle for people accustomed to dealing with copper wiring.

In air-blown fiber installation, fiber is blown into a microconduit using portable blowing equipment. This technique can speed installation and reduce costs. The fiber itself, called jet fiber, tends to be a bit more expensive than other types, but the decreased installation costs make it equal to other types of fiber. Jet fiber is particularly useful for fiber to the home. Microconduit that holds the fiber is installed first, requiring no special optical expertise. Later, if desired, jet fiber can be blown in through the microconduit.

Trenching, where the streets are torn up to lay cable, requires a backhoe, jackhammer, and other heavy equipment.

"In the groove" fiber is deployed by cutting a groove in the roadway and installing fiber in that groove. Such installations are less disruptive to roadways than trenching.

Aerial cable placement requires equipment similar to that used by telephone companies to string wires—in fact, the same poles are often used where permission can be obtained. Additionally, some systems, including Alcatel's, enable aerial cable to be installed without turning off power lines.

In sewer installations, special robots are used to install fiber and to maintain the conduits and sewers where fiber is deployed. Sewer installations involve minimal disruption to streets, an advantage for Metropolitan Area Networks (MANs). Sewer deployments were pioneered in Japan and have spread to Europe and North America.

Testing and Management Equipment

Fiber optic testing is the process of verifying the performance of fiber optic components, links, systems and networks and troubleshooting problems. Tests may include measuring the power a fiber gives off or testing the continuity or optical loss of fiber, cable, connectors, and splices. Determining the information-carrying capacity of the fiber or cable is called bandwidth or dispersion testing.

Manufacturers like Digital Lightwave and FOTEC (Fiber Optic Test Equipment Company) make equipment for testing fiber optic networks.

Management and monitoring of optical networks may use both hardware and software solutions. Equipment may be protocol or technology specific, for SONET- or DWDM-based networks, for example.

Location or Physical Plant

Fiber optic networks may have termination points or hubs on a single campus. Compared to copper LANs, optical LANs require far fewer hubs and wiring closets. At George Washington University, discussed in Chapter 6 (*Optical Networking and the Corporate Network*), a campus-wide copper LAN would have required some 160 hubs, one every 100 meters. The optical LAN the university deployed instead required only 11 hub closets that served 80 buildings. Because optical networking equipment doesn't generate heat, its environmental needs are modest as well. Optical networks save space and money. Because their administration is centralized, fiber optic networks tend to look more like a telco's central office architecture than like a traditional LAN in terms of their physical plant requirements.

Software

Software used in optical networking includes network management software and software for order management and billing. An important emerging category is operation support systems (OSS). These systems provide a range of services to support emerging offerings like bandwidth-on-demand, including billing and accounting.

The OSS market is growing. According to Dataquest, the market will grow from $18 billion in 2000 to more than $30 billion in 2003, which does not include IT hardware or consulting that supports the sales of such systems. See Table 2.2 for a list of OSS vendors.

Typically, internal staff have handled the functions performed by OSS. In some cases, functions were handled through static means that are now proving inadequate for offerings like bandwidth-on-demand. Visio drawings of networks and Excel spreadsheets projecting demand are static entities that quickly fall out of date. As Web-based provisioning of services becomes more common, OSS, with its dynamic view of network elements and customers affected by the workings of those network elements, is increasingly a requirement. Relying on the memory of operations staff to give an up-to-date picture of the network is not adequate for complex offerings like bandwidth-on-

Table 2.2 OSS Vendors

Telcordia Technologies	www.telcordia.com
Eftia	www.eftia.co.uk
Orchestream	www.orchestream.com
Syndesis	www.syndesis.com
Kabira Technologies	www.kabira.com
Netcracker	www.netcracker.com
MetaSolv	www.metasolv.com
Opticom	www.getiview.com

demand, which typically support advanced services like VPNs, videoconferencing, and more.

While carriers are the primary market for OSS, complex enterprise networks may benefit from operation support systems as well.

Although OSS is an important tool, providers are slow to adopt new software solutions—many are just starting to implement billing and provisioning systems. According to Neil Baimel, chairman and co-founder of service assurance technology provider Syndesis, "Most companies aren't in a position in their life cycles to even think about adopting automated provisioning technology. Some are just getting into implementation of billing and order management systems, while others are further along and keeping up with provisioning and activation—mostly by throwing people at it" (Schwartz 2001).

For an in-depth treatment of operation support systems, see *OSS Essentials*, by Kornel Terplan (Wiley, 2001).

Software is an important area for optical networking providers as well as corporations deploying optical networks on a large scale. Despite the demand, the traditional ways of handling these functions are slow to give way to more advanced methods, and it will be some time before they are widely deployed. For example, of the metro Ethernet providers, only Telseon offered Web-based provisioning of bandwidth as of August 2001.

Protocols

Standards bodies like the ITU, IETF, and IEEE have a number of protocols in place to govern how fiber is used to transmit information. Fiber is technology neutral, like an empty pipe, meaning you can use any of a number of rules (protocols) to send data across fiber. SONET and ATM are the most widely implemented (mostly by telcos), but Gigabit Ethernet is also gaining ground, particularly for campus, LAN, and metro deployments.

ATM

Asynchronous transfer mode (ATM) is a high speed transmission technology for multiplexing and switching. It is connection-oriented, making it ideal for voice traffic.

ATM is deployed with SONET. ATM is particularly good at carrying multiple data types, including voice, video, and data. It should be noted, however, that IP can also handle multiple data types.

ATM's ability to carry multiple data types and guarantee *quality-of-service (QoS)* makes it an ideal technology for high-capacity fiber-optic networks. Further, the wide-scale deployment of ATM by carriers means that the companies with the largest optical networks routinely use ATM. But ATM can be used at any level of an optical network. ATM over SONET is the architecture of choice for George Washington University's fiber optic LAN. At an even more modest scale, ATM is being deployed frequently for passive optical networks that carry fiber to the home, allowing such networks to carry voice, video, and high-speed data services.

SONET

Synchronous optical network (SONET) is a standard for optical-fiber transmission, designed to transport many digital signals with varying capacities. The standard was first published in 1988 with ANSI, and a version called *synchronous digital hierarchy (SDH)* has been adopted by the ITU for the European market.

SONET is the dominant protocol on optical networks and ensures that equipment from multiple vendors works together properly. SONET networks are typically deployed in a ring topology to provide redundancy. It is known for its Automatic Protection Switching, in which failures in one ring are automatically sensed, and the system shifts to its protection ring (which is normally kept idle) within 50 milliseconds. SONET runs at a variety of speeds, starting at OC-1, 51 Mbps. Currently, the fastest speed offered by SONET is OC-192, just slightly less than 10 Gbps.

For more information on SONET, see *SONET* by Walter Goralski (McGraw-Hill, 2000).

Ethernet

Ethernet is a local-area network (LAN) protocol that uses a bus or star topology and supports data transfer rates of 10 Mbps to 10 Gbps. It uses carrier-sense multiple access with collision detection (CSMA/CD) as the access method, implemented at the Physical Layer in the ISO Open Systems Interconnection Reference Model. Ethernet and Fast Ethernet (100 Mbps) can run over fiber or over copper infrastructures. Gigabit Ethernet and 10-Gigabit Ethernet, described next, have more relevance to optical networking. If any type of Ethernet is run over fiber, however, speeds can be upgraded at a later time simply by replacing interface cards.

Gigabit Ethernet

Gigabit Ethernet is a version of Ethernet that supports data transfer rates of 1 gigabit (1000 megabits) per second. 10-Gigabit Ethernet supports 10 Gbps, similar in speed to the fastest SONET speed currently available, OC-192. In fact, so that SONET-based networks can be easily interfaced with 10-Gigabit Ethernet networks, the standard includes two interfaces: one that runs at exactly 10 Gbps and one that runs at OC-192 speeds, which are just slightly slower.

Gigabit Ethernet can run over high-quality copper (Category 5 Enhanced), but some copper infrastructures may not be able to support it. It must be tested on a case-by-case basis. 10-Gigabit Ethernet cannot run over copper at all.

Whatever the speed, there are advantages to deploying the same protocol all along a network. It means that high-speed WANs can be managed as easily as Ethernet LANs, building on existing skill sets. Since it interfaces well with SONET and since metro providers and traditional telcos are offering Gigabit Ethernet services, Ethernet is becoming an important standard for optical networking from the home to the LAN to the WAN to the enterprise. Even backbone providers may increasingly deploy this protocol since optical Ethernet equipment costs are typically one-tenth of their SONET counterparts. Broadcom is one of the suppliers of Gigabit Ethernet and 10-Gigabit Ethernet components for optical networks.

IP

Internet Protocol (IP) was designed for use in packet-switched networks (like the Internet). Optical internets deploy IP over fiber. The capacity of such networks can be further expanded using DWDM. If desired, *Multiprotocol Label*

Switching (MPLS) can provide ATM-like quality of service (although some IP-over-fiber advocates would rather maintain excess bandwidth to accommodate the bursty nature of IP traffic than use a quality-of-service mechanism of any kind). High-speed routers decide which path the IP bits will take across the backbone.

Although optical internets, discussed in Chapter 4 (*Optical Internets*), use IP over fiber, they do require the use of a framing protocol. Choices include SONET framing or Ethernet framing. SONET framing can be used without expensive SONET equipment. Since optical internets often interface with Ethernet-based networks, Ethernet framing is often used with such networks.

TCP

Transmission Control Protocol (TCP) is deployed with IP-based networks. TCP guarantees end-to-end transmission of data. If a data link is congested, TCP begins retransmitting packets more slowly until the congestion clears. This feature of TCP is often called "layer 3 restoral" and is considered a viable alternative to SONET's protection bandwidth. IP routes around damaged nodes that might exist in the network. Combined with TCP's guaranteed packet delivery features, these features make *TCP/IP*-based optical networks a viable alternative to SONET and its protection bandwidth for environments where SONET is considered cost-prohibitive or overly complex.

MPLS

Label switching involves identifying and marking IP datagrams with labels and forwarding them to a modified switch or router, which then uses the labels to switch the datagrams through the network. The labels are created and assigned to IP datagrams based upon the information gathered from existing IP routing protocols.

Multiprotocol label switching (MPLS) applies label switching to large-scale networks and gives IP-based networks the fast switching capabilities of ATM and Frame Relay (FOLDOC 2001). MPLS is considered an important standard for allowing packet-switched TCP/IP networks to behave like circuit-switched networks for particular applications. If premium services are to be offered over optical networks, MPLS may be the technology deployed to ensure QoS for those applications.

Although MPLS is often associated with QoS, it is in fact more closely related to traffic engineering. IP standards such as Differentiated Services (Diffserv) provide more traditional quality-of-service and class-of-service features. MPLS sets up an explicit pathway while DiffServ provides a framework where certain types of traffic receive preferential treatment over other traffic. The two standards are complementary rather than competing. Because MPLS brings ATM-like functionality to IP, it is appropriate to deploy for IP-based optical networks when desired.

Network Layers

Network functionality is divided into layers, also referred to as *protocol stacks*. The seven-layer protocol model for Open Systems Interconnect, designed by the ISO (International Standards Organization), is often used as a reference for talking about networks. TCP/IP in fact has a four-layer model, as shown in Figure 2.1. First we will discuss optical network functionality in terms of the OSI model.

Each layer defines a function, not a protocol. For example, there are many applications and many application protocols at the application layer (OSI) or application services layer (TCP/IP).

Each layer passes information down to the next layer. It is only at the physical layer that data is transmitted to another networked system, then passed back up through the protocol stack on that system where it is then processed.

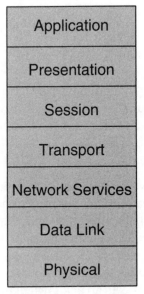
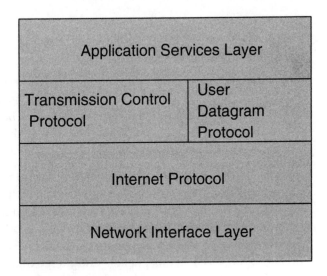

Figure 2.1   OSI and TCP/IP protocol stacks.

The Application Layer

The Application layer provides specific services, like file transfer or Web applications. The application layer takes data and converts it into a format understood by the receiving system, then hands it off to the Presentation layer.

The Presentation Layer

The Presentation layer deals with the form of the data. For the most part, TCP/IP applications handle the functions of both the application layer and the presentation layer. MIME, used for e-mail attachments, is an example of data formatting that could be thought of as taking place at the Presentation layer. The Presentation layer also handles data that is compressed or encrypted.

The Session Layer

The next layer down is the Session layer, which maps the connection between applications on remote systems. This layer captures user passwords, turning off the local echo so that when you type a password, it isn't displayed. All the data accumulated so far, referred to as the Protocol Data Unit, is now handed down to the Transport layer. (One note of difference for TCP/IP: The mapping of the connection between applications under TCP/IP occurs at the Transport layer instead of the Session layer.)

The Transport Layer

The Transport layer is the first layer that is truly thought of as part of the network. It's the job of the Transport layer to guarantee end-to-end delivery of data. Circuit-switched networks, like ATM-based networks or the telephone network, establish an end-to-end path for data to travel. For a voice call, it's the path between you (the caller) and the person you're calling.

TCP/IP is, by contrast, a store-and-forward network. There is no predetermined path for data to follow (although MPLS can provide this functionality). Under TCP/IP, each message is divided into packets which are then sent over the network. The Transport layer, then, is particularly important for TCP/IP-based applications. Applications that require a guaranteed delivery of packets use TCP. TCP sends packets and then expects to receive an acknowledgment. If the packet isn't received, TCP resends it until it gets an acknowledgment.

The protocol monitors for congestion and, if it finds congestion, starts retransmitting packets at a lower rate of speed until the congestion clears.

The other Transport layer protocol used on the Internet is the User Datagram Protocol. Applications that do not require the overhead of TCP—or the guarantees it offers—use UDP instead. UDP is often used for applications that value delivery speed above precision, such as streaming media where timely delivery of packets is more critical than acknowledgment of each packet of information.

The Network Layer

The next layer down is the Network layer, which handles addressing and delivering the data. Internet Protocol works at the Network layer. The Network layer handles both connection-oriented and connectionless protocols.

With a connection-oriented protocol, like ATM or frame relay, for example, only the first packet has the complete address. That packet blazes its way across the network. All subsequent packets have the address of the virtual circuit, the pathway created by that first packet. Every packet will follow the same route.

IP-based data is connectionless. Each packet has the full address and, depending on how the network is working at the time, each packet may take a slightly different route to its destination. At that point the data is reassembled in the proper order.

Routing protocols come in at the Network layer.

The Data Link Layer

Error-checking is the next step in the processing of data in the protocol stack, and this is handled in the Data Link layer, at least in protocols like ATM and frame relay. The packet is framed and error checked at this level. TCP/IP typically doesn't use Data Link layer protocols.

The Physical Layer

The lowest layer in the protocol stack is the Physical layer. Here at last is where transmission protocols like SONET, Ethernet, T-1 and DSL come into play. DWDM is also implemented at the Physical layer.

Although brief, this discussion of network layers may help you understand how data is passed down through the protocol stack. On the receiving system, data is handed back up through the layers until it reaches the application layer there. For more details on how particular networking protocols work, see the resources cited in Appendix A.

Security

Unlike copper, the non-conductive nature of optical fiber makes remote detection of a signal being transmitted within the cable impossible. Copper wire emits radiation that allows for signals to be intercepted, permitting eavesdropping without physical access to the medium. The only way to detect a signal in an optical network is to access the optical fiber itself—requiring intervention that would certainly be detected by a surveillance system. Built-in security makes fiber attractive to government, banks, and any industry with major security concerns.

Network Design

Network design is an important consideration to control costs and ensure an error-free, reliable system. You will need to consider initial and future network usage to determine how much fiber to lay and how to deploy it. Design of fiber optic networks is a book unto itself: See, for example, *Fiber-Optic Communication Systems* by Govind Agrawal (Wiley, 1997). Without going into too much detail, common topologies include the following (see Figure 2.2a–d):

Point to point. Used to interconnect two points (like a main university campus and a branch campus).

Ring. As in SONET, used for multipoint connections and where redundancy is needed (four fiber rings are deployed, with only two active at a time).

Tree. Each fiber site connects to its nearest adjacent partner using a point-to-point link. Tree topologies are cheaper than ring, yet more flexible than point to point.

Star (or hub and spoke). A more resilient topology than tree, in which all remote sites connect directly to a single central hub site.

Mesh. Mesh improves on point-to-point topology by providing each node with a dedicated connection to every other node.

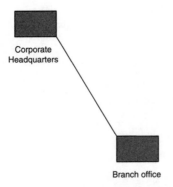

Figure 2.2a   Point-to-point topology.

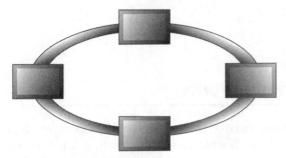

Figure 2.2b   Ring topology.

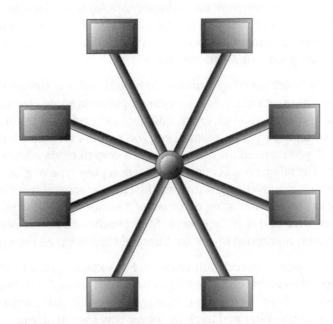

Figure 2.2c   Star topology.

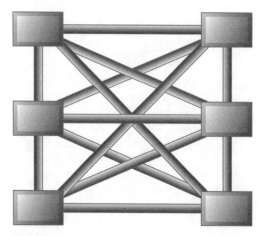

Figure 2.2d   Mesh topology.

How Optical Networking Works

In optical networking, data is carried at the speed of light (slowed slightly according to the medium through which it is being carried, whether air, glass, or plastic). In most cases, the light pulses are carried over hair-thin optical fibers. In wireless optical networking, described in Chapter 6, *Optical Networking and the Corporate Network*, lasers beam data from one building to another through the air. Data carried on fiber, however, is the most common method by far, and its deployment ranges from office buildings to the backbone networks of the telecommunications giants.

The light in optical networking is not ordinary light, but highly concentrated laser light. The fiber, although glass, is not ordinary glass (in some cases, plastic is used in place of glass, but it can carry data only over relatively short distances). If you beam light through regular glass, you would find that it loses a lot of its strength. The glass used for fiber optics is a very pure glass with a high silica content. The silica core is coated with a less pure type of glass called *cladding,* which guides the light toward the core, keeping it from escaping. On top of this is a polymer coating that makes it easier to handle the fiber and protects it from wear and tear. Of course, fiber bundles do not consist of just one strand of fiber; numerous fibers are bundled together (see Figure 2.3).

Along each fiber, light pulses encode information. For example, on a fiber carrying data at 1 Gbps, the lasers flash one billion times per second, sending pulses of data down the fiber. Fibers are typically deployed in pairs, with data traveling one way over one fiber and back the other way over another.

Regeneration

Optical signals eventually weaken through a process called attenuation. According to fiber optic expert Jeff Hecht, "Light signals traveling through even the most transparent optical fibers fade to undetectable levels after a couple hundred kilometers." (1999b) Because of attenuation and the need to route data, light signals must periodically be translated into electronic format and then back into optical form, a process known as *regeneration*. The signal is regenerated at its original strength and sent back on its way.

Compared to data traveling at the blazing speed of light across fiber, the conversion from optical to electrical and back again slows down data considerably; further, it takes what could be a pure optical network and requires building repeater huts with controlled environments and power requirements. Research is ongoing about how to reduce if not eliminate this conversion; see Chapter 8, *The Outlook for Optical Networking*, for details on all-optical networking.

Erbium to the Rescue

The periodic conversion of data from light back into electronic format helps routers direct it to its destination and network operators monitor it when necessary. What if there is a long-haul network and no routing is needed between segments? Can the problem of attenuation be dealt with without requiring electronic regeneration?

An element called erbium is used to amplify the signal, strengthening it and allowing it to remain in optical format. Light of a certain frequency meets the erbium molecules, which get excited and generate more light of that frequency. These amplifiers are called Erbium Doped Fiber Amplifiers (EDFA),

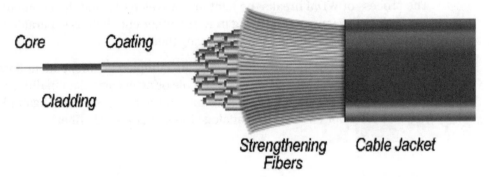

Figure 2.3 Structure of a fiber optic cable.

Copyright 2000. Courtesy of University of Oregon *Computing Center News*.

and they have been instrumental in enabling another innovation in optical net-working: *wavelength division multiplexing (WDM)*. EDFAs allow for signals to be amplified without breaking them out and regenerating them separately, a particularly important feature for WDM, discussed next.

Dense Wavelength Division Multiplexing (DWDM)

Fiber's inherent capacity, as discussed in Chapter 1, *The Optical Networking Revolution*, is phenomenal. Even so, much of the research in this area has attempted to squeeze yet more data through a single strand of fiber optic cable.

The greatest breakthrough in this area is WDM. With WDM, light is separated into various frequencies (or colors, if you think in terms of a prism). Each of these frequencies can carry the same amount of data that the fiber as a whole did, multiplying its capacity and improving the network's flexibility. In the mid-1990s, carriers broke the light into four wavelengths and then into eight. At this point (eight wavelengths or more), it is called *dense* wavelength division multiplexing (DWDM). Soon 16 wavelengths became available, with Ciena offering the first commercial system in 1996. Now 64- and 80-channel systems are fairly common for carrier deployment and in the laboratories. Further, each channel is capable of carrying more data. So a fiber with 40 wavelengths that can each carry 10 Gbps has a throughput of 400 Gbps. Nortel introduced a system in summer 2001 that can carry 6400 Gbps, 16 times the 400 Gbps throughput.

To multiply fiber throughput, you need only add DWDM equipment. Because EDFAs amplify data of a given wavelength or frequency without having to break out the frequencies separately (demultiplex them), they have also been instrumental in enabling DWDM.

The process of WDM breaks the light into wavelengths and then combines it into a single stream, multiplexing it. At the other end, light is separated back into discrete wavelengths (demultiplexing them).

It is important to note that wavelengths are completely independent data streams. They can carry different protocols or even carry data in different directions. WDM makes it possible to mix traffic types, such as Gigabit Ethernet, SONET, fiber channel, and analog video, over a single fiber.

Perhaps even more important than WDM's ability to multiply fiber's capacity (after all, how many organizations are running into capacity problems with fiber?) is the flexibility it offers. Because there are multiple paths through the fiber, courtesy of the wavelengths generated by WDM, carriers have more flexibility in connecting sites. For example, suppose that two sites want to exchange traffic in a VPN directly, bypassing other sites on the same fiber network. To do this apart from WDM would require the use of a different, dedicated connection. With WDM this can be achieved using a different wavelength.

Dense wavelength division multiplexing has breathed new life into existing fiber and expanded the capacity of new fiber deployments as well. It is as though a two-lane highway had been transformed to efficiently carry thousands of lanes of traffic, and the number of lanes keep expanding. Commuters would appreciate it if scientists could take these breakthroughs and apply them to the traffic problems in metropolitan areas. At any rate, DWDM, with the flexibility it offers to create different routes from a single fiber and its ability to multiply fiber's capacity, has caused the cost of transmitting data over optical networks to drop precipitously. Organizations with legacy fiber, such as telcos, have seen the most important impact from these advances. However, it must be noted that not all existing fiber can benefit from DWDM; some legacy fiber cannot handle DWDM because of limitations in the fiber's optical window.

Coarse Wavelength Division Multiplexing (CWDM)

Dense wavelength division multiplexing and the EDFAs that help enable it in the long-haul are expensive technologies. What if you want to multiply the capacity of fiber over a shorter distance? Are there cheaper alternatives?

The answer is *Coarse Wavelength Division Multiplexing (CWDM)*, sometimes called Wide Wavelength Division Multiplexing. This technology packs fewer wavelengths into its spectrum with greater space between them (see Figure 2.4). Because it requires less rigid tolerances, it is cheaper and more effective for multiplying the capacity of fiber over shorter distances. It also typically doesn't work with EDFAs. If the need to exploit the capacity of fiber is sufficient or distances are longer, at a certain point it makes economic sense to invest in DWDM and EDFAs.

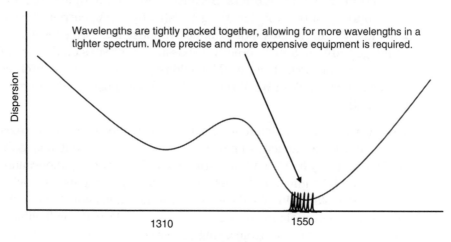

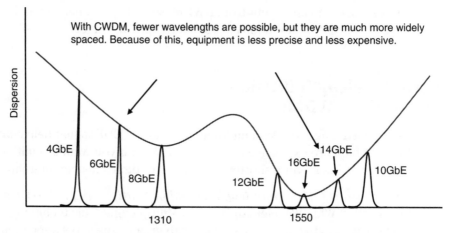

Figure 2.4   DWDM versus CWDM.
Copyright 2000. Courtesy of CANARIE.

Conclusion

With a bit of background under our belts about how optical networks operate, we now turn to the application of optical networks in the real world. Optical networks have spread from telcos outward to cities, corporations, and homes. Chapter 3, *Optical Networking and Telcos*, discusses the deployment of optical networks by carriers.

CHAPTER 3

Optical Networking and Telcos

N ot surprisingly, telecommunications companies (telcos) represent the largest users of optical networking. In 1982, MCI (now WorldCom) was an early adopter of more efficient but then-experimental single-mode fiber, using it for its network. Two years later, in 1984 Sprint deployed the first nationwide fiber optic network using single-mode fiber. AT&T, which had planned to use the older multimode style of fiber, followed suit.

To date, optical innovations follow this trend. Backbone networks, which have the greatest need to expand capacity, adopt new technology first and it spreads outward to the network edge over time. This dispersion has happened with single-mode fiber, DWDM, and is currently in the very early stages with all-optical components that reduce the need for electronic regeneration. Since optical networking innovations have generally helped squeeze more and more bandwidth out of existing fiber, telcos, as the biggest users of such networks, stand to gain greatly from these improvements.

Given the high demand from telcos and other long-haul providers for increased bandwidth, it is not surprising that the biggest pipes are expected to see the fastest growth. Darryl Schoolar of Cahners In-Stat Group in Scottsdale, Arizona states that OC-192s will see a compound annual growth rate of 27 percent between now and 2004. The next size down, OC-48 lines, will see an even faster growth rate: 46 percent for the same time period (Cope 2001).

In addition to efficiency gains from deploying the fastest optical technologies, competition also drives telcos' adoption of optical networks. There's a race on to see which telco has the fastest network, and breakthroughs are regularly heralded in press releases. Since optical networking is an increasingly popular topic, telcos also boast about their implementation of the latest and greatest optical technology.

There are many players in the world of telecommunications, including access network providers, many different levels of carriers, and, of course, customers. In order to understand how telcos are using fiber, and the direction of future services and technologies, it is important to describe the participants, beginning with carriers.

Telecommunications Companies

Carrier in simple terms refers to a company that provides telephone and data communications between points in a state or in one or more countries. In this section we will talk about telecom providers, including ILECs, CLECs, IXCs, global carriers, and emerging carriers.

Incumbent Local Exchange Carriers (ILECs)

Some background on the telecommunications industry may help explain the confusing distinctions between carriers in the United States. In 1983, AT&T gave up an anti-trust fight with the U.S. government by agreeing to relinquish control of its monopoly on local telephone service. It retained rights to the then-lucrative long distance business, but local business was split up among the Bell operating companies (BOCs), which were grouped into holding companies collectively known as the *regional Bell operating companies (RBOCs)*.

After a few years, the RBOCs asked the Federal Communications Commission (FCC) for the right to enter the long distance market. The Telecommunications Act of 1996 gave RBOCs a piece of the long distance business on the contingency that they allow other companies to compete for local phone service. An *incumbent local exchange carrier (ILEC)* is a telephone company in the United States that was providing local service when the Telecommunications Act of 1996 was enacted.

A local exchange refers to the local central office of a carrier. Lines from homes and businesses terminate at a local exchange. Local exchanges connect to other local exchanges within a local access and transport area (LATA) or to interexchange carriers (IXCs) such as long-distance carriers AT&T, WorldCom, and Sprint.

ILECs include Verizon, SBC Communications, BellSouth, Altell, and Broadwing. In many cases the ILECs own the local facilities and a certain amount of existing fiber. Rather than building out their networks themselves, however, they may lease fiber from dark fiber providers such as Metromedia Fiber Network. Regardless of whether they own or lease their local loop infrastructure, ILECs have control over who uses it and can charge competitive local exchange carriers (CLECs) to gain access to it.

Broadwing is an example of a company that operates both as an ILEC and as an emerging carrier with a nationwide fiber infrastructure. Broadwing was formed by the merger of fiber company IXC Communications and Cincinnati Bell. It provides local phone service to over one million customers in the Cincinnati area.

Competitive Local Exchange Carriers (CLECs)

After the passage of the Telecommunications Act of 1996, which forced ILECs to open their local loop networks, competitors could provide services to end-users. At least, it was the intention of the legislation to foster competition. Actual progress in the area of local loop competition has been considerably less impressive.

Where local loops have been opened, competitive local exchange carriers (CLECs) often collocate their equipment in the central office facilities and use existing local loops to deliver services. They pay ILECs for this privilege. In some cases, the prices charged by ILECs make it difficult for CLECs to offer competitive pricing to end-customers.

The Association for Local Telecommunications Services (ALTS) reports that there were about 375 CLECs as of February 2000 which provided 10.4 million access lines, up from 5.5 million in 1998. A few include WinStar, Teligent, and Nextlink. NextLink uses both its own fiber lines and fixed wireless to provide diversified broadband services to customers. The company has fiber optic networks in 49 U.S. cities and offers everything from local and long-distance phone service, to high-speed Internet access and Web-hosting (Rugaber 2001).

Although many CLECs use ILEC wireline facilities for their last-mile connections, WinStar and Teligent use fixed wireless equipment to provide broadband telecom services to businesses. By placing hubs and dish antennas on building roofs to transmit their signals, these companies can provide services while circumventing the last-mile issue. However, the fact that wireless companies are considered CLECs makes it somewhat difficult to tell where competition for traditional wireline local phone service (or data services) is really in place. Additionally, many ISPs have registered as CLECs but in fact are still not able to provide services.

Five years after the passage of the Telecom Act, the FCC reported in May 2001 that the number of phone lines served by CLECs had grown 93 percent in

2000. CLECs now service 16.4 million U.S. phone lines, 8.5 percent of the 194 million lines in the country (FCC 2001).

CLECs still gain access to ILEC infrastructure only with difficulty, but ILECs aren't the only roadblocks to competitive access. According to ALTS president John Windhausen Jr., " . . . building owners often resist competitors' requests to provide broadband wireless and wireline services to commercial tenants and apartment-dwelling families. Finally, many cities make competitors' lives miserable by imposing franchise fees and onerous regulations that are unnecessary and anticompetitive" (Guerra 2001).

CLECs are also involved in providing DSL as well as local telephone service. This may involve three parties: the CLEC, the ISP, and the ILEC that controls the local loop. The CLEC installs the necessary equipment in the ILEC's *central office (CO)*. Then the CLEC wholesales the DSL access to an ISP, which in turn markets the service to home and business users. Conflict often ensues. According to Jerry Sullivan, president and CEO of Kite Networks: "The CLECs' and ISPs' DSL business cases are dependent on the good graces of a potentially hostile competitor, namely the RBOC, which will also, in most cases, be marketing its own version of DSL service to the end-user. For anyone to believe that this arrangement will end positively for all parties involved can often require a large leap of faith" (Sullivan 2001). Sullivan believes that the slow rate of DSL rollout is attributable not only to problems with the technology, such as its distance sensitivity, but to these complex and conflicting relationships among DSL providers.

InterExchange Carriers (IXCs)

Interexchange carriers in the United States are long-distance providers; they tend to have established international networks and are the single largest consumers of fiber optic infrastructures. Because of their extensive use of optical networking, we focus especially on them in this section. Although IXC is a more precise term, the main telecommunications providers are often referred to simply as telcos. We'll use that term in the following discussion.

Telcos face the unenviable task of being all things to all people. They offer a wide array of products and services, including plain old telephone service (POTS), wireless, optical connections, data services, broadband, and even e-commerce consulting. The demand for these products varies tremendously. The demand for POTS is relatively flat, growing at a very slow pace. Meanwhile the demand for traditional data products such as frame relay and ATM has exploded, growing at 100 percent per year, according to AT&T. Given the disparity in these growth rates, it is not surprising that the proportion of data traffic overtook voice traffic over the public telephone network in 1999.

Data Services

According to Gary Smith, CEO of Ciena, the burgeoning demand for data services has left telcos struggling to keep up with the demand: "With voice traffic, you can linearly anticipate the growth, year on year. It's a statistical forecast. And all of a sudden, all of this data comes along which scales at a frightening pace, wants huge amounts of bandwidth, and is very unpredictable. So you've got a fundamental shift taking place." Smith continues with his perception of how the telcos are struggling to meet the demand for data services: "If you go into a lot of these carrier sites, what they've got is a load of Post-It notes with all the numbers, and they have to wander around with them to be sure these cables are plugged in the right place. A lot of it is cobbled together and it has to be because of the explosive growth. You're using voice architecture to cobble together the huge demand of data. And it was never designed for it" (Wolinsky 2000).

The increased demand for data services is partly reflected in the delays to get private lines. According to the Yankee Group, it took an average of 60 to 90 days to provision an OC-3 line in 1998 but by 2000 it took 180 to 240 days. Delays vary considerably depending on the area of the United States and the relative demand there.

Legacy Infrastructure

Telcos need to support a variety of services to meet all their customers' needs. Although they are generally eager to adopt new technology that improves the efficiency of existing networks, they are hampered by their legacy infrastructure. As AT&T's Dado Vrsalovic quipped in a 1999 article in the *Industry Standard*, "God made the world in six days and rested on the seventh day, but that was only because he didn't have an installed base. I cannot stop the world and start from the beginning. I would like to, but I'd be without revenue for the year" (Krause 1999). The telcos' need to depreciate very expensive equipment over 20 years or more means that although IXCs are big, they can not always be agile in deploying new technologies. Although upstart carriers such as Global Crossing and Enron have built innovative optical internets, telcos can not follow suit by abandoning their existing infrastructure to build a network from scratch.

Trend toward IP-Based Backbones

Long distance, the traditional bread-and-butter of telcos, is a failing industry in the United States. Although we can respectably describe demand as flat, the real picture is even worse. Telcos are in a difficult position because they must refocus their business on providing data services. Demand, as mentioned earlier, is strongest for IP services. Vorhees, New Jersey-based analyst firm CIMI predicts that the demand for IP data services will grow from 25 percent of all data services to 87 percent by 2010 (Williamson 2001). For this reason, telcos are increasing their support for IP. For the most part, however, they are still using ATM to provide sufficient QoS for voice calls.

Since the demand for voice is so low, telcos increasingly want to move business voice traffic to their IP-based networks. It is the desire that telcos have to consolidate, rather than a demand from business, that is generally driving any movement toward voice and data convergence. Telcos are making it possible to run traffic over existing data lines using existing PBX equipment and stress the positive features of VoIP, such as the ability to plug and unplug phones and have them register automatically without any reconfiguration of PBX equipment. Telcos may ultimately have to offer corporate incentives to nudge companies to merge their voice and data infrastructures. Read *Converged Networks and Services* by Igor Faynberg, et al. (Wiley 2000), for an in-depth look at the technologies and business issues surrounding convergence of the PSTN and the Internet.

To continue our examination of how the telcos are deploying optical networking, we'll first take a look at what the established carriers are doing, including AT&T, Sprint, and WorldCom. Then we'll look at emerging carriers and their use of fiber optic technology.

AT&T

AT&T is the original telco, the grandfather of them all. The company has been through many transformations, from its government-mandated breakup in 1983 to its current divestiture into four separate companies, a process not expected to be complete until 2002. AT&T's CEO, C. Michael Armstrong, is forthcoming about the rationale behind this move. When asked, "Why break up AT&T?" Armstrong replied, "To understand that, first you have to understand that in 1997 82 percent of our business was long distance and it was going to go away" (Rosenbush 2001). Few people understand the evaporation of the long-distance market and the fact that carriers now have to diversify in order to continue to make a profit. In particular, carriers must move away from an emphasis on traditional voice and move toward wireless and data, which is comprising more and more of the company's traffic. AT&T's fiber optic network is ever-expanding. As of June 2001, 98 percent of the company's traffic travels over fiber optic cable; the remainder travels via microwave, radio, and frame relay. The company has some 61,000 route miles of fiber in the continental United States. Some 45,000 miles of that is long-haul fiber in the network's backbone while the other 16,000 route miles handle metro or local services which extend into 71 major markets.

AT&T's IP-based network was acquired from IBM in 1998 and had been called (up to that point) the IBM Global Network. In January 2001, AT&T announced a coast-to-coast optical IP backbone running at OC-192. With throughput of 10 Gbps, the network quadruples the capacity of the previous backbone. The network connects Boston, Chicago, Los Angeles, New York, St. Louis, and San Francisco (see Figure 3.1). Most of AT&T's backbone runs at OC-48, although it is capable of OC-192 when the demand warrants it.

In addition to this infrastructure, the company is in the second year of a two-year build of what it refers to as its "next generation network." This new network runs an additional 16,500 route miles, much of it overlaying existing routes. The $1 billion investment will first be deployed in 30 major metro areas, which the company predicts will generate 80 percent of the demand for high-bandwidth services. This network uses the latest generation of single-mode fiber, with more than 300 strands per cable. It handles OC-192 and will handle OC-768 as that standard becomes finalized and demand warrants its deployment.

In terms of Wave Division Multiplexing, as of June 2001, the company is deploying 64 to 80 channels. Some segments of the network are using more wavelengths than others, depending on the demand, according to Thomas

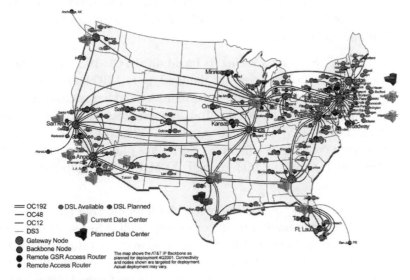

Figure 3.1   AT&T's IP network.

Copyright 2001. Reprinted with permission of AT&T.

Afferton, AT&T's District Manager of Advanced Transport Technology and Architecture Planning. Later in 2001, the company will be deploying WDM systems capable of handling 160 wavelengths.

In terms of architecture, AT&T is migrating its network toward IP, partly in response to the phenomenal growth in IP traffic. IP is the company's fastest growing segment of traffic, with a steady growth of 200 percent per year. Other data traffic, such as frame relay and ATM, are growing at 60 percent per year. Voice traffic, although it is growing, sees a very modest annual increase of 5 to 6 percent.

IP runs over SONET in a form referred to as Packet over SONET. The company has substantial investment in SONET equipment and has no plans to retire it. In the metro area, AT&T can interface Gigabit Ethernet services with SONET and allow that traffic to be carried seamlessly across its existing network.

The division of AT&T into four business units is unlikely to affect any of this very much. AT&T Network Services, which runs the network, will have contractual relationships with each new business unit and each of the units will run traffic over AT&T's existing network.

Sprint

Sprint had its beginnings in 1899, when it was known as the Brown Telephone Company in Abilene, Kansas. In 1984, Sprint deployed the United States' first nationwide fiber optic network (see Figure 3.2). The company played a role in the Internet before its commercialization when, in 1991, it managed the link between the U.S. backbone NSFNET and research and education networks in Europe and elsewhere.

Like AT&T, Sprint is moving its backbone to OC-192. According to Bob Azzi, vice-president of engineering, demand for OC-192 has occurred only recently (Brown 2000). Some customers are interested in purchasing OC-12 lines and a few are interested in OC-48s. Today much of its backbone runs at OC-48, using Packet over SONET in some cases and ATM over SONET in others. DWDM is deployed on Sprint's backbone. Sprint has plans to increase its backbone speed to 40 Gbps by 2002. Using DWDM, this throughput could be increased to 3.2 Tbps.

Sprint has been conducting research on its Internet backbone routers to find out whether its backbone is performing well. After sampling routers for three years, it found out that its backbone is operating with a great deal of excess capacity and that there are no significant delays in the backbone routers sampled. According to Sprint's distinguished scientist of traffic monitoring, Christophe Didiot, "The idea is to keep the network simple and robust with complexity at the edges and the fastest possible backbone. . . . So to

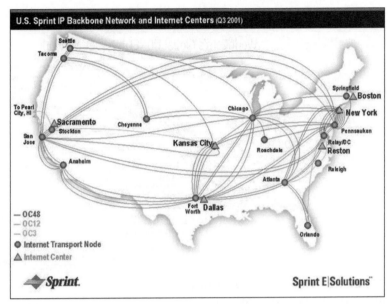

Figure 3.2   Sprint's Internet network.

Copyright 2001. Courtesy of *Broadband Week.*

make it a highly efficient network, what we have to do is overprovision the backbone. In fact we don't use more than 50 percent of the links, but this is not because we don't have customers. It's because we want the network like this" (Brown 2001).

WorldCom

A third major U.S. telecom player is WorldCom, based in Clinton, Mississippi. WorldCom invests about $8 billion per year in its network, which provides services in 20 countries. The network includes some 48,000 miles of fiber optic cable in North America, including connections to 100 cities and 35,000 office buildings. In Europe, WorldCom has some 7,000 miles of fiber. (See Figure 3.3.)

As with the other telcos, the voice business for WorldCom is receding. In 2000 some 28 percent of the company's business was POTS, and its annual rate of decline is 6 to 8 percent. Its market for data services is growing at 40 percent per year and is projected to reach $66 billion by 2003. The company's market for Internet services is growing at 60 percent annually, for a total of $56 billion in the same timeframe (Shaff 2000).

Because of declining growth in traditional telephony, the company announced plans in June 2001 to divest into two separate companies: MCI Group, which handles consumer and small business telephone and Internet access services,

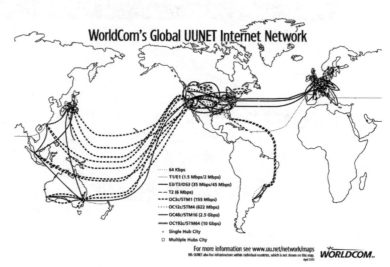

Figure 3.3   WorldCom network map.

Copyright 2001. Courtesy of WorldCom.

and the WorldCom Group, which handles the meat of the company's data and Internet business as well as corporate telephony.

Although MCI was forced to divest its Internet backbone when it merged with WorldCom in 1998 (the backbone was sold to Cable & Wireless), it still owns an important Internet service provider, UUnet. The UUnet backbone runs at OC-192 and parts of its network are architected as an optical internet, described further in Chapter 4.

WorldCom is also actively working with new optical technologies. In March 2001, the company worked with Siemens to create a throughput of 3.2 Tbps over a single fiber with 80 wavelengths, each running at 40 Gbps.

Emerging Carriers

Emerging carriers face a different set of challenges from established telcos. Telcos bear the weight of a legacy infrastructure and the requirement that they provide a wide range of services while emerging or upstart carriers are unfettered by the past. They build shining new networks using the latest technologies and can often offer their services for less as a result. But new, especially in a volatile market, is not always good. The sheer number of upstart carriers indicates that the market will see further consolidation, and companies purchasing data services from these carriers today may well wonder what the future holds for them. Upstart carriers lack the solid customer base that the telcos have and they lack "mindshare." For many of these carriers, it will be a struggle to survive.

There are indications, however, that the emerging carriers are gaining ground, particularly in terms of fiber optic infrastructure used for long-distance services. According to research from Robertson Stephens, in 1996, 72 percent of the long-distance fiber optic infrastructure was deployed by Sprint, AT&T, and MCI. In 1999, their proportion dropped to 30 percent, with newer carriers such as Qwest and Williams making up 29 percent of the fiber and utilities deploying 16 percent.

The new technology, lower prices, and new services that these carriers offer prove quite attractive to certain market segments. For example, although telcos continue to sell bandwidth in terms of traditional leased line increments (T-1, T-3, OC-3, and so on), some of the emerging carriers, such as Yipes, offer more flexible products, allowing bandwidth to be purchased in 1 Mbps increments and to be augmented on demand.

Who are the customers of upstart carriers? In some cases, such as Global Crossing and Williams, they are carriers' carriers, selling their services to others in their field. In other cases, such as Yipes and Broadwing, they sell services directly to companies, developers, and ISPs (which could be considered another class of carrier themselves). Problems can arise, however, if a company mixes this model by selling both to carriers and to end customers because by selling to end customers they wind up competing with their other customers, the carriers.

This section briefly summarizes some of the best-known upstart carriers and their deployment of optical networking technologies. In some cases, the new carriers offer innovative products and services that the telcos will eventually offer as well. In others, the new carriers represent leaner organizations with newer technologies and compete on that basis.

Qwest Communications

Qwest was founded in 1996. Using old railroad grades for right-of-ways, Qwest built a 25,500-mile long IP-based fiber optic network while helping other carriers build similar networks. Qwest installed two conduits in most parts of its network. Qwest, as well as other carriers, is using the first conduit while the second conduit is reserved for future use.

Qwest's backbone network runs at OC-192 nationwide, the only carrier with its backbone currently running at that speed from end to end. The Abilene backbone, an Internet2 backbone network providing nationwide high-performance networking capabilities for more than 180 Internet2 universities in the US and

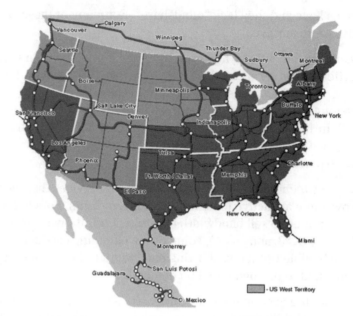

Figure 3.4 Qwest network map.

Copyright 2001. Courtesy of Qwest.

Puerto Rico, is provisioned from Qwest's network. The Abilene backbone is an OC-48 connection running over Qwest's OC-192 backbone.

Qwest is similar to a legacy telco in some respects. It uses Nortel DMS 250 voice switches, just like the mainstream telcos do. And its core infrastructure is SONET-based. Although at first the company offered VOIP in the form of its Q.talk plan, it now offers traditional circuit-switched telephony in addition to a variety of data services. Qwest is moving towards advanced services in several areas. In 2002, Qwest is installing next- generation switches instead of additional DMS 250s. Among other things, this will enable Qwest to carry packet-based voice traffic. The carrier is moving into wavelengths as well: its Qwave product allows customers to purchase dedicated 2.5 Gbps and 10 Gbps wavelengths.

In June 2000, Qwest purchased an RBOC, U S WEST, adding its 40,400-mile PSTN network to its stables. (As an ILEC, Qwest may not provide interLATA service originating in any of the company's 14-state local-service region until Section 271 approvals are gained.) KPNQwest, Qwest's European joint venture with Dutch telecom company KPN, is building a high-capacity, European fiber optic network that spans 12,500 miles. Once this is complete, Qwest will have 113,000 network miles around the world.

Qwest is also moving into the metro market with an initiative called Qwest Local Broadband. Qwest will work with established metro players in some areas and install fiber rings in others to provide voice and data services.

Qwest Local Broadband, currently in 24 of 27 major metro markets in the US (all of which are outside of its 14-state local service territory), will offer DSL and fixed wireless as well as fiber optic connections.

Williams Communications

Although Qwest has built its fiber-optic network on railroad grades, Williams Communications built its network using decommissioned pipelines, providing a natural conduit for cable. The pipeline idea isn't surprising given that its parent company, Williams, has been in the oil and gas pipeline business for more than 80 years and is the largest volume transporter of natural gas in the United States.

Williams Communications is hard to classify as a new carrier since it is as old as the deregulation of the telephone industry. It is definitely an upstart, however.

In 1985, Williams started laying fiber optic cable in its pipelines. In 1994, its WilTel subsidiary was one of the top 4 providers of high-capacity data and one of the top 5 providers of long-distance services. In January 1995, Williams sold its WilTel subsidiary to LDDS, which eventually became part of WorldCom. In the process, it sold all but 9700 route miles of its fiber. However, it reentered the business in 1998 and now has more than 33,000 route miles of fiber, the fourth largest fiber optic network in the United States. It has capacity on TAT-14, the newest of the transatlantic cables and recently completed an IP-based OC-48 network that runs Packet over SONET.

Williams sells exclusively to carriers, such as ISPs and others. In terms of innovative services, Williams allows customers to lease wavelengths on its

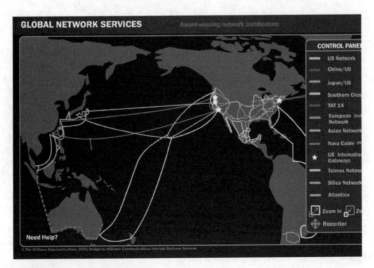

Figure 3.5 Williams network map.

Copyright 2001. Courtesy of Williams Communications Group.

DWDM network and is in the process of offering software-based provisioning. Because of its wealth of bandwidth, Williams is also involved in live broadcasts through its Vyvx service. Williams carries live broadcasts of media and sports events as well as being a business-to-business video broadcast provider. The service carries 65 percent of all live broadcasts and 80 percent of all professional football, baseball, basketball, and hockey broadcasts.

Broadwing

Broadwing is an upstart carrier that was created from the merger of telco Cincinnati Bell and IXC Communications, a fiber optic provider. The company has some 18,500 route miles of fiber, with three main rings. Each optical switch is connected to three fiber routes, ensuring a highly reliable mesh topology.

Broadwing has been working with all-optical, or should we say *more* optical, networking. On its long-haul DWDM circuits, the company claims that it can send a signal for 3200 to 4000 kilometers without regeneration. The company built an all-optical interoperability lab in September 2000.

Broadwing's backbone runs at OC-48. According to the company, it was the first to offer 10 Gbps optical wavelength service. The company offers a range

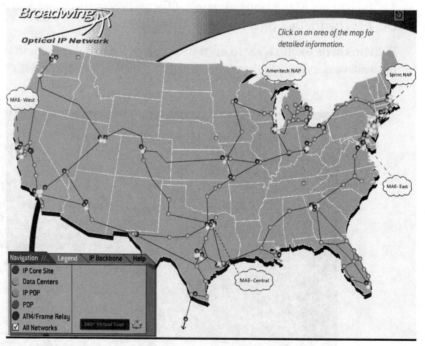

Figure 3.6   Broadwing network map.

Copyright 2001. Courtesy of Broadwing.

of data, voice, and consulting services to its clients in 137 of the top 150 metropolitan areas.

Global Carriers

Although several of the IXCs have international networks, global carriers are more focused on international operations than they are on providing services in any one country. Level3, 360Networks, Cable & Wireless, and Global Crossing all fall into this category.

Global Crossing

Global Crossing, based in Hamilton, Bermuda, has been laying fiber worldwide since it purchased optical internet carrier Frontier in 1999. The company completed its core network in June 2001. It has 101,000 route miles worldwide on five continents, covering 27 countries and with connectivity into 200 cities. Global Crossing exchanges traffic with many other networks through private peering as well as having points-of-presence (POPs) at all major Internet exchange points. It is a truly international optical network. Because of its international character, Global Crossing has a great deal of undersea fiber, an important investment. Unlike dark fiber, undersea fiber requires an upfront investment in all electronic and optical components.

Global Crossing is a carrier's carrier, but it also sells to end customers such as the British government, for which it will deploy a private network linking the nation's 240 embassies worldwide. Actually, 135 will be linked via fiber optic cable while the remaining 105 will require satellite links, which are good for difficult-to-reach locations or places too remote for fiber optic cable to be cost-effectively deployed.

Like Qwest, Global Crossing is involved in next-generation network research. Global Crossing partnered with the National Science Foundation and Internet2 to build AmPATH, a network that rings South America and provides connectivity to U.S. research networks in Miami.

International Telecom Companies

So far, our discussion of telcos and fiber has focused largely on U.S.-based companies. But telcos in other countries are having a substantial impact on world markets for fiber, including Deutsche Telecom, France Telecom, British Telecom, Telefonica (Spain), KPN in the Netherlands, Telia in Sweden, and NTT in Japan.

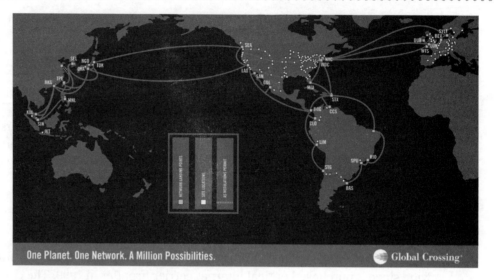

Figure 3.7 Global Crossing's network.
Copyright 2001. Courtesy of Global Crossing.

Deutsche Telecom (DT) is building out its fiber optic network with help from Global Crossing, leasing dark fiber from that company's Pan European Crossing network. DT is building an international fiber optic network called T-GlobeNet that will ultimately link 90 cities in 40 countries. The company's Internet service, T-Online, is the largest online service in Europe, with 8.3 million customers. DT also purchases dark fiber and wavelengths from 360Networks.

NTT not only deploys fiber optic infrastructure throughout that country but is also focused on various areas of fiber optic research. NTT is also active in deploying fiber to the home (FTTH) in Japan.

Sweden's Telia recently purchased some of the U.S. assets of a major backbone provider, AGIS. But Telia already had its own fiber optic network, with 200 points of presence in 45 countries around the world. Telia's fiber optic deployment also played a role in developing Sweden's advanced fiber optic infrastructure. The company has several public peering points in the United States and is in the process of upgrading its backbone from OC-12 to OC-48 speeds; the network is capable of OC-192 speeds.

Conclusion

Telcos and other carriers are important customers for optical networking vendors. Because of their economies of scale, they are the most likely to experi-

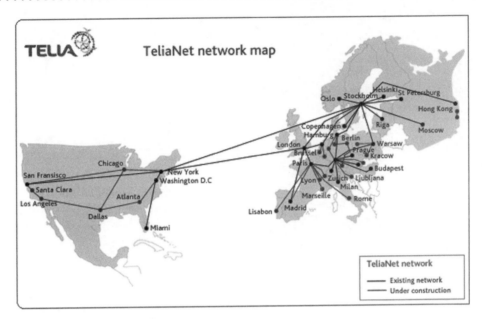

Figure 3.8   Telia's Fiber Optic Network.

Copyright 2001. Courtesy of Telia.

ment with the latest optical networking technologies. All-optical networking, largely a future trend discussed in Chapter 8, "The Outlook for Optical Networking," will come to the carriers' long-haul networks before it reaches other optical networking market segments.

Despite their scale, which allows for innovation, carriers with a significant amount of legacy equipment find themselves unable to move quickly into new markets and new ways of doing business. Telcos are only with difficulty offering bandwidth-on-demand, a feature offered routinely by the metro providers discussed in Chapter 6, "Optical Networking and the Corporate Network."

The burgeoning demand for data means that telcos whose primary market a few years ago was voice traffic have had to completely switch gears. Whether they can do so successfully will largely determine how well they can adapt to this rapidly changing marketplace. Chapter 4, "Optical Internets," examines optical internets, an architecture built from the ground up to handle data rather than voice traffic.

CHAPTER 4

Optical Internets

Optical internets represent a radical architecture. Rather than using traditional physical layer services such as ATM or SONET, optical internets run IP directly over fiber. Such networks are also referred to as All-IP networks or IP/DWDM networks. By running IP directly over fiber, optical internets gain incredible efficiency and significantly reduce costs.

Although some consider optical internets to be an experimental architecture, they are already being deployed. Canada's advanced Internet research organization, CANARIE, deployed the first optical internet, CA*net3, in 1998. Other organizations with optical internets either deployed or in the planning stages include Sprint, Frontier, Global Center, Enron, Teleglobe, Cogent, and Hermes. The popularity of Gigabit Ethernet, discussed briefly in this chapter and in more detail in Chapter 6, "Optical Networking and the Corporate Network," has made optical internets even more prevalent. In many ways, optical internets are the precursors of the optical Ethernet architecture.

Sri Nathan, vice-president of network architecture at Qtera Corp. in Boca Raton, Florida defines an optical internet in this way: "A true optical Internet will link the service layer to the transport or photonic layer without any intervening device or layer whatsoever. In this model, the transport of data packets is done over a purely photonic backbone" (Matsumoto 2001). It directly connects the network link layer, in the form of dedicated wavelengths, to a high-speed router.

Note that although optical internets eliminate the cost and overhead of running SONET and ATM, they are not all-optical networks in the sense of using only all-optical components. In fact, to reduce costs, they are likely for the foreseeable future to continue to rely on electrical regeneration.

Why an Optical Internet?

The primary motivator for deploying optical internets is the cost savings and the efficiency of such networks. For new network deployments, optical internets yield capital cost savings of 50 to 90 percent when compared with SONET or IP/ATM/SONET networks. Their operating costs are approximately 60 percent less. In part the savings comes from eliminating expensive SONET equipment; a SONET add-drop multiplexor (ADM) for a backbone network can cost $1 million.

The impressive cost savings of optical internets is rivaled by their efficiency. Optical internets carry IP-based traffic. Most networks to date are designed to carry voice traffic. By matching the network design to the traffic type, new efficiencies can be realized.

The most fundamental difference between IP-based networks and voice networks is that IP-based networks are packet-switched and connectionless. Their characteristics are quite different from connection-oriented voice networks. Packet-switched networks divide traffic into packets which are routed across the network by devices called routers. A single message may consist of many packets, and in transmission, different packets may take different routes through the network.

A second difference between IP traffic and voice traffic is the size of the data transmitted. Voice traffic is fixed in size but IP transmissions may be of any size at all. A computer may send a great deal of IP traffic or it may send none. On voice networks, each call consumes the same amount of bandwidth: approximately 64 Kbps for the length of the call. These calls are aggregated (or multiplexed) into a single data stream. The local exchange traffic (which is aggregated voice traffic) is then multiplexed into intercity loops and finally onto national backbones. Once a link is saturated with all the 64-KB voice calls it can handle, you get the familiar Mother's Day message that "all circuits are busy." A voice call is a circuit, connecting you directly to the other party for the length of the call. IP does not set up circuits but sends packets across the network. The design of a connectionless network is fundamentally different from a connection-oriented network such as the Public Switched Telephone Network (PSTN).

Despite these differences, most IP traffic rides across the telephone network. This traffic flow creates needless inefficiencies. As we have seen, voice traffic is predictable. We know how much bandwidth a single phone call will consume and can plan accordingly. By contrast, IP traffic is often described as "bursty." (See Figure 4.1.) Any computer can use as much bandwidth as it needs at any time. Surprisingly, however, if you look at patterns of IP traffic, it appears to follow certain patterns and is therefore described as "self-similar." So IP traffic in general uses a certain amount of bandwidth and then there are bursts of greater bandwidth usage.

What happens when a network link gets congested during such bursts? If there is not enough bandwidth, TCP/IP itself is designed to handle these conditions. All computers on the congested line begin resending packets at a slower rate until the congestion has cleared. Computers will not get an "all circuits are busy" message from the Internet in general. It is true, however, that particular Web sites can be overwhelmed with traffic and thereby paralyzed when undergoing either a legitimate traffic surge (a good response to a Super-Bowl ad) or a denial-of-service attack. But that still wouldn't keep users from reaching other Web sites during such times.

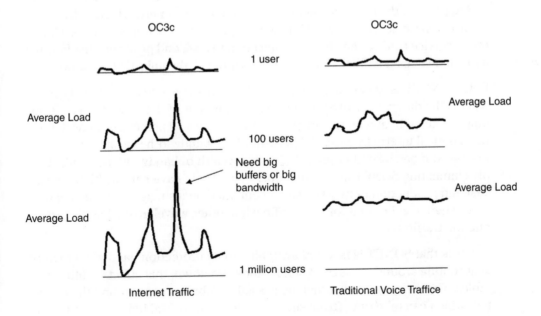

Figure 4.1   Internet traffic is bursty.

Optical internets generally handle bandwidth overload by having so much bandwidth available that bursts are not a significant problem. If the links are ever saturated, the network can simply fall back on TCP/IP's own built-in congestion handling. But that is not often the case. For example, Cogent's optical internet's average load is 10 percent of capacity, leaving considerable room for any sudden bursts of traffic. By having bandwidth to spare, IP traffic's bursty patterns can be easily accommodated.

Why SONET Is Inefficient for IP Traffic

As a technology designed for voice networks, SONET has design principles that do not fit IP traffic well. SONET retains fully half of its bandwidth for emergencies. If there's a cut in one fiber ring, a second ring stands ready and can be brought online in just 50 milliseconds. Most of the time, therefore, half of the bandwidth in a SONET ring is idle. By eliminating SONET, optical internets immediately gain 50 percent more bandwidth. If a problem occurs, such as a fiber cut (called a "backhoe fade" because such cuts are often the result of construction accidents), IP is designed to route around damage. It is not a ring architecture; rather, it offers any-to-any connections. One of the design principles of the Internet was to allow it to survive a nuclear war which could destroy perhaps half of the network's nodes. One often hears of network providers going down for several hours. Although the providers' customers are certainly out of service (unless they have a connection to a second provider), the Internet as a whole does not break down. It "routes around" the links that are down.

Both SONET-based networks and optical internets have excess capacity. So what is the difference? In SONET's case, 50 percent of the bandwidth is never tapped except in an emergency (and then the other 50 percent is unavailable). In an optical internet's case, 100 percent of the bandwidth is available *if it's needed*. But because fiber provides such a wealth of bandwidth by itself, simply eliminating SONET means that optical internets have bandwidth to burn. Test and production networks can be combined on a single fiber; a dedicated wavelength can be used for test traffic while other wavelengths handle production traffic.

It is true that SONET is faster at switching to its protection bandwidth than IP is at routing around damage. When IP nodes go down, this affects routing tables. These changes must then be passed to other routers around the Internet, which can take time (from several minutes to several hours depending on how strategically the router is situated).

IP Traffic Is Not Symmetrical Like Phone Traffic

In a telephone conversation, I talk and you talk back (or at least we both have the capability to talk). Even if all conversations are not the ideal of perfect give-and-take (we've all had that experience), telephone traffic is clearly symmetrical, and information sent and information received are generally assumed to be equal.

Nothing could be further from the truth with IP traffic. It is asymmetrical and, depending on where you are in the network, the transmit (or Tx) traffic could exceed the receive (or Rx) traffic by a factor of 16 to 1, particularly close to Web server farms. On the other hand, nearer to end users, receive traffic greatly exceeds transmit traffic; the asymmetrical pipes offered by DSL and cable modems seem more like true broadband to end users as a result of this traffic pattern. If IP networks sit on top of symmetrical phone networks, one link will be congested while the other is significantly underused.

Although most networks assume symmetry of traffic, optical internets have an opportunity to be more efficient. Since traffic patterns at any given point in the network tend to be similar over time, a network administrator with knowledge of the local pattern could set up an optimal proportion of send wavelengths to receive wavelengths. In this way, even more bandwidth efficiency is gained. Although custom-configuring wavelengths for sending and receiving is not possible with today's equipment, the ability to optimize the network for the local traffic patterns could provide further bandwidth efficiencies for optical internets in the future.

Owning Your Own Fiber — Being Your Own Carrier

Optical internets in many cases represent an important paradigm shift. Traditionally, organizations buy service from larger carriers. Even ISPs typically do not build their own networks. But optical internets require new deployments. One of the best ways to get the cost advantage is to lay your own fiber and build your own network. Alternatively, dark fiber can be leased and lit. And with Gigabit Ethernet, described in Chapter 6, providers are beginning to offer service on optical internets. Frankly, SONET equipment is simply too expensive for building out infrastructure when there are alternatives like Gigabit Ethernet available.

Customer-owned fiber is an important revolution. Although in the United States we typically look at telephone lines as public utilities, there is no question when we get a bill for service that someone else owns the infrastructure. Optical networking in general, and optical internets in particular, put owning the infrastructure within reach for many types of organizations. Rather than leasing a line between branch offices, one could own the fiber that connects them and, beyond installation and maintenance, not pay anyone for that service. As more providers adopt the optical internet approach, it is possible to purchase service from them. But the importance of customer-owned fiber—and its ultimate impact on telcos—cannot be underestimated. Chapter 5, "Optical Networking and Urban Planning," explores this concept in more detail.

More Flexible for Customers

It is less expensive and less trouble to hook up sites to optical internets than to connect them to a SONET-based network. Although a SONET network must break out a circuit for a customer using SONET equipment at a central office (CO), an optical internet can break out a circuit where it is most convenient, using a Gigabit Ethernet or 10-Gigabit Ethernet switch. This points out a fundamental architectural difference between optical internets and more traditional optical networks; optical networks are generally built using traditional telecommunications equipment whereas optical internets function far more like high-speed LANs. This LAN similarity is another key to the network's cost savings.

Architecture of an Optical Internet

With foundational concepts in place, it is appropriate now to examine the architecture of an optical internet. It is possible to incorporate SONET or ATM, but the following basic architecture does not use either.

The simplest—and most efficient—optical internet will run fiber between 10-Gigabit Ethernet switches and high-speed routers. Regeneration, if the network is large enough to require it, is handled using electronic transponders. It can be difficult to find transponders that are not designed for SONET, although this is becoming less of a problem over time.

Using Gigabit Ethernet is not as efficient as SONET in one respect. Ethernet places 8 bits in a 10-bit block, which ultimately accounts for a greater than 25 percent inefficiency in the network, according to Bill St. Arnaud, Senior Director of Network Projects at CANARIE. 10-Gigabit Ethernet was specifically designed to work with DWDM networks, so it addresses this efficiency problem.

Using Ethernet as a basis for an optical internet is an interesting approach. Whether you're dealing with a nationwide backbone (as in Cogent's case) or a metropolitan area network, the same technology that is used on the LAN can be extended to the larger network. Given the increasing speed of LAN technologies, what was once unthinkable has become an emerging practice. When George Gilder predicted that Ethernet would kill ATM, Ethernet's inventor, Bob Metcalfe, balked. However, this is one case where Metcalfe, who is famous for literally eating his words about such things as an Internet meltdown, really did change his tune. Ethernet is a viable technology for the larger network infrastructure.

Ethernet offers efficiencies, too. Rather than remapping packets to SONET or ATM, packets can be transmitted as they were originally packaged by their hosts. New locations can be easily bridged by using LAN technologies rather than requiring more sophisticated connections with traditional telecom networks.

Ultimately, optical internet architecture calls for an asymmetric traffic flow that matches (roughly) the typical flow of traffic. Optical equipment cannot handle such a data flow, as it was engineered for the symmetrical data flows of voice networks. Instead, these efficiencies are being explored on test networks such as CA*net3. For now, this experimentation consists of turning off some lasers in order to create an asymmetrical flow, clearly an undesirable approach for production networks. Ultimately, equipment that allows for the direction of wavelengths to be configured to match the asymmetric patterns of traffic flow is needed. Such equipment is not available today.

Disadvantages of Optical Internets

Despite their efficiencies, optical internets have drawbacks as well. For one thing, optical internets typically carry only IP traffic, although optical internet designers such as Bill St. Arnaud state that other types of traffic (SONET or ATM) could be carried on dedicated wavelengths if desired and if the investment in equipment for handling those technologies was made. There is no reason that an optical internet couldn't carry other types of traffic in addition to IP, if desired.

Another disadvantage is that optical internets must handle service disruptions by another method. While SONET offers protection bandwidth and a 50-ms switchover, optical internets cannot compete. IP will route around damage and as such has its own protections. MPLS, which promises a 50-ms (or faster) switchover rivaling SONET, is an emerging standard, but some analysts question whether it will not be as difficult to implement as ATM itself. Although MPLS offers competitive capabilities for an IP network, it also shares ATM's complexity. Currently, optical internets such as Cogent's use Layer 3 restoration techniques to provide a switchover of 1 minute or less.

Optical internets do not offer the same class-of-service capabilities that ATM does. But with the rich bandwidth of an optical internet, class of service is not needed, since each application has all the bandwidth it needs. If service level guarantees are needed, customers can be assigned dedicated wavelengths to ensure that their traffic will not compete with anyone else's.

For conservative network designers, perhaps one of the biggest disadvantages of optical internets is their experimental nature. This is becoming less of a problem as optical internets gain a track record of their own. CA*net3 is obviously a success, and commercial providers such as Cogent and Yipes are beginning to take a lead in the field, taking full advantage of the economic and efficiency advantages that optical internets offer to provide customers with LAN-speed Internet access far more cheaply than traditional carriers can.

Case Study: Canada's Leading-Edge Research Network: CA*net3

Although there are research networks around the world, including Internet2 in the United States, none is as innovatively designed as Canada's CA*net3. Although most research networks use some part of an existing network, CA*net3 was built from scratch as an optical internet. For example, Internet2 is provisioned from Qwest's network under a five-year agreement. Although Internet2 has a great deal of bandwidth, there is no real innovation in the network's design. This is where CA*net3 differs considerably.

CA*net3 is a true optical internet, running IP over DWDM. There is no SONET and no ATM (although SONET is used for framing, this requires no SONET equipment or overhead). Optical amplifiers are placed every 50 km with regenerators every 2500 km. At the regeneration point, wavelengths can be broken out and connected to a high-speed router. All the optical equipment comes from Nortel and Cisco routers are used. When CA*net3 was deployed, it was difficult to find equipment that didn't rely on SONET. Nortel and Cisco engineers had to work together onsite at CANARIE to interface their products directly rather than using SONET equipment as an intermediary.

Bill St. Arnaud, Senior Director of Network Projects for CANARIE, conceptualized CA*net3. CANARIE had already deployed a research network called CA*net2, but the organization realized that provisioning an existing network did not build on Canada's strengths in optical networking. A research network could not only offer research into new applications by providing universities with high-speed connectivity, but it could also research new network designs in cooperation with Canadian optical vendors.

CANARIE, the research consortium that funds CA*net3, partnered with several vendors in order to build the network. Bell Nexxia, a subsidiary of Bell Canada, manages the infrastructure for CA*net3's primary route, a provision that will change with CA*net4 because in practice, CANARIE has found that it can see network problems before its carrier partner does. Further, Bell Canada uses traditional SONET equipment that it adds on to the network, so in effect, Bell Canada has only half of the wavelengths available since it retains the remaining half for protection bandwidth. CANARIE utilizes all its available wavelengths with CA*net3.

Deployed in 1998, CA*net3 is the first nationwide optical internet. At the time CA*net3 was deployed, several other companies were experimenting with the architecture. Michael O'Dell, then at UUnet but now Director of V-One, was also working with optical internet trials in sections of that ISP's network.

The government of Canada has been generous in funding CA*net3 and now plans are underway for CA*net4, which will be an optical internet that is wholly owned by the Canadian government. CA*net4 will experiment with massive peering with other ISPs, allowing the government to save about 50 percent of its Internet access costs.

Case Study: Stan Hanks's Work In Optical Internets

Stan Hanks has seen the Internet go through many changes. When he started working on the Internet's predecessor, the ARPANET, the network encompassed just 64 hosts. Hanks now operates a consultancy called Network Mercenaries, where he advises venture capitalists and startups about next-generation networking tools and technologies.

Hanks calls optical internets "IP on glass": "The 'IP on glass' catch-phrase clearly describes this architecture, which allows IP bits to be placed directly on fiber for high-speed transport to their destination. This eliminates intermediate protocols, simplifies the architecture, lowers costs, increases reliability and reduces errors" (Hanks 1999). Hanks began experimenting with optical internets at MFS Communications in 1991. MFS concentrated on building metropolitan area networks, and Hanks was working with encapsulating Ethernet frames in IP datagrams using the generic routing encapsulation (GRE) protocol, which he was instrumental in developing. A company with two locations in New York City wanted to get a leased line between its LANs. Hanks attempted to sell them a point-to-point Ethernet solution, saying "Think of it as an extension cord for your Ethernet." But the concept of metro Ethernet, which is coming into its own some

continues

continued

10 years later, was too novel, and the company didn't accept it. But Hanks continued to work with running IP directly over fiber, running TCP/IP across multiple FDDI rings. Hanks also engaged in pilot projects to interconnect metro areas using DS3s. However, since no one else was doing this at the time, he faced the same difficulties mentioned by Bill St. Arnaud; the equipment wasn't available to do what he wanted to do.

Hanks continued his work with optical internets when he joined Enron Communications in 1993. They wanted to "prove that you can run big networks on nothing but packets and glass, so to speak." Enron was in the process of building a network that could handle real-time broadcast quality transmissions over a long-haul optical internet.

Creating such a network could be approached in two ways: either build it or use existing fiber from other companies. Enron took the second approach. Rather than build all the network infrastructure itself, the company built routes that no one else wanted to—understandably so, if you consider that these routes went over the Rocky Mountains, over the Sierras, and through the Everglades. With these routes in its pocket, Enron could trade with carriers for capacity on routes it didn't own. The company began deploying the network in 1998 with a sizeable portion up by 1999. Enron's network encompasses more than 20,000 route miles of fiber.

While Bill St. Arnaud views excess capacity as an alternative to quality of service (QoS) measures, Hanks has a different philosophy. Particularly since Enron's vision is the delivery of real-time broadcasts over its network, Hanks used MPLS to create ATM-like functionality for its optical internet, allowing for virtual circuits to be created across the network. Hanks sees these QoS measures as fundamentally important, working from the assumption that dropping so much as a packet is never acceptable. To date, only MPLS, which effectively makes a TCP/IP connection work like a circuit-style connection, employs this assumption. DiffServ (which, incidentally can be used complementarily with MPLS) works on the premise that it is acceptable to drop packets occasionally. With MPLS, network managers set up label switch paths (LSPs) and monitor the load on them to see if additional links need to be brought online.

Other innovations that Hanks was involved with at Enron included the development of a methodology and software to permit forward scheduling of bandwidth over the company's optical internet. Using this approach, the company could commit that it would have a particular amount of bandwidth available on the following Tuesday and intelligently make that commitment to the customer. If requested capacity was already committed, the company would be aware of it and turn the customer away.

Hanks also helped bring the idea of the commoditization of bandwidth to Enron, a topic discussed further in Chapter 8, "The Outlook for Optical Networking." Hanks felt that contracts for communications services took too long to negotiate and once negotiations were complete, there was no penalty if the service wasn't delivered on time. By standardizing elements of the contract, as is the case with commodities trading, deals could be done far more quickly. Further, the party supplying the bandwidth would have to supply it on time or face the penalties stated in the contract. Enron already had experience in commodities trading and a balance sheet to execute the plan.

The groundwork of people like Hanks, St. Arnaud, and others in developing optical internets created a framework for a new type of optical networks without the overhead of SONET. Without their work, optical Ethernets, further discussed in Chapters 5 and 6, would not be such an important trend in optical networking today.

Conclusion

Optical internets yield unparalleled efficiencies for handling IP-based traffic. This architecture, rather than SONET, is driving the most exciting advances in optical networking today, including municipal optical networks, described in Chapter 5, and corporate optical networks, described in Chapter 6.

Optical Networking and Urban Planning

C ities are in a strategic position to create a leading-edge infrastructure that will drive economic growth, encourage competition for telecommunications services, and reduce the costs of those services. The term *information superhighway* was so overused a few years ago that even a mention could cause audible groaning. Despite the worn-out metaphor, thinking of networks as essential infrastructure has merit. Cities and towns can attract businesses in part based on their networking capabilities. Just as roads and public utilities provide needed infrastructure, so does broadband network access. As Chicago's Mayor Daley says, companies locating or expanding in Chicago "are always asking about the type of telecommunications infrastructure that's available" (Cope 2000a).

Chicago has committed to a 10-year investment in its network infrastructure, a project known as CivicNet. Dr. Joel Mambretti, director of the International Center for Advanced Internet Research at Northwestern University and chairman of Chicago's Request for Information Subcommittee, put it this way: "For any city economy to be successful in the 21st century, they absolutely have to have modern digital communications. Asking if any other cities would do what Chicago is doing is like asking if any other city should have a telephone system in the 1950s or a power system" (Metannikov 2001). Communications infrastructure is just as important as other essential utilities like roads, power lines, sewers, and telephones. And Chicago is far from alone in recognizing this requirement.

Cities Compete for Business

When publishing firm Total TV Network considered a move from Plano, Texas, to Durango, Colorado, the move was derailed when the company discovered it could not get T-1 lines in Durango. The city's lack of bandwidth turned away two other firms as well in 2001. An investment in infrastructure can drive city growth, just as lack of infrastructure can limit growth.

The metro market for optical networking is a popular topic these days as carriers attempt to serve corporations in urban areas. This chapter focuses specifically on municipalities of all sizes and their use of fiber to create a leading-edge infrastructure that will stimulate economic growth, provide unlimited bandwidth for government and schools, and potentially become a new source of revenue. It is clear that bandwidth can stimulate growth, but the central question is, who should deploy, control, and maintain the fiber?

Fiber Deployment: Carriers versus Municipalities

Fiber-based metropolitan area networks are nothing new. Many original metropolitan area networks (MANs) were deployed by telcos and are old enough now that they need to be upgraded or replaced. However, technology advances and lower costs are shifting the balance of economics and power from carriers to cities.

New MAN Technologies

MANs today use a Gigabit Optical Ethernet architecture or even 10-Gigabit Ethernet, which makes their throughput comparable to OC-192. This is the basic fiber throughput before you consider breaking the light into wavelengths using CWDM. If you combine a 16-wavelength CWDM system with 10-Gigabit Ethernet, the throughput would be 160 Gbps. And unlike the telcos' expensive optical networks that use DWDM and SONET, these MANs are inexpensive to deploy, with a payback of two to five years. Optical Ethernet is 10 times less expensive than SONET.

In addition, new MANs are more like traditional LANs—requiring few special skills to operate. This makes new optical MANs perfect for organizations like governments and school districts to deploy.

Clearly, fiber has become cheaper to deploy and easier to manage. What else is driving municipalities to deploy their own MANs rather than leaving it to carriers? Two considerations are the disruptions caused from fiber installations by multiple carriers and vendor lock-in.

Tearing Up the Streets

The problem with fiber is not that no one wants to install it, at least in larger cities. The problem is that there are so many carriers as a result of the deregulation from the Telecommunications Act of 1996 that many, many companies are looking to dig up city streets and lay fiber. According to KMI Corp.'s research, some 85 million miles of fiber were installed in the United States between 1980 and 2000. The impact of the Telecom Act, however, is dramatically illustrated when you consider that more than two-thirds of that fiber was installed after 1996. In the year 2000 alone, some 33 million miles of fiber were installed.

This profusion of fiber installations has put pressure on cities, and in some cases cities are imposing strict regulations in response. In Washington, D.C., an ambulance was stuck in a traffic jam caused by carriers trenching fiber. As a result of the incident, Washington declared a temporary halt to all fiber optic construction, even for carriers with jobs in progress. The U.S. capitol now limits trenching on certain streets to twice in five years. Plans must be filed with the city two years in advance of trenching. Many other municipalities have declared moratoriums or restrictions on fiber builds. Not only do fiber builds disrupt traffic patterns, but they reduce the life of the roads. If a roadway is cut, its useful life is cut in half. Subsequent cuts follow the same pattern, halving the life of the street again. No wonder cities are reacting strongly—and reluctantly—to myriad requests for trenching fiber. In response, cities may take one of three approaches: becoming a roadblock to fiber deployment through restrictive regulations, creating their own network to obviate the need for additional fiber deployments, or coordinating the efforts of various carriers to attempt to minimize street disruption from fiber installations.

Vendor Lock-In

Networks have traditionally been built by carriers. The problem with this scenario is that it obviates competition. If carriers build the infrastructure and provide the service across it, those who use the network are essentially captive to the vendors; no other vendor can afford to duplicate that infrastructure. The U.S. approach to date has been to force incumbent carriers to open their networks to other service providers, but this is problematic as well. It creates disincentives for the incumbents, who are left with no competitive reason to upgrade their networks; further, the incumbents who do open their networks then charge their competitors higher prices and may take measures to ensure that their service is superior (for example, giving routing preference to their own network traffic). If a given carrier is the only one providing a service, there are additional risks; in the ever-changing telecom market, providers in business today may go out of business tomorrow.

Consider what happened when DSL provider NorthPoint Communications was sold to AT&T in March 2001—without its customer base and without any warning for existing DSL customers. A hundred thousand customers—primarily businesses—lost their broadband service overnight. For people like Jan Kalandra, owner of four New York City hotels, the loss of broadband access resulted in a significant loss of business, estimated at $2,000 to $3,000 per week as business guests would go elsewhere upon finding out that the hotels' broadband services were out. It can take six weeks or longer to get a new DSL connection, leaving these customers in the lurch. Such is the problem with vendor lock-in.

So what is the solution for municipalities who need an optical network infrastructure to attract business, but want to avoid disruptions and vendor lock-in? Lay your own dark fiber. By installing an open-access fiber bundle with many strands, cities can lay fiber once and provide many carriers with access to the fiber, which in turn creates a competitive environment. In most cases, cities own the rights-of-way, making them likely candidates for either installing open-access fiber or encouraging its installation. If fiber is trenched at all—and there are technological alternatives to trenching—the job is done once to create an infrastructure for both the private and public sector's use.

Dark Fiber

What is *dark fiber*? Building a new optical network entails installing fiber, usually far in excess of the capacity immediately needed. Because many of these fiber strands won't be used for a while (and thus will not be lit with lasers so that they carry data), such installations are referred to as dark fiber.

Dark fiber is flexible. It can be lit using any technology, depending on the carrier's and customer's needs. Fiber has a lifespan of at least 20 years, unlike other telecommunications technologies; fiber installed 20 years ago is still useful today. The components that light the fiber are what change.

Since installation represents a high proportion of the costs of deploying a fiber optic network, it makes sense to overbuild, installing more fiber than there is an anticipated need for. The cost differential is very small between installing a 96-strand fiber bundle and installing a 144-strand fiber bundle. The more potential capacity, the more potential users of the network can be accommodated.

The company that installs the fiber also maintains it. In addition to the initial capital cost of the fiber installation, an annual maintenance fee is paid, typically about 5 percent of the capital cost of the fiber. Technically, the installer owns the fiber, but the groups installing it purchase an indefeasible right of use (IRU) on the fiber for 20 years on average. This IRU is considered an asset rather than a service. It can be sold, traded, or leased. It can also be depreciated as an asset over 20 years, providing a far greater tax advantage than traditional telecom services.

Advantages of Dark Fiber

What advantages does dark fiber offer for municipalities? The advantages include both economic and technological benefits. We'll also explore the drawbacks to this approach.

Economic Benefits

Deploying dark fiber provides numerous economic benefits, including providing a new revenue stream, attracting private sector economic development, and offering competitive prices for telecommunications services.

Recouping Costs through Leasing

Depending on the business model used, the costs of laying fiber may be recouped through leasing it to businesses, institutions, carriers, and ISPs. This provides an important, ongoing secondary revenue stream other than taxes. There is some controversy about this approach, since it arguably puts cities in the telecommunications business. Depending on local regulations, some jurisdictions may restrict cities from leasing fiber to others.

Attracting New Business

Leading edge network infrastructure can draw businesses to large cities, but it can also be used by smaller municipalities to attract businesses. While at one time it was important that businesses locate in an urban area, e-business has changed this requirement. The location of bandwidth is more important in some cases than the traditional urban geography of the past. Smaller cities with a leading-edge infrastructure can offer competitive pricing for offices and housing and a higher quality of life than many urban areas, allowing these regions to attract more businesses. Quality of life is in part determined by the quality of schools, libraries, hospitals, city-owned utilities, and emergency services such as police and firefighter responsiveness. By implementing a fiber optic network for these institutions, they can all improve their technology-based service offerings and improve the quality of life in the city, creating further economic incentives for businesses to locate and expand there.

Cities Attract Business

Attracting new businesses and encouraging the expansion of existing businesses was a prime factor in the building of Dublink, a citywide network in Dublin, Ohio. Since the installation of Dublink, AirTouch Cellular has expanded its business in the city and several Fortune 500 companies have relocated there.

South Dundas, a small town near Ottawa with many commuters, expects its fiber optic network to attract 20 to 40 new jobs per year. The town also hopes to encourage telework. According to Tom Morrow, president of the South Dundas Chamber of Commerce, "We feel, as a chamber of commerce, the day has come where bandwidth and connectivity is as basic as a telephone line was a few years ago" (Pilieci 2000).

When Johnson & Johnson decided to build a WAN that would link all its plants, company officials looked skeptically at the plant located in Iroquois, Ontario. The plant was so remote that it would be cheaper to close the plant than to build out the WAN to reach it. When city officials heard of this, they decided to deploy a fiber optic infrastructure. Johnson & Johnson kept its plant there, and the area was able to attract other businesses as well.

Small towns can be revitalized by dark fiber installation. To start, by attracting businesses, small municipalities improve their tax base. Further, high-speed networks in schools can pave the way for upgrading the technology skills of the population and decreasing youth outmigration, which has affected so many towns adversely. Workers can use the infrastructure to telecommute, rather than commuting or relocating, allowing them to remain residents of the smaller town with its lower cost of living. Telemedicine over fiber networks can provide small-town hospitals with access to specialists in urban areas.

Encouraging Competition

Open-access fiber increases the competition among carriers, driving down bandwidth costs while simultaneously increasing bandwidth per user. Competition also provides greater security for customers; if one provider goes out of business, another can be easily procured. Competition results in a dramatic savings in telecommunications costs for both the public and private sector. Further, with a municipally owned infrastructure, the local loop costs are guaranteed to not increase over time, providing even greater advantages in the long term.

Owning the fiber changes the balance of power in relationships with carriers. If a carrier builds out to City Hall, for example, it is unlikely that another carrier, even one with lower prices, could afford to build that infrastructure a second time. Even if the carrier provides solid short-term incentives, similar to cellular providers who offer consumers a so-called free phone for signing a contract, in the long term, vendor lock-in is both risky and likely to backfire economically. The institution becomes, in essence, captive to the vendor.

The Economics of Fiber

Despite a false perception that fiber is expensive to deploy, prices have fallen significantly. The one-time cost of installing fiber is about $25,000 for a given facility, such as a school, or about $400 per month to lease it. An OC-3 connection to a school would cost between $3,000 and $6,000 per month, making the annual cost for such a connection more expensive than the one-time cost of the fiber, which can then be depreciated as an asset, providing tax advantages over telecommunication services (St. Arnaud 2001b, p. 5).

The typical return-on-investment for dark fiber occurs between one year and 18 months, though some installations can take as long as 3 to 5 years to recoup their initial investment. The Victoriaville school board in Quebec began laying fiber between schools in 1991 with a one-time capital cost of $2 to $7 per meter. The school board participated in several condominium fiber arrangements to obtain the needed fiber to connect all its schools. The effective cost for each school to have essentially unlimited bandwidth is $80 per month, which includes both the capital cost and the annual maintenance of the fiber.

Technological Benefits of Dark Fiber

Certainly the prime technological benefit of fiber is the bandwidth capacity it provides. DSL and cable modems are effectively stopgap measures, offering short-term quasi-broadband solutions. The capacity of a single fiber pair is some 600,000 voice circuits, compared with two for a phone line.

Fiber offers some other technological advantages. Unlike copper, it cannot be tapped easily. It can be strung 20 times farther than copper, allowing organizations to greatly reduce the number of wiring closets they use. Since fiber optic devices are largely passive, there are fewer electrical components to repair, another cost savings.

From WAN to LAN

Because of fiber's extremely high capacity, organizations can gain substantial economic and logistical benefits by decentralizing their networks. In the case of a school district, rather than having a LAN at each school, the LAN-like bandwidth of the fiber optic network makes it possible to move all servers to a central location, significantly easing administration. Backups can be handled centrally. LAN administration staff can be reduced, or at the very least travel costs between buildings can be saved, as all administration of servers can occur in-house. Using technologies such as Gigabit Ethernet or 10-Gigabit Ethernet, the familiar LAN technology is extended to the WAN, allowing organizations to capitalize on their existing LAN expertise. Again, Ethernet technologies and equipment cost far less than traditional SONET or ATM equipment, making them very attractive for such networks.

In addition to the benefits of centralized computing services, organizations can also aggregate their network traffic, allowing them to jointly pay for a single connection to an ISP rather than having each school connected separately. Although the example here discusses schools, concepts apply equally to municipal buildings (which are often spread across a town) or to any other organization's multiple locations. The city of Stockholm, Sweden, moved from having WAN links connecting locations to using fiber to recentralize the network and make it, in essence, one big LAN. The cost savings from recentralizing its network allowed it to pay for itself even more quickly than it otherwise would have.

Organizations that want to outsource some of their servers, particularly Web servers, find that a fiber optic network makes outsourcing even more attractive, because all servers can be reached at LAN-like speeds.

No Obsolescence

Although Ethernet technologies are attractive financially, dark fiber is actually technology-agnostic. It is simply a transmission medium. Any technology can be used to light the fiber. If an organization wants SONET or ATM, they can finance the equipment and add it to their fiber strands. The fiber itself does not need to be replaced as technology evolves, since it is just a conduit for light; only the components that determine the speed and capacity need to be changed.

Some argue that fiber optic infrastructure investment is foolhardy when communications technology is changing rapidly. In fact, fiber has only increased in capacity while solutions such as wireless are clearly limited to last-mile applications. It is a myth that wireless has anywhere near the capacity of fiber. According to Bill St. Arnaud of CANARIE, one strand of fiber can provide more bandwidth than all the satellite and wireless systems in Canada. Further, wireless often costs more to deploy than anticipated and doesn't have the lifespan that fiber offers. Meanwhile, since municipal fiber optic networks should pay for themselves over the course of five years or less, in the unlikely event that a new technology appears to make the network obsolete, it will have already paid for itself.

Explore New Applications

More bandwidth allows organizations to consider adopting new, bandwidth-intensive applications such as telemedicine and distance education. Cities and schools can experiment with videoconferencing or deploy VoIP. Especially in schools, which typically do not have phones in each classroom, the fiber optic network provides the ability to expand the phone system without costly private branch exchange (PBX) equipment while significantly reducing the school or municipality's existing phone costs.

Disadvantages of Dark Fiber

While fiber is a good investment, both economically and technologically, there are circumstances in which it doesn't make sense to deploy. Building a fiber optic network is a longer-range plan; it can take as long as two years to put such a network in place. Some ambitious networks take even longer. In the case of Chicago, the city is planning for a 10-year build so that the network will reach every area and every street in the city.

If a company is only renting or moves its location frequently, fiber is not a good investment. It works best for fixed institutions that do not anticipate moving after installing the infrastructure. Companies with small bandwidth needs, for example, less than 1 Mbps, that don't expect growth are also not good candidates for fiber. Despite the quick payback on fiber optic investments, it does not always make sense. If an organization cannot project a return on investment (ROI) in five years, fiber is probably not the best solution.

However, for municipalities, fiber installation is a choice that can empower economic growth and offer control over services. City networks tend to connect fixed locations, making them good candidates for fiber deployment.

Customer-Empowered Networking

So far, we've discussed dark fiber, and the benefits gained by cities that deploy their own fiber-based MANs. It is clear that we have reached a point in networking where it's no longer the best idea to allow carriers to own the infrastructure. What is the next step?

When municipalities own the cables that terminate at a carrier-neutral facility, it is called *customer-empowered networking*. There are several paradigms for achieving customer-empowered networking, but all make one fundamental change. The carrier no longer owns the infrastructure in the metro area and instead focuses on long-haul networks. With customer-empowered networking, multiple carriers are available, and switching carriers is a matter of changing a cable in a patch panel at the carrier-neutral facility where the local network terminates.

There are several models of customer-empowered networking that cities are using today. Before we start describing the models, it should be noted that these categories are not hard and fast; some deployments may mix elements of the models. The first model we will look at is *municipal fiber*.

Municipal Fiber

With municipal fiber, the city owns and deploys the network for its own use and the use of related institutions needing bandwidth, including schools, hospitals, and fire and police departments. With municipal fiber, the city owns the network. In some cases, depending on the regulations in the area in question, the city may be able to lease fiber to third parties, creating a new revenue stream that can pay for the investment in the network. Sometimes an accusation of the local government acting as a telco is leveled at proponents of this model. However, the government is not providing services, just a conduit for the services. The conduit can be thought of as a highway of sorts, and no one questions the right (or responsibility) of governments to provide roads that are accessible to all. The analogy does break down, however, because no governments lease roads specifically to certain groups or companies. As a result, municipal fiber builds are often built strictly to serve the bandwidth needs, present and future, of the government and related institutions. School districts or utilities may also build their own networks following this model.

Condominium Fiber

A second model is *condominium fiber*. In this model, numerous organizations join forces to install the citywide network with each organization bearing a portion of the cost and splitting up the maintenance fee, which applies to the whole fiber bundle, not to individual strands. This arrangement is very similar to what one finds with physical condominiums. Customers own a condo in the building and then share maintenance fees with all the other owners. In this case, rather than owning a housing unit, the customers own strands of fiber.

Those parties interested in building the network form a consortium. Consortium members get in on the ground level (before construction of the network) and thereby get preferential pricing, just as condominium units are less expensive when purchased before the building is complete than afterward.

Condominium fiber paves the way for a natural partnership between the public and private sectors. Various organizations may participate. However, it is important that one larger organization with substantial financial backing take the lead. This organization becomes the *anchor tenant*. In many cases, the municipality serves as the anchor tenant since the city has buildings to connect over a relatively large geographic area, from hospitals to schools to municipal buildings. The anchor tenant determines the topology of the network, taking into account the needs of all consortium members.

Open-Access Fiber

The third model, *open-access fiber*, takes yet another approach. It is usually driven by a municipality that recognizes the need for leading-edge infrastructure. The city offers the installer of the fiber access to rights-of-way to build the network. This is the approach Chicago has taken with CivicNet, but in that case the city has gone even further. The company (or, more likely, companies together) that win CivicNet's business will be awarded the city's telecommunications budget for a period of 10 years. In Chicago's case, this represents an annual budget of $32 million for 10 years for a total of $320 million. In addition to rights-of-way, the city has substantial underused fiber in place that can be used by the company or companies deploying the network. The city serves as an anchor tenant; other businesses will also be involved in the creation of CivicNet and certainly in its use. In the case of the province of Alberta and its high-speed SUPERNET, the province is providing all the assets that Chicago allocates to CivicNet (rights of way, telecom budget, and existing fiber) along with a one-time capital investment from the government. The province-wide scale of the project makes this investment necessary.

Some open-access fiber projects are corporate rather than city-driven. Companies sell municipalities on the idea of a fiber optic network, obtaining right-of-way permission. The companies then install and own the fiber, which they in turn lease to carriers and other enterprises. CityNet Telecommunications, based in Silver Spring, Maryland, follows this paradigm, as did the Fishel Company with its building of Dublink, a network for Dublin, Ohio.

CityNet can build fiber optic networks with a minimum of street disruption: It is the first U.S. company to deploy fiber optic networks in sewers. As part of its arrangement with the city, it offers a small share in the gross receipts of the network's profits, up to 2.5 percent. It uses robots to clean, inspect and prepare sewers for fiber optic deployment. Since sewers run throughout the city and into each building, they can serve as a natural conduit for data. CityNet's arrangement with the city also includes ongoing cleaning and inspection of city sewers throughout the life of the contract, typically a 25-year IRU. CityNet has deployed networks in Indianapolis, Albuquerque, and Omaha. For more information on CityNet's deployment methods, see Chapter 8, *The Outlook for Optical Networking*.

Other third parties, such as utility companies, may also become involved in fiber optic deployment. In Hamilton and Sudbury, Ontario, hydroelectric companies own and deploy open-access fiber optic networks.

In each of these arrangements, municipalities can be agents of change. But so can large corporations, utilities, or school systems. Table 5.1 summarizes the differences between these models of customer-empowered networking.

Whether or not cities enjoy direct economic benefits from the deployment of dark fiber, it makes sense for them to be instrumental in the deployment of a city-wide fiber optic network. For one thing, cities can play a key role by coordinating the interests of carriers and local businesses who will lease the fiber. And, of course, cities have a great interest in local economic development, which fiber optic networks play a strategic role in stimulating.

Even cities that choose not to take a central role in deploying or encouraging the deployment of dark fiber can still facilitate the use of fiber by insisting that any street repair include installation of conduit for fiber. As a good example of proactive city planning, San Diego used geographic information systems (GIS) to map all the fiber in the city, including information about what buildings are fibered and what carriers serve those buildings. In this way, the city serves as a clearinghouse for information about city networks (even though it doesn't centrally control them).

Carrier-Neutral Exchanges

Having the MAN terminate at a carrier-neutral exchange (also known as a carrier-neutral hotel or sometimes a collocation facility) provides the maximum flexibility for those who own the network. This concept came from research institutes and universities, which would meet at GigaPoPs, neutral telecom facilities with links to multiple carriers.

Carriers (and some fiber installers) may offer to build out the infrastructure on behalf of their customers. But, this commits the city to doing business with the carrier who creates the infrastructure. Few other providers can afford to compete if they have to duplicate existing infrastructure. Customer-empowered networking relies on the concept of a carrier-neutral facility with a *meet-me room* where lessees of the fiber strands can connect to any carrier who offers services there. Further, this facility typically has strong security and backup power to ensure that networks remain running even in adverse circumstances.

Table 5.1 Models of Customer-Empowered Networking

	WHO OWNS THE FIBER?	WHO PROFITS FROM LEASING?	ADVANTAGES
Municipal fiber	The city	The city, if the network is built for commercial as well as public use	Leading-edge infrastructure for public sector and possible revenue source
Condominium fiber	Consortium members in proportion to their usage of the network (an anchor tenant would own more fiber strands than other tenants, for example)	The consortium divides the profits proportionally to ownership	Good opportunity for public-private partnerships in creating an effective network
Open-access fiber, municipal-driven	The installer	Generally the installer, but depends on contract with the city	City offers its telecommunications budget to installer as well as rights-of-way to gain a leading-edge infrastructure
Open-access fiber, corporate driven	The installer	Primarily the installer, but city may receive a small share	May offer other benefits, such as cleaning and maintenance of sewers for the term of the IRU

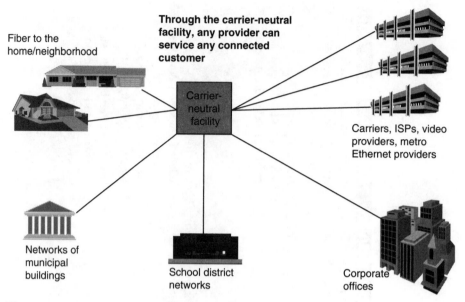

Figure 5.1   Customer-empowered networking.

A simple change to an optical patch panel allows customers to switch providers at will. Figure 5.1 illustrates customer-empowered networking.

Owning part of the infrastructure makes an enormous difference in what services the carrier provides. Since the carrier need only provide service from the neutral facility outward, the costs of leasing a line from a carrier are eliminated; each company or municipality instead owns the portion of the network it would typically have leased. The price difference between leasing, for example, a T-3 line from a carrier which would then install the line versus owning a part of the network is substantial. Further, the cost of the fiber optic network can be amortized while telecom services, such as leased lines, cannot be, providing a significant tax advantage.

Deploying a Customer-Empowered Network

So how should municipalities and other organizations interested in developing such a network proceed? Of course, the exact methodology depends on the model being used. This procedure (based on St. Arnaud, 2001b) can be used as a guideline.

First, the organization needs to find out whether others are interested in a condominium fiber arrangement. After establishing the participants in that group and choosing one participant to serve as an anchor tenant, the group should form a consortium. Before issuing a request for proposal (RFP), the group may want to invest in an independent engineering survey, which will later help in evaluating RFP responses. In developing the RFP, the group should evaluate other similar documents which have been issued. Appendix A, *Recommended Resources*, lists some of the documents that a consortium may want to review in developing its RFP.

The next step is to issue the RFP. The anchor tenant should issue the RFP rather than the consortium. The RFP should state that all respondents must

➤ Have a carrier license

➤ Have liability insurance

➤ Be willing to do an overbuild and make excess fiber strands available for a set period and a set price

➤ Be willing to contract with each member of the consortium individually (although the RFP sets up the terms and conditions for all members)

The respondents should be evaluated based not only on price, but on the services they offer. For example, what happens if adds, moves, or changes must be made? For minor modifications, such services are typically included in the maintenance fee. How quickly will the installer respond in the event of a break in the fiber? In what timeframe will the installer be able to complete the job?

After awarding the contract, the installer will typically order the fiber (because of possible delays) and at the same time do an engineering study which will entail drawing detailed diagrams of the entire fiber installation.

Deploying a dark fiber network is an important step for a city, and it should be completed in a timely fashion to reap the maximum benefits. However, since it is a long-term investment, considerable up-front research must be done to ensure that the project meets the needs of the participants.

Municipal Optical Networks: Today and Tomorrow

In the United States alone, there are more than 400 cities considering municipal fiber builds or in the process of deploying them. If one considers North America, the number is far higher because Canada has been proactive in installing fiber optic networks. For example, Montreal is the city with the most fiber optic cable installed in North America, as Stockholm is in Europe. Indeed, Quebec as a province has taken a leadership role in developing its high-speed infrastructure.

MTUs and Developers

Carriers are constantly asking permission of cities to install fiber. Perhaps the second most frequent request is from carriers who want to wire multi-tenant units (MTUs).

Owners of these MTUs face the same kinds of issues cities do, but on a smaller scale. Allowing a single carrier to wire the building creates the same type of vendor lock-in described earlier. One approach is for the developer or owner to wire the building and then allow multiple carriers into the equipment room. A still more elegant solution is to connect to a nearby carrier-neutral facility, providing all tenants with a choice of carriers and more competitive access costs while reducing congestion in access ducts and equipment rooms. For major corporate businesses, fiber connections to two separate carrier-neutral facilities provides a further competitive advantage, since a second data path is available in the event of a fiber cut in the first connection. MTU owners may wish to become part of a condominium fiber build to make it more cost-effective to connect their buildings to such facilities. Hotels and leading-edge housing developments may also want to follow the same strategy.

Table 5.2 lists some of the cities and larger areas (provinces, counties) with municipal fiber plans or fiber already in place. In some cases, particularly in Canada, the project is not undertaken by the city but by school systems.

Some cities are advanced enough that they are moving to the next stage: fiber to the home (FTTH), a subject discussed in detail in Chapter 7. Palo Alto, California, which has a municipal-owned fiber utility, is one such example. The city is considering a rate of $90 per month for a 10-Mbps connection and $170 for a 100-Mbps connection.

What motivates cities to deploy fiber? It's usually to create municipal integration, allowing the police departments, fire departments, ambulances, 911, and public works to share a high-speed network. Such is the case for Vancouver, British Columbia's network. BarrieNet, in Barrie, Ontario, will take advantage of its integrated network provide firefighters with instant access to building schematics. Barrie plans ultimately to use the network to move towards e-government. In other cases, cities have more bottom-line reasons for deploying high-speed fiber optic networks. Ottawa's main goal in participating in a condo fiber build is to reduce its telecom costs.

Fiber optic builds differ in their motivation and leadership and even in their technology. Some municipalities are building hybrid networks of coaxial cable and fiber. In some cases, rather than the municipality leading the way, it is a

Table 5.2   Cities with Fiber Builds in Place or in Progress

CITY
South Dundas, Ottawa
Spokane, Washington
Albuquerque, New Mexico
Ashland, Oregon
Provo, Utah
Indianapolis, Indiana
Omaha, Nebraska
Chicago, Illinois
Glasgow, Kentucky
Toronto, Ontario
North York, Ontario
Victoriaville, Quebec
Canberra, Australia
Ottawa, Ontario
Kanata, Ontario
Edmonton, Alberta
Sudbury, Ontario
Hamilton, Ontario
Montreal, Quebec
Vancouver, British Columbia
Barrie, Ontario
Braintree, Massachusetts
Cedar Falls, Iowa
Dublin, Ohio
Harlan, Iowa
Holland, Michigan
Wadsworth, Ohio
Laval, Quebec
Stockholm, Sweden
Umea, Sweden

continues

Table 5.2   Continued

WIDER INITIATIVES
Alberta (province-wide)
Grant County Public Utility District, Washington
King's County, Washington
Quebec
Simcoe County, Ontario

utility company. And, in still other cases, the school system takes the initiative in developing a fiber optic network. These categories are described next.

Hybrid Fiber/Coax Builds

Rather than deploying a pure optical network, a number of cities install a hybrid architecture that blends coaxial cable with fiber. Especially since coaxial cable for television connects to most homes, this type of architecture is appealing. While it is not a pure optical network, it is worth noting that cities are doing this in growing numbers.

During the 1994 elections in Cedar Falls, Iowa, the citizens approved the establishment of a municipal communications facility by a 71 percent margin, allowing the city to offer communications services. The hybrid fiber/coax network will ultimately reach all businesses and residences with both voice and data services. Cable TV and cable modem service will also be offered. And, in Harlan, Iowa, the town is developing a hybrid fiber/coax broadband network to offer not only common services such as cable television but Internet access, telephone services, and telemedicine.

While from a technology standpoint, a hybrid fiber/coax network cannot provide all the speed that pure fiber can, such an infrastructure still moves communities in the direction of true broadband services. It is particularly important that cities take an active role in promoting broadband since it may be many years before commercial interests provide such services in more rural and remote areas, effectively hobbling their economic progress in the meantime.

Utilities and Fiber Deployment

For a variety of reasons, utility companies often take the initiative in building a citywide fiber optic network. For one thing, they have access to the rights-of-way already, and given that they already have utility poles throughout the city, stringing the fiber for the network on the same poles presents little difficulty and requires a relatively small investment. Even more germane, utilities often have fiber optic networks in place, and offering fiber to third parties is a natural extension of those networks.

Companies in need of broadband have begun to recognize utilities as potential providers of high-speed networking services. In 1997, Palo Alto, California-based WebTV arranged to get high-speed data services from the City of Palo Alto Utilities fiber optic network, connecting five of its downtown buildings to the fiber optic network and in turn connecting the utility's network to the Palo Alto Internet Exchange. This not only gave WebTV a new broadband connection, but it provided redundancy with its existing connections.

Often the fiber optic network is designed not only to provide a new revenue stream for the utility but to help the company (or the city) become more efficient; Holland, Michigan's network will not only improve the electric utility itself but will provide automated meter reading for connected businesses. The new network will offer advanced networking for the government and will incorporate schools, hospitals, and businesses as well. Often these initiatives start out to benefit the utility company and then expand. In Braintree, Massachusetts, the Braintree Electric Light Department originally deployed a fiber optic network between its generation facility and its administration offices. The network has now evolved into a comprehensive network for the city.

The original motive for Provo City Power's network was to automate the traffic lights across the city, improving traffic flow. But why not expand the vision? According to Mary DeLaMare-Schaefer, Provo City Power's director of marketing and customer service, "We're going to have to build [a fiber optic network] for ourselves anyway. We said, 'Hmmm. If we're going to build it for ourselves, maybe we should think about building it for all of our residents.' So that's how we began to explore the concept"(Cruz 2000). Whatever motivates these networks in the beginning, the benefits they offer are myriad and far-reaching.

Glasgow: The Most Wired Town in Kentucky

For small towns, deregulation is not a dream come true. In effect, deregulation means that companies can charge rural areas what the market will bear. In a city where there is a sufficient profit motive for several carriers to establish services at a reasonable price, private companies do so. In smaller towns, there is less motive to establish affordable service, and as a result, the prices tend to be much higher. This is particularly true of cable services.

continues

continued

Glasgow, Kentucky, recognized this early on. In 1962, the town created its own electric utility, following the tradition of U.S. municipalities that did so under the encouragement of President Franklin Delano Roosevelt during the Great Depression. In 1986, Glasgow began contemplating a broadband network. Its electric utility needed a fiber optic network to remain efficient. With a high-speed backbone, the electrical systems could be fully automated, monitoring meters and allowing for real-time rate calculation.

But that was a large investment for a small electric company. When it sought to justify the investment, the town decided that since fiber optic cable had bandwidth to spare, it could double as a cable television delivery mechanism. The town then built the nation's first broadband municipal network, a hybrid/fiber coax network, and began offering cable TV services at cost. This positioned the town perfectly to become a broadband ISP in 1995 as demand for such services arose.

As the need for bandwidth increased, so did the proportion of fiber in the network. Today, it is half coax and half fiber. For businesses, Glasgow leases direct fiber connections running at 100 Mbps. The city will soon offer Gigabit Ethernet services to businesses.

Because all of these services are run on a nonprofit basis, the prices are far lower than typical market prices. Cable television costs $18 per month for 60 channels. Even more remarkable, cable modems running at 10 Mbps cost only $14 per month. About 30 percent of the area's households receive high-speed Internet service.

William Ray, Superintendent of the Glasgow Electrical Plant Board, states that Glasgow's network has impacted the local economy in several ways. First, he estimates that some $30 million has remained in the local economy through retained earnings. Since residents and businesses pay lower prices for telecommunications services, this substantial sum has been freed up for other local spending. Additionally, the network has paved the way for home-based entrepreneurs and helped attract large industrial businesses to the area. Ray has written extensively about the role of utilities in networking. See Appendix A, *Recommended Resources*, for details.

In Australia's capital, Canberra, the water and power utility has deployed open-access fiber and is in the process of deploying fiber to the home; the same water and power lines that facilitate municipal networks will ultimately reach the whole city.

In Canada, hydroelectric plants have been instrumental in building municipal fiber networks. The Sudbury Regional Network, SureNet, is owned and operated by Sudbury Hydro, which has been a supplier of dark fiber since 1997. Although it is utility led and owned, the effect of the network is the same as any fiber build: stimulating the local economy. SureNet has resulted in 750 new jobs in the area. Hamilton, Ontario's Hamilton Hydro and UTILiNK further illustrate this trend, supplying dark fiber to the municipality and leasing excess strands to other carriers. The optical network provides cable television as well as a high-speed data services. UTILiNK is a private company that helps utilities make the transition from providing electricity and using their fiber optic networks internally to becoming bandwidth providers.

The utilities enjoy a rapid return on investment; Toronto Hydro and Electric Company recouped its investment in fiber installation in less than three years. Dark fiber creates an additional revenue stream for hydroelectric plants; North York Hydro in Ontario connected two McDonald's restaurants as a pilot project, using 2 kilometers of fiber. The restaurants lease the fiber on a long-term contract, generating revenue for the utility.

In some cities, such as Edmonton, Alberta, the fiber optic networks serve college campuses and provide longer-haul services than a typical municipal build does. EPCOR, formerly Edmonton Power, leases dark fiber to the Northern Alberta Institute of Technology to link four of its campuses. The utility also supplies fiber to businesses and other carriers.

Schools and Fiber: Addressing the Digital Divide

The lack of broadband can hinder economic progress for a community, but it also impacts students of area schools, who become digital have-nots without adequate experience with technology to be competitive in the marketplace upon graduation. The tension between wired schools, usually in more affluent suburban areas, and schools with backward technology and little to no Internet access, often in inner cities or rural areas, has been termed the digital divide. While communities often take the lead in broadband network development, in some areas schools are playing a more significant role.

To date, however, schools in the United States have been addressing their broadband needs primarily through the government's E-Rate program, funded by the FCC. This program provides $2.25 billion in annual funding for wiring schools to the Internet via broadband. The amount of money a school receives is based on the number of students who receive free lunches at school or the proportion of parents below the poverty level.

Case Study: An Optical Network for All of Chicago

Chicago's CivicNet is an effort to create a citywide infrastructure for both public and private use. Given market forces, the private sector would have wired downtown Chicago, further increasing real estate prices in that segment of the city. But what about city offices? What about an abandoned warehouse in a lower-rent part of the town?

According to Joel Mambretti, director of the International Center for Advanced Internet Research at Northwestern University and chairman of Chicago's Request for Information Subcommittee, "The CivicNet project is the world's most ambitious optical metro net project" (2000). Whether Mambretti's assessment is true for the entire world, there is no doubt that CivicNet is the most ambitious municipal networking project in the United States.

Chicago's purpose in creating CivicNet is to transform the economics of the city as well as provide some 1600 agencies and government entities with a high-speed network. Importantly, CivicNet will do this at no increased expense to the city. The city, for its part, offers its infrastructure: "In addition, the value of existing dark fiber, rights of way, and available conduit and duct space owned by the City constitute a significant in-kind contribution toward the construction of the CivicNet infrastructure" (City of Chicago 2000, 7).

In addition to offering its rights-of-way and existing fiber resources, Chicago has placed quite a carrot in front of the vendor or vendors who will build CivicNet: a $32 million annual telecommunications budget for a period of 10 years, combining the telecom spending of all its agencies into a single contract. From the city's standpoint, the deal was irresistible. Chicago would gain a high-speed infrastructure, both for public and private use while not spending any additional funds or doing the work itself.

While many metro projects work to fiber the downtown area, an area of high-rents and deep corporate pockets that is attractive to the private sector, CivicNet will connect all of Chicago. The fact that the 1600 government entities to be connected include Chicago's public schools by definition means that the network will be dispersed all over the city. In addition to schools, it encompasses all city offices, the Chicago Transit Authority, the Chicago Housing Authority, the City Colleges of Chicago, and the Chicago Park District. Connecting all these entities alone means that the network could encompass 3 million city residents and businesses (City of Chicago 2000, 10). The city serves as an anchor tenant for the network.

Not only will CivicNet unify the city's own communications infrastructure, which is currently fragmented, but it will change the desirability of real estate in some areas of the city. An old office building in a less-desirable part of town, if it has high-speed connectivity, suddenly becomes a far more valuable piece of real estate, attractive to startups and other businesses.

CivicNet documentation and those working on the project speak of the network as a "public-private partnership." This partnership has many facets. A private company—or more likely a group of private companies—will build out the network (City of Chicago 2000, 6). These partners can be referred to as "provider partners." It's also a public-private partnership because private industry will be using the network. These fellow users could be thought of as "network user partners."

Traffic from the city's segment of the network, called the Government Network in the city's Request for Quotation document, and the private sector network, referred to as the Open Network, will be separated, although at this stage in the project the exact means of separating it is unclear. CivicNet is still in the bidding process at this writing.

The process began with a voluminous Request for Information, issued in November 2000. Although starting with an RFI is an unusual approach, it was appropriate for a project where the city wanted the input of the private sector to inform its requirements. The RFI repeatedly encourages respondents to take a creative approach, even though requirements are laid out in some detail. (CivicNet's RFI is available online at www.chicagocivicnet.com; viewing the document requires registration. For any city considering a project of this nature, the RFI serves as a model document worthy of review.) Some 500 organizations received the RFI, and 75 organizations responded to it.

Respondents are not easily categorized. Because of the scope of the project, there were a variety of ways companies could respond. Businesses might provide a low-cost means of network construction in order to gain access to fiber. They could provide financing in exchange for use of the fiber to selected locations (a business) or throughout the network (a carrier). Venture capital is also welcomed.

The company or consortium of companies that wins the telecommunications budget to create CivicNet, though, must have some particular characteristics and capabilities. In addition to being technically capable of carrying off a project of this scale, the city needs both a carrier (for itself) and a carrier's carrier. The carrier's carrier will make the Open Network available to a variety of carriers, creating competition for private sector business on that portion of the network. The project also paves the way for smaller carriers to compete effectively to service the Open Network since the infrastructure will be in place rather than requiring a large capital investment to build it.

continues

continued

Part of the challenge in pulling the project together will be that companies that are traditionally rivals must work together on CivicNet. The city is taking a wise approach, however, in ensuring that the infrastructure will be city-owned rather than carrier-owned, enabling carriers to compete for business on it rather than monopolizing it. However, there is potential for abuse; certainly the carrier's carrier might not in fact provide other carriers with equal access to the private portion of the network; third-party arbitration procedures will probably need to be put into place to ensure competition.

In fact, CivicNet will not be a monopoly even for fiber in Chicago. Carriers wanting to build their own fiber infrastructure can apply to the city for a permit.

It is also important to understand where the network stops. The last mile to private sector homes and businesses won't be automatically connected. While the network will be close by to almost everywhere, minimizing the cost of connecting to it, the last mile itself must still be addressed through other means.

The city clearly understands the benefits of owning its infrastructure. The RFI likens the current method of paying for telecom services to paying rent while CivicNet will enable the city to be "in a position of building equity, with the eventual result being lower or stabilized costs." The infrastructure could even become "at some point a revenue source for the City" (City of Chicago 2000, 8).

A Request for Qualifications was issued in May 2001 and was due by July 2. From the respondents to the RFQ the city selected a short list of potential applicants. These applicants then responded to the Request for Proposal. The final details of the project will be settled and the award will be made in late 2001, with construction beginning in 2002.

Among the requirements for the network is that it be built on IETF standards rather than ITU standards, making it in effect an optical internet. This optical network, then, will be built on Internet standards rather than having a traditional circuit-switched architecture. According to the RFI, "To some degree, the new model is increasingly driven by IETF architectural specifications, based on its vision of multiple autonomous peering networks using a common set of protocols, rather than simply ITU architectures based on hierarchies and gateways." The RFI also makes it clear that this type of an architecture is more desirable not only because of open standards, but because it better fits modern network traffic patterns: "Research has demonstrated that communications architecture based on central offices is optimal when approximately eighty percent of traffic is local, which is true for voice services. However, Internet traffic, primarily (over ninety percent) consists of access to remote locations" (City of Chicago 2000, 6).

However, although a modern network infrastructure is clearly desired, not all the city's existing fiber resources fit into this category. The companies that build CivicNet will be faced with migrating older portions of the network, based on

SONET, to this new architecture with minimal disruption. In the short term, the companies will have to maintain this architecture. A transition plan is required as part of the response to the RFQ.

Although the infrastructure that will connect the 1600 buildings that are part of the government's portion of CivicNet will be a fiber optic network, the broadband options offered to the private sector need not be fiber immediately. Fiber to the home, for example, would be cost-prohibitive to put in place for every residence in Chicago. Instead, according to Doug Power, CivicNet project manager, the infrastructure will be hybrid for the near-term, making use of fiber, wireless broadband and existing copper.

In addition to being based on IETF standards, CivicNet will be a converged network, handling Internet access, data services, digital voice, and digital video. Voice and video will run over IP and the network will use Diffserv for QoS issues. It will include DWDM support and will offer Gigabit Ethernet and Ethernet services, at least at the edge. Physically, the city wants the least disruptive installation possible, minimizing the impact on traffic as well as other inconveniences that residents will have to endure during the network build.

CivicNet will make Chicago attractive not only to existing businesses, but has the potential to transform its economy and draw businesses from around the country to enjoy its leading-edge infrastructure. Since it is a long-term project, it's impossible to gauge the economic impact of the network at this point, but it is certain that CivicNet will be the envy of many cities throughout the United States as well as throughout the world.

Despite the funding behind this program, it has several drawbacks. The demographics tend to favor inner-city schools. Rural schools, which are underserved by broadband providers, may have fewer students at poverty level but are just as likely to lack high-speed Internet access. Further, E-Rate effectively locks the schools into a particular carrier, which receives the funding for building the connection to the school and for the telecommunications services provided by that connection. In this way, E-Rate benefits incumbent carriers and obviates competition. Further, the broadband being subsidized is at best pseudobroadband such as DSL, a continuing investment in a relatively short-lived copper rather than long-term fiber optic infrastructure.

A few other government programs also address broadband connectivity for rural and low-income areas. Legislation under consideration in the United States would offer a 10 percent tax credit for carriers who offer 1.5 Mbps services to rural and low-income areas and a 20 percent tax credit for 22 Mbps services, giving carriers an incentive to move into areas that might not be economically attractive to them. Further aiding rural areas are the Rural Utility Service Loans, some $100 million in available treasury rate funds for connecting communities of up to 20,000 residents; this program, however, is currently only a one-year pilot.

All these programs share the same drawback, however. They provide incentive and funds to incumbent carriers, which then effectively lock schools in as permanent customers, since upstart carriers are unlikely to be able to duplicate the infrastructure cost-effectively.

Canada's approach is more empowering to schools (and communities). Canadian schools, particularly in Quebec, are either planning or have deployed dark fiber. In Quebec, some 75 percent of the school districts have either installed or are in the process of installing dark fiber networks, an initiative that is part of the larger Canadian public grid project. The Victoriaville school board connected its schools via fiber starting in 1991. Paybacks for these initiatives are even more rapid than for municipal builds, falling in the six-month to two-year range, partly because the scope of the effort is narrower. Recentralization of the network for easier and more cost-effective administration is an important factor in accelerating this payback. The Laval School Board, in cooperation with the City of Laval and QuebecTel, is participating in a condominium fiber build that will connect 45,000 students, 2500 teachers, and 160 educational and municipal institutions.

In Canada, as we have seen, there is tremendous government support for this type of innovative communications architecture. It is likely that all of Canada will be linked by fiber optic cable before the United States even stands back and evaluates the flaws in its approach to broadband funding. However, not all U.S. cities and schools are following a typical U.S. model. For example, in

Alberta SUPERNET: Connecting Municipalities Province-wide

Rural areas of the Canadian province of Alberta suffer from the same problem that most rural areas have. There is no economic incentive to create a high-speed network in an area where there are relatively few users. And, if carriers do create such a network, it comes at a high price, far higher than urban areas pay. To help Alberta reach its potential—ultimately the government wants the province to become "a world leader in information and communications technology"—the government decided to invest in a high-speed Ethernet-based fiber optic network that will connect more than 420 communities province-wide (Government of Alberta 2000). SUPERNET will connect all schools, hospitals, libraries, government facilities, and public institutions at speeds of 10 and 100 Mbps. The facilities, and public institutions at speeds of 10 and 100 Mbps. The network will be built over three years, starting in late 2001 and ending in 2004 (with perhaps a bit of work stretching into 2005).

SUPERNET is being built by a consortium of companies led by Bell Intrigna. The network will be managed by AXIA, which will ensure that all carriers have equal access to its capacity. The group of companies listed in Table 5.3 won the contract to build the network after an RFP process. The RFP was issued in February 2000 through the province's online bidding system and closed April 4, 2000. From the 10 respondents, a shortlist was created, followed by a two-phase best and final offer process. The government of Alberta then awarded the contract on October 31, 2000.

Table 5.3   SUPERNET Participants

PARTICIPANT	WEB ADDRESS
360 Networks	www.360networks.com
AXIA IP Services Ltd.	www.axia.com
BCE Emergis	www.bceemergis.com
Bell ActiMedia	www.bellactimedia.com
Bell Intrigna	www.bellintrigna.com
Bell Nexxia	www.bellnexxia.com
Cisco	www.cisco.com
Microsoft	www.microsoft.com
Netricom	www.netricom.com
Nortel Networks	www.nortel.com
Telesat Canada	www.telesat.ca
Total Telecom	www.totaltelecom.com
Wi-LAN	www.wilan.com

Competitive, open access for all providers is a key part of SUPERNET's architecture. According to Ken Hewitt, "Bell Intrigna's offer of a fiber condominium to the government of Alberta played an important part in their winning the RFP. Their offer included an invitation to competitive players to participate in the fiber build as well as an affirmation of their continuing commitment after the build to provide local and open access to the fiber. All these offers on their part combined to become an important factor in their receiving the bid" (Cook 2001).

continues

continued

SUPERNET is not simply a public sector network. It will be accessible by businesses and residential users as well. Further, any provider can connect to SUPERNET using the meet-me room at the point-of-presence (POP) in each community. This allows smaller ISPs to compete on a new playing field since they need not build out their infrastructure to enjoy the services of the high-speed network and to attract customers they will in turn connect to SUPERNET.

In terms of models, SUPERNET represents a variation on Chicago's approach. In addition to a 10-year telecommunications budget commitment of $108 million and in-kind contributions of the province's existing fiber, Alberta is making a one-time capital investment of $123 million in the network. In the RFP, one of the options for respondents to consider was the possibility of building the network without a capital commitment from the province. Because the population is so geographically dispersed, however, it makes sense for the government to make this investment in its infrastructure.

Further, Alberta will enjoy considerable cost-avoidance from building SUPERNET. Hospitals, schools, and other public agencies are all funded by the government. Their communications needs would have increased drastically over time. Now those expenditures will be limited to equipment, like video-conferencing systems, rather than network builds or high-cost network services in remote areas. Much of the capital investment could be viewed as a shifting of costs from one budget area to another. And, since the network investment represents a capital cost, it can be depreciated over the long term (20 years or more), providing tax advantages.

Another unique aspect to SUPERNET is the concept of a base network and an extended network. The base network will be owned by Bell Intrigna and perhaps, over time, other private parties. In these areas, there is already adequate competition for high-speed Internet access. The extended network is where the government is making its investment. In these areas of the province, there is no high-speed access at competitive prices. Ultimately, as competition is introduced, the base area of the network will expand and the extended area will shrink.

Some communities in Alberta are very remote. Even with SUPERNET, there may not be competitive interest in providing affordable access. If no other provider offers affordable access at urban rates, Bell Intrigna guarantees access for those communities. Currently, the rates are, for businesses, 256 Kbps for $160 per month or less, 10 Mbps for $320 per month or less, and 100 Mbps for $445 per month or less. Home users will have at least one broadband option (cable modem or DSL) for about $25 per month. Currently, only 30 of the 420 communities connected by SUPERNET have affordable high-speed residential service; after SUPERNET is completed, all the communities will have this type of access.

For commercial access, businesses that want a high-speed connection will have to pay a fee to get connected to the SUPERNET POP in their area. SUPERNET does not cover the last mile for businesses, but the benefits of connecting will override the one-time charge of installing connectivity from the business in question to the POP. To ensure the greatest possible competition, businesses will need to make sure that they do not lock themselves into a particular provider when they get connected.

Again, because of the geography of Alberta, SUPERNET is a long-haul network. Although it is an Ethernet-based optical network, SUPERNET will employ DWDM rather than the cheaper CWDM; the long-haul nature of the network justifies the cost. MPLS will be used for traffic engineering.

Some towns are so remote that it is impractical to offer fiber optic access to them. The network will be approximately 95 percent fiber optic and 5 percent wireless, using high-speed fixed wireless connections in areas too remote for fiber. Because of fiber's ability to scale at a low cost, it is the predominant solution for the vast majority of the network.

Essentially, SUPERNET levels the playing field for businesses that need high-speed access as well as providing greater government services, including telehealth, to areas that are currently too remote to enjoy the benefits of, for example, greater access to specialists in urban areas. Specialists can be consulted via the high-speed network in real-time, and when patients need to go to urban areas for treatment, medical records can be transferred quickly (currently patients often stay in a hotel in the area waiting for their medical records to arrive). The infrastructure also provides benefits for government and education. Smaller towns that offer a high-quality infrastructure and low cost of living may become attractive areas for new businesses to locate. Although high-tech infrastructure is just one kind of infrastructure, the potential is that SUPERNET will transform Alberta both economically and socially over time, allowing the province to become a high-tech magnet area.

1999 in Spokane, Washington, the school board put in dark fiber linking all 50 of the schools in the district. And, some U.S. cities, including Chicago, are following a much more empowering model of networking.

Conclusion

Municipalities have a unique opportunity before them. By creating a leading-edge network, they can distinguish themselves from the surrounding area and benefit their citizenry on a number of levels. The economic health and well being of an area can be positively impacted by this investment in an infrastructure that is just as vital to a modern community as roads, sewers, and other utilities.

CHAPTER 6

Optical Networking and the Corporate Network

H ow do optical networks impact the corporate network? First we must consider that corporate networks typically have several basic levels with distinct needs:

- ➤ The network in each corporate office building (LANs)
- ➤ A campus network that connects buildings in a single location or area
- ➤ A WAN connecting remote offices
- ➤ Corporate Internet connections

In this chapter you will find discussions of corporate optical networking needs and trends from LAN to WAN to Internet connectivity. Before delving into these levels of the corporate network, however, we will examine the relevance of two different technology options for the corporation: optical Ethernet and SONET. Finally, the chapter describes applications and services to consider, including quality-of-service issues, storage area networks, and convergence of voice and data on a single network.

Technology Options for the Enterprise

Several technologies may be used for corporate optical networking. We'll discuss the two most prominent: optical Ethernet and SONET. Of these options, the only one that can span all the networking needs of the enterprise is optical

Ethernet. SONET serves WANs and, traditionally, provides connectivity to the Internet through leased lines.

Gigabit Ethernet

Ethernet is the most common LAN technology. With 320 million ports, Ethernet runs more than 85 percent of corporate LANs today, according to IDC (Intel 2001). Competitors such as Token Ring have faded into near obscurity as Ethernet has become the dominant standard in corporate networking.

The advent of Gigabit Ethernet has expanded Ethernet's role from a LAN technology to a corporate backbone, campus, or even WAN technology. Now 10-Gigabit Ethernet, slated to be ratified as a standard in March 2002 but already deployed in 2001, puts Ethernet on par with the fastest SONET speed currently available, OC-192. We are beginning to see carriers with optical Ethernet backbones that span the United States. David Isenberg, telecom expert, former AT&T engineer, and president of the consultancy isen.com, explains how the scope of Ethernet has expanded:

> Ethernet started as a local area networking protocol—but now it mirrors the extent to which the definition of local is expanding and expanding and expanding. When Ethernet started, 100 meters was how far it could travel, that was how far the two furthest computers on a network could be apart from each other. Today it's a thousand kilometers, so imagine a "local" area network that's a thousand kilometers in diameter. Pretty good. All of a sudden it starts looking like long distance, so you start wondering: Why do we need anything else here, when we have Ethernet and it's cheap and it has all kinds of economies of scale that stem from the fact that you're stamping out millions and millions of Ethernet circuits a year? (Moritz 2000a).

Ethernet's familiarity is a major draw for corporations to consider it as a broader technology, extending the LAN to the WAN. According to Phil Edholm, CTO of Nortel Networks, "The beauty of optical Ethernet is that it handles the data in Ethernet size and form from end to end. It doesn't require that complexity of tearing the packet apart at the enterprise level and then handing it over to the telecom" (Scanlon 2001).

Where does Gigabit Ethernet make sense? Most corporate networks include a mix of speeds, often aggregated through trunking. At this point, Gigabit Ethernet to the desktop is overkill since most desktop PCs cannot handle that speed. But Gigabit Ethernet certainly makes sense not only as a backbone technology but for connections to critical servers, which will soon be able to handle gigabit speeds as I/O interfaces such as InfiniBand and PCI-X become more common. The technology is also becoming important for *storage area networks (SANs)*, described later in this chapter.

Gigabit Ethernet does not necessarily entail optical networking, although most deployments are fiber-based. Within a building, Gigabit Ethernet can run over CAT5 copper wire or over fiber optic cable. (CAT5 wire must be tested to see whether it can handle Gigabit Ethernet. Older copper typically cannot. Newer CAT5 Enhanced is a better choice for Gigabit Ethernet.) Between buildings, however, the choice is more clear-cut; distance constraints on copper usually dictate the use of fiber between buildings. 10-Gigabit Ethernet is another story, however. Even newer CAT5 copper can handle only 4 Gbps, which is inadequate by definition for 10-Gigabit Ethernet. 10-Gigabit Ethernet is a fiber-only solution.

10-Gigabit Ethernet

10-Gigabit Ethernet is designed for fiber optic networks. As such, it will initially be deployed in corporate backbones. Although the market for 10-Gigabit Ethernet is young, several companies have projected the demand for such networks. In 2000, the market for 10-Gigabit Ethernet was only $33.7 million, but it is projected to reach significant revenue levels ($3.6 billion) by 2003, according to market researcher Gartner Dataquest. (See Figure 6.1.) Another market research firm, IDC, measures the market in terms of the number of ports shipping. That firm projects that approximately 230,000 10-Gigabit Ethernet ports

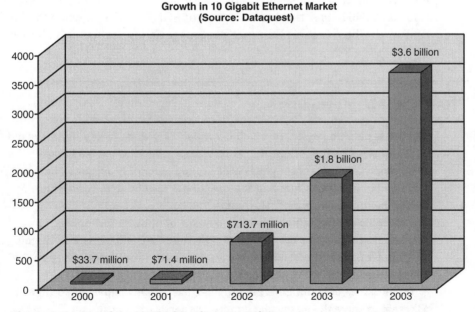

Figure 6.1   Growth in 10-Gigabit Ethernet market.

Copyright 2001. Courtesy of Gartner Dataquest and *Network World*.

will ship by the end of 2001 and that in 2004, over 4 million ports will ship (Hochmuth 2001c).

In terms of corporate spending, it's clear that Gigabit Ethernet currently has the edge over 10-Gigabit Ethernet, not surprising given 10-Gigabit Ethernet's limited availability. According to the 2001 *Network World* Spending Survey, 36 percent of companies planned to invest in Gigabit Ethernet equipment in 2001. The proportion planning to invest in nascent 10-Gigabit Ethernet equipment is much smaller, only 6 percent (Gaudin 2001). However, as prices drop and standards solidify, 10-Gigabit Ethernet will play a greater role in corporate budgets and corporate networks.

In addition to providing more bandwidth for saturated network backbones, 10-Gigabit Ethernet will be used for bandwidth aggregation. Various network speeds are often aggregated into a single pipe. When aggregating LANs, the combined bandwidth can overwhelm Gigabit Ethernet; 10-Gigabit Ethernet will provide a more robust solution for such networks.

10-Gigabit versus Gigabit Ethernet

How do Gigabit Ethernet and 10-Gigabit Ethernet compare? In terms of framing and traffic, they are identical. 10-Gigabit Ethernet is pure Ethernet. Unlike Gigabit Ethernet which can run at half duplex or full duplex, 10 Gigabit Ethernet runs only at full duplex. There are some changes in the physical and data link layers. For seamless integration with SONET networks, the WAN PHY runs at 9.58464Gbps, the precise speed of SONET OC-192, while the LAN PHY runs at 10 Gbps. Gigabit Ethernet's autonegotiation feature, which turned out

10-Gigabit Deployments

The Swiss particle physics research institute CERN plans to deploy 10-Gigabit Ethernet soon, as it predicts that its current Gigabit Ethernet backbone will be obsolete by 2002. According to CERN's group leader of IT, Jacques Altaber, "We will need to inject 10-Gigabit in the core of our backbone to connect our backbone routers together" (Hochmuth 2001).

University of Southern California's director of network technology, James Wiedel, also eagerly awaits 10-Gigabit Ethernet: "We will be looking at going to [10-Gigabit Ethernet] when it arrives on the scene. I could start using 10-Gig today" (Hochmuth 2001).

Intellispace, a Gigabit Ethernet provider, has already deployed 10-Gigabit Ethernet to serve the increasing bandwidth needs of its customers.

to be more trouble than it was worth, was eliminated from the 10-Gigabit Ethernet standard.

10-Gigabit Ethernet also carries data over longer distances. Over single-mode fiber, 10-Gigabit Ethernet can carry data for 40 kilometers; compare that to 5 kilometers for Gigabit Ethernet. See Table 6.1.

Optical Ethernet versus SONET

As we move from the corporate campus into the WAN and the Internet connection, the traditional choice for optical networking is SONET. Companies leasing lines from the phone companies may not even be thinking in terms of SONET, but it is typically the technology behind the service, particularly for higher speed connections.

As discussed in Chapter 4, *Optical Internets*, SONET has a great deal of overhead (by design, half of its bandwidth is always idle). It is inherently more expensive than Gigabit Ethernet. And, the difference in expense isn't marginal; SONET can be about 85 percent more expensive than Gigabit Ethernet. A study by the Dell'Oro Group found that 10-Gigabit Ethernet cost $950 per gigabit in 2001 and will drop to $485 per gigabit in 2004. By contrast, SONET networks running at the comparable speed, OC-192, today cost $7653 per gigabit and will cost $3134 per gigabit by 2004 (Light Reading 2001).

SONET equipment is far more expensive than Gigabit Ethernet, but the number of emerging providers with managed Gigabit Ethernet offerings will put

Table 6.1   Distances for 10 Gigabit Ethernet over Fiber

PHY TYPE	DESCRIPTION	FIBER TYPE	MAXIMUM DISTANCE (METERS)
10GBase-SR	850-nm serial LAN	Multimode	65
10GBase-LX4	1,310-nm WWDM LAN	Multimode	300
10GBase-LR	1,310-nm serial LAN	Single-mode	10,000
10GBase-ER	1,550-nm serial LAN	Single-mode	40,000
10GBase-SW	850-nm serial WAN	Multimode	65
10GBase-LW	1,310-nm serial WAN	Single-mode	10,000
10GBase-EW	1,550-nm serial WAN	Single-mode	40,000

nm = nonometer, WWDM = wide wave division multiplexing

Copyright 2001. Courtesy of *NetworkWorld*.

price pressure on the traditional carriers. And, some companies may be hesitant to purchase service from newer providers, questioning their economic stability. However, the price and the flexibility these providers offer may be hard to resist in the long term. Rather than ordering increments of bandwidth such as T-1, T-3, and OC-3, as is the case with SONET, Gigabit Ethernet providers offer bandwidth in 1 Mbps increments. Flexible provisioning for special occasions is available. In some cases, providers actually encourage customers to use more bandwidth by giving it away as a promotion for a limited time. (Yipes Communications falls into this promotional bandwidth category.)

When discussing convergence, it's important to note that SONET was created for switched voice traffic, although it can carry any protocol type. Gigabit Ethernet on the other hand is best for data, and particularly IP-based traffic. ATM is often used with SONET to provide quality-of-service. IP offers nothing truly comparable, but with abundant cheap bandwidth, some companies have chosen to forgo explicit QoS measures in favor of bigger pipes. For those seeking ATM-like functionality for IP networks, MPLS can provide it.

SONET is well-known for its protection bandwidth. As mentioned in Chapter 4, however, keeping half the bandwidth idle in case of a fiber cut is ultimately inefficient. There are other ways to provide resilience in a network that take a few more seconds to switch over, but the Internet itself was designed to route around damage, so its protocols offer built-in protection. SONET's protection bandwidth helps only if there is a cut in the local fiber loop. If part of the carrier's network goes down, it still appears to the corporate network as an outage. Maintaining redundant connections with different providers is the best policy to ensure uptime, whether one uses a traditional SONET service or a managed Ethernet service.

Ethernet and SONET are both framing protocols. It is possible to use SONET framing, as Cogent and CA*net3 do, without using expensive SONET equipment or architectures. This configuration is typically called Packet over SONET.

With SONET, upgrading a line to obtain more bandwidth takes at least 20 days as engineers manually configure cross-connects. By contrast, Gigabit Ethernet services can be provisioned remotely within hours, in some cases by customers using a Web-based interface.

Passive Optical Networking

Passive optical networks (PONs) are making inroads into corporate networks. PONs may be offered by telcos to compete with managed bandwidth services. In a PON, all active optical components are removed, making it a less expensive form of optical networking than traditional SONET networks. What runs over the PON can be either SONET and ATM or Ethernet, depending on the company's needs. In addition to incumbent local exchange carriers, new carriers are beginning to offer PONs to businesses. However, as a technology, it is more competitive with DSL than with managed Ethernet services. Vendors in the PON market include Quantum Bridge and Terawave. Passive optical networks are currently more prevalent in the FTTH market, as discussed in Chapter 7, *Fiber to the Home.*

Optical Networking and the Corporate LAN

Optical networking impacts the corporate network at many levels. The first area of the corporate network to examine in detail is the LAN. Within a corporate building, there could be numerous LANs. But, for the purposes of this discussion we will talk about all the interconnected networks inside a given building as a corporate LAN.

It makes sense to upgrade certain connections to a faster speed of Ethernet, as mentioned earlier. The connections to critical servers, for example, may justify Gigabit Ethernet, especially as the price per port has dropped precipitously.

Fiber versus Copper and Gigabit Ethernet

Clearly, 10-Gigabit Ethernet requires fiber optic cable. But what about Gigabit Ethernet?

As mentioned, Gigabit Ethernet can be run over copper, provided that it is state-of-the-art CAT5 wiring. If older copper wiring must be upgraded to accommodate Gigabit Ethernet, then it makes sense to consider installing fiber instead of simply upgrading the older copper infrastructure. If you have copper that will support Gigabit Ethernet, it does not make sense to pull copper wiring and replace it with fiber, even though fiber definitely has long-term advantages that we will discuss next.

There are limitations to running Gigabit Ethernet over copper, including distance, which is why copper is a good solution for corporate LANs, but not a good solution for the corporate campus or corporate WANs.

Fiber in the LAN: Does Fiber to the Desktop Make Sense Yet?

There is a market for fiber to the LAN, but it is limited to date. Fiber offers longevity and an obsolescence-proof infrastructure, and the market is growing, although it is still small. According to Charlottesville, Virginia-based Communications Industry Researchers, the market for fiber to the desktop stood at $40.3 million in 2000 and will expand to $233 million by 2003.

There is considerable controversy about when to upgrade the corporate LAN to fiber. Is it worth pulling out your current copper infrastructure and installing fiber?

Certainly, in the long run, fiber is the infrastructure of choice. Neither wireless nor copper can provide the bandwidth that fiber can. But whether that migration needs to happen today is questionable. The important thing, as mentioned earlier, is to consider fiber when performing network upgrades. If you need to upgrade to CAT5, it makes sense to skip a generation and move directly to fiber. This was the strategy taken at George Washington University (GWU), which chose to install a fiber infrastructure in 1996.

Why consider fiber now? For one thing, the cost is now comparable to copper. A 1998 survey by Sage Research Inc., indicated that 70 percent of companies would deploy fiber if the price were the same as copper. And, in fact the price is very nearly the same. For GWU to wire its network with copper would have cost an estimated $250,000. To deploy fiber instead cost just $5,000 more. Kevin Wilcox, Assistant Vice President of Technology at Fiserv of Brookfield, Wisconsin, also reported that upgrading his 1100 PC LAN to fiber cost about the same as a copper upgrade (Cope 2000b).

Costs versus Efficiencies

Individually, however, components for Gigabit Ethernet cost more if they accept both fiber and copper connections than do the equivalent copper-only components. However, fiber introduces some important network efficiencies that level out the costs. Because fiber can carry data over a longer distance, fewer hubs are required. Rather than having wiring closets on each floor, for example, all the connections can run back to the central computer room. All patch panels can be placed in a central wiring closet. Workgroup switches and routers for each floor can be eliminated. This not only saves space and money but simplifies the network architecture. GWU put in 11 hub closets for 80 buildings. Deploying copper instead would have required 160 hubs, one every 100 meters.

The benefits of consolidation were critical for GWU because space was tight. But the flexibility to easily manage adds, moves, and changes is another clear advantage.

Experience is another factor to consider when deciding between copper and fiber deployment. Most organizations have a great deal of experience with

Fiber Advantages for Fiber-Crossroads

Robert Miller, Senior Information Technology/Information Systems Manager at Fiber-Crossroads, cites ease of change as a prime benefit of the company's fiber-based LAN: "Having one location to troubleshoot user problems or administer moves, adds, and changes has proved to be of tremendous benefit. It greatly improves our department's overall effectiveness."

Space savings were also an important factor in the project, according to Stan Potts, account manager for XO Spec, the company that helped install the fiber optic LAN: "The fiber solution also allowed Crossroads to maximize its usable space on each floor. Compared to a traditional copper architecture, fiber allowed us to minimize the dedicated space for telecommunication cross-connections. As a result, Crossroads was able to utilize that space for other purposes" (Wages 2001). The high-speed LAN also accelerates product development cycles, according to Miller: "On average, our users can expect to transfer 10 Mbytes in 3 seconds on our network. This enables Crossroads engineers to reduce the design time for a particular server or software package and improve time-to-market on Crossroads' products" (Wages 2001).

copper. Although newer fiber, such as 3M's Volition, is far easier to install, there is still a learning curve to deploying a different cabling infrastructure. Hiring experts in fiber installation may be cheaper in the long run as they may offer warranties of up to 20 years for fiber that they install and certify.

Fiber is an investment for the long-term. Its speed and capacity are unsurpassed. If bandwidth demands are increasing rapidly, investing in a copper infrastructure that will probably last only five years does not make sense, particularly when fiber could be deployed for the same price. GWU projects that the fiber it installed will provide enough bandwidth for at least 10 years. In terms of immediate benefits, fiber yielded a 60-fold increase in speed.

Optical Networking and the Corporate Campus

Optical networking makes a great deal of sense for a corporate campus. There are two approaches. The first and more robust is to link buildings together via fiber installed either underground or on poles. The second approach is to deploy wireless optical networking between buildings that are in a line of

Why Not Fiber?

Despite the advantages of fiber to the LAN, it doesn't make sense for every organization. Even organizations undergoing infrastructure upgrades may choose to stick with copper.

Bob Folsom, Director of Network Administration at Mrs. Field's Cookies, states, "We didn't have the time to put in fiber, and we didn't need it to the desktop" (Hochmuth 2000). Instead, the company deployed CAT5e cabling in its new facility.

Other organizations, such as e-Media, just don't see a need for the bandwidth fiber provides. According to Brendan Wiese, Vice President of Infrastructure Development, "The decision to go copper instead of fiber was a backwards-compatible decision. All of our servers don't need Gigabit Ethernet. Some of our Web servers, like [advertising] servers, that only serve up text, don't justify the cost of Gigabit Ethernet" (Hochmuth 2000).

sight from one another. Rapid installation is the main advantage of wireless deployment.

Linking Buildings with Fiber Optics

Fiber is often deployed in a ring. However, this can make it difficult to add a building. A better topology is a star. Using a star topology, you can add in buildings later as needed without substantially disrupting the network.

Even if you link buildings with fiber for a corporate campus, there are two approaches, depending how far away from each other the buildings are. You can either install fiber, light it, and maintain it yourself, or you can buy service from a metro provider, particularly if the buildings are in different parts of the city. The metro carriers described later in this chapter may be helpful if you take the latter approach.

In terms of network architecture, you may wish to deploy Ethernet throughout. Certainly this is the most straightforward and inexpensive approach and leverages in-house LAN expertise. Gigabit Ethernet makes the most sense between buildings to keep LANs throughout the campus humming at the highest possible speed; 10-Gigabit Ethernet may also be a consideration if traffic requirements are already high. Further, the upgrade from Gigabit Ethernet to 10-Gigabit Ethernet involves simply swapping out components, not a network upgrade, if fiber is in place. For connections between buildings, fiber is usually already installed.

Making the campus network like a LAN allows for a less hierarchical approach to networks. LANs are relatively flat, but WANs are typically hierarchical and aggregate traffic to provide the greatest usage of available bandwidth. With optical networking, the high bandwidth capacity allows the campus network to resemble a LAN more than a WAN. Optical networking is clearly an important solution for the corporate campus.

Wireless Optical Networking between Corporate Buildings

Another option for optical networking between buildings is wireless optical networking, also called free space optics. In this scenario, lasers mounted on roofs or at windows can beam data at speeds of up to 2 Gbps. Although this type of optical networking is limited in scope—buildings must be in a line of sight with each other and no more than 3 km apart, depending on the vendor—it is incredibly fast to deploy, taking only hours. As is the case when you install fiber and light it yourself between buildings, you own the infrastructure, so there is never a charge beyond the initial investment in the equipment and any maintenance and upgrades that requires. No carrier charges are involved. Despite the absence of fiber, this is true optical networking, as data is beamed from building to building via lasers.

The lasers deployed in wireless optical networks do not harm the environment in any way. They are safe for animals, buildings, and even the human eye. ANSI defines eye safety standards for wireless optical networks, but nonetheless, this is an important criteria to consider when evaluating these products.

Because they are in the light spectrum rather than in the radio spectrum, there is no difficulty with government regulation of frequencies. The only pitfall is that fog or heavy rain can interfere with data transmission. Options include boosting the power of the laser when it's foggy or using shorter lengths than those strictly supported. Even with these measures, fog can sometimes interfere. To address this pitfall, companies offering wireless optical equipment often provide a lower-speed backup option, typically radio frequency or microwave backup. Further, if a plane or helicopter crosses the data path, it can temporarily interfere with data transmission. Having a redundant topology allows data to be rerouted if one path is temporarily blocked.

Unlike microwave data service, there are no frequency licenses or towers to deal with. The laser devices are simply installed in windows or on roofs and aimed at one another. Since buildings can sway slightly and change shape with shifts in temperature, the aperture is spread, hitting a wider area. Over a one-kilometer distance, the laser spreads two meters. A wider spread doesn't weaken the signal; on the contrary, it makes it more reliable.

Table 6.2   Companies in the Wireless Optical Networking Market

COMPANY	WEB ADDRESS
AirFiber Inc.	www.airfiber.com
Canon U.S.A. Inc.	www.usa.canon.com
Cisco Aironet	www.cisco.com/warp/public/cc/pd/witc/ao350ap/
fSona, Inc.	www.fsona.com
LightPointe	www.lightpointe.com
Optical Access, Inc.	www.opticalaccess.com
Terabeam, Inc.	www.terabeam.com

Wireless Optical Networking Providers

Who are some of the companies providing solutions? Table 6.2 lists companies that offer wireless optical networking equipment.

AirFiber

AirFiber, funded by Nortel and Qualcomm, deploys roof-based transceivers in a mesh topology, ensuring that there is no problem if a single beam is blocked. Up to four transceivers can be deployed per roof. The mesh topology is more complex than some other approaches but ensures reliability. And, according to the company, this technology can work for distances of up to 200 meters. AirFiber uses SONET/ATM protocols.

How fast can AirFiber transmit data? At 200 meters, speeds up to 622 Mbps (OC-12) are available per node. To increase the throughput, simply deploy more transceivers per rooftop. The cost for AirFiber equipment is $30,000 per building.

Terabeam Internet

Terabeam Internet is a joint venture of Lucent and Terabeam. Terabeam has been particularly noted for pushing the envelope with wireless networking speed. Speeds of 140 Gbps are being tested, while speeds of 1 to 2 Gbps are routinely possible. The slowest link offered by the company is 5 Mbps.

Terabeam currently offers service in Seattle and five other U.S. cities. Unlike AirFiber, Terabeam's equipment does not require access to the roof, instead relying on 20-inch window-mounted transceivers. Buildings can be located up to 3 kilometers apart using Terabeam's technology.

Optical Access

Optical Access of Chatsworth, California, a wholly owned subsidiary of MRV Communications, offers wireless optical equipment that ranges in speed from

100 Mbps to 1 Gbps. It can beam data at distances of up to 2.3 miles. A pair of 100 Mbps transceivers costs $20,000. To help with any disruptions due to interference from fog, a 10 Mbps radio backup is available for an additional $5,000. In order to ensure that service is not disrupted, most customers implement two pairs of lasers for redundancy.

Wireless optical access provides a last-mile option for connections that need to be deployed more quickly than a fiber-based optical network. However, these networks are not everywhere and do not currently allow for the extension of optical Ethernet from the corporate network into the campus network.

Connecting the Corporate Network to the Internet or WAN

After networking the campus and local offices in the metro area, corporations face more challenges: connecting the corporate offices in a WAN and obtaining high-speed Internet connectivity. Since these topics are related, both in terms of the providers being used and in the technologies deployed, we will discuss them together.

In general, there is a bandwidth gap between corporate offices and the Internet backbone. LANs run at a high speed, and Internet backbone speeds can be measured in terabits per second. The connection between the corporate office and the larger network, however, is often a bottleneck. According to Ron Young, co-founder of Yipes Communications, "Everyone knows there's this serious bottleneck between fast local area networks and terabit fiber criss-crossing the country. When four out of five businesses have slower than T-1 access, no wonder the promise of the Internet isn't being realized" (Scanlon 2001).

Options for Connecting the Corporate Network to the Internet or WAN

Companies have several choices in building out their networks. They can lease dark fiber and create their own WAN, obtain traditional SONET services (T-1, DS-3, OC-3) from carriers or ISPs, or obtain service from an emerging carrier that offers metro Ethernet services.

Selecting a protocol for the WAN in part depends on what will be done with the connection. If the network carries both voice and data, and QoS is an important concern, SONET and ATM may offer the best combination. If the network will mainly carry data, Gigabit Ethernet is far less expensive to deploy, at less than half the price of SONET. Further, more companies are moving to VoIP. Combine Gigabit Ethernet (or 10-Gigabit Ethernet) with the bandwidth capability of fiber and the amount of available bandwidth may make the QoS measures offered by ATM unnecessary. We will discuss QoS issues later in this chapter as we examine the convergence of voice and data on the corporate network.

As mentioned earlier, Ethernet offers various other benefits worth considering. Having a single protocol from the LAN to the WAN can leverage the company's local skill set effectively and allow management of the WAN to be brought in-house. Further, the lack of protocol translation between the LAN and the larger Internet or WAN provides a more seamless interface and obviates the need for equipment to translate between SONET and Ethernet framing.

Leasing Dark Fiber

Since the early 1990s, large enterprises have been creating WANs by leasing dark fiber rather than obtaining service from traditional carriers in fixed increments. This is particularly true of financial institutions, whose stringent security requirements drove them to lease fiber, light it themselves, and manage their networks from end to end. In some cases, these companies can save money by purchasing services from Gigabit Ethernet providers. Depending on the terms of the lease on the fiber, however, they may need to maintain their existing arrangements. Additionally, the relative newness of the providers described in this chapter may cause larger corporations to shy away from them (thus reinforcing the status quo), fearing that a new provider may go out of business. Additionally, if these companies are leasing dark fiber, the network infrastructure that is currently in place is likely to be SONET-based, so Gigabit Ethernet may not be attractive.

If leased fiber is already in place, its capacity can be multiplied by using WDM. Companies may lack expertise to do this, but hiring people with this skill set, either as consultants or on a full-time basis, can be more cost-effective than procuring and lighting additional fiber along the same route. Developing expertise with DWDM, or less expensive CWDM, can help companies exploit the full potential of their optical networks.

Obtaining WAN and Internet Service from Carriers

About 80 percent of businesses in the United States are connected to the Internet with a T-1 connection (1.5 Mbps), which is slower than some cable modems. Further, businesses face serious delays in obtaining services in many areas of the country. To obtain an OC-48 can take up to a year in New York; having a T-3 line installed to connect offices in Manhattan and New Jersey takes more than six months, up to 200 working days. These delays are often unacceptable, especially as corporate bandwidth demands are doubling each year.

A number of metro providers have been popping up to fill this gap and to provide more flexible service than the traditional SONET speeds offered by carriers. Service is generally available more quickly and in more flexible increments, a feature referred to as *bandwidth on demand*. Further, after these connections are installed, additional bandwidth can be added either temporarily for a special event, such as a videoconference, or simply to upgrade the connection to reflect growing bandwidth needs. These increases in speed may be self-provisioned either through the provider's Web site or through a call to the provider. While getting a higher speed connection may take months through a traditional carrier, higher speeds, even temporary ones, can be obtained in 24 hours or less through these metro providers.

These Gigabit Ethernet providers are changing the market. Consultants like Tim Weis from TeleChoice recognize what is happening to the market: "It's coming down to cost. You can get 100 meg[abits per second] for a grand from providers like Cogent, get $14 per megabit per month from XO, or pay $1200 per month for a T-1 (1.5 Mbps) line from an ILEC" (Everitt 2001). Gigabit Ethernet providers have a different business model. As Scott Berry, Director of Product Development and Marketing at Metromedia Fiber Network, states, "Fundamentally, people are needing more and more bandwidth. Our business

---

Buying Bandwidth on Demand

By using newer carriers that offer bandwidth on demand, companies can obtain more flexible connections. Matt Kesner, CIO at Fenwick & West, a Palo Alto-based law firm, explored traditional telco offerings initially: "We talked to all the major telecom carriers. They suggested a DS3 or OC3 as the two options. It seemed like those two options were a huge step up in bandwidth—much more than we needed" (Moore 2001).

Fenwick & West almost signed a contract with a telco for $18,000 per month, more than a 10-fold increase from the $1500 per month it was paying for a T-1 connection. Kesner investigated the newer carriers, including Yipes.

The offering from Yipes matched their bandwidth requirements more closely: "They could bring fiber [to us] and bring in the bandwidth in the increments we wanted, starting at 10 Mb, which was closer to what we needed" (Moore 2001). Further, Yipes installed the service in 10 days, faster than the telcos' range of 30 to 60 days. The service costs Fenwick & West $6,000 per month along with a one-time installation fee of $1,000.

model is: Don't pay by the bit. Take fiber in. Pay by the month. Pump all you want" (Greim Everitt 2001).

Of course, obtaining service means that your offices must be located where metro providers have deployed their networks and that you are within a certain distance of their fiber loop. Those that offer short-term month-to-month contracts, such as Cogent Communications, have additional stipulations. For Cogent to connect a building to its network, there must be 25 tenants interested in service.

Most of the metro providers offer IP services over Ethernet, meaning that no translation need occur between the LAN and the WAN. Some publications have taken to calling such providers *EtherLECs*. A few, including Cogent, offer bandwidth on demand over IP but use SONET framing rather than Ethernet framing. Cogent's service does not require the installation of expensive SONET equipment, however.

The difficulty with metro providers, however, is that they truly serve only the major metro areas and typically only the downtown (most profitable) areas of those metro regions. Companies that want to connect all their branch offices may find it difficult to obtain WAN service from a single provider.

Evaluating Carriers

Companies interested in Gigabit Ethernet carriers, then, should evaluate them based on such factors as the geographic regions they serve, any limitations placed on locations connected within a service area, the terms of the contract, and, of course, cost.

Other requirements that you should examine include:

➤ **Protocol support.** Do you need only Gigabit Ethernet or do you need to support SONET and ATM as well? Some providers, such as GiantLoop, support multiple protocols.

➤ **Security.** What security measures are taken to protect your traffic? Does it travel over the commodity Internet? Is VPN service available, and is there an extra charge for using it?

➤ **Network reliability.** What does the carrier offer in terms of service level agreements (SLAs)?

➤ **Bandwidth flexibility.** Is true bandwidth on demand offered? How quickly can more capacity be brought online? Is it available temporarily or only as a permanent upgrade? Is there a Web-based interface through which you can provision your own bandwidth as needed?

➤ **Traffic segregation.** Is your traffic separated from that of other companies? How is the separation achieved? Does it travel over different fibers? Different wavelengths? Are virtual LANs (VLANs) used?

➤ **Monitoring and reporting.** One complaint regarding Gigabit Ethernet services is the inability to verify that the speeds being touted are in fact available. You should be able to monitor and receive reports regarding your actual bandwidth usage. You should be able to verify that you are receiving the bandwidth you are paying for. Traditional SONET services offer leased lines at various speeds. A T-3 is a T-3, and there's no question of how much bandwidth is available. New carriers need to provide the same type of assurance for their services.

Table 6.3 lists some of the carriers that have come on the scene.

Broadwing

Broadwing has a nationwide network, so it is not strictly a metro provider. Further, it was born of a merger between telco Cincinnati Bell and fiber provider IXC Communications in 1999. Broadwing does offer Gigabit Ethernet

Table 6.3 Metro Providers

CARRIERS	WEB ADDRESS
360 Networks	www.360networks.com
AT&T	www.att.com
Broadwing	www.broadwing.com
Cap Rock Communications	www.caprock.com
Cogent	www.cogent.com
GiantLoop	www.giantloop.com
Global Crossing	www.globalcrossing.com
Intellispace	www.intellispace.net
Level 3 Communications	www.level3.com
Looking Glass Networks	www.lglass.net
Metromedia Fiber Network	www.mmfn.com
Telseon	www.telseon.com
XO Communications	www.xo.com
Yipes	www.yipes.com

services in some metro areas, installing Gigabit Ethernet equipment at the customer's premises. Rather than signing up for a certain amount of bandwidth, Broadwing allows companies to pay for their average bandwidth usage per month, even if their traffic bursts into the gigabit per second range at times during the month.

Telseon

Based in Palo Alto, California, Telseon offers optical Ethernet services in 20 metro areas. In addition to its U.S. markets, it is currently undergoing an international expansion. Telseon offers Web-based provisioning and class-of-service differentiation. In addition to Gigabit Ethernet services, Telseon offers hosting as well as colocation for public servers requiring high-speed access. It is focusing on Web-hosting providers and application service providers (ASPs) in particular, which both require high bandwidth and availability.

Yipes

Yipes, based in San Francisco, offers optical Ethernet services, including bandwidth on demand. Currently, it has Web-based provisioning in beta testing and uses NetScreen to keep corporate traffic separate. This traffic separation is available for two of its services, Yipes WAN, which features a VPN, and Yipes WALL, a managed firewall service. Yipes WAN connects corporate locations in two areas served by Yipes, so clearly it will not work for all WAN services. Other products include Yipes NET for high-speed Internet access and Yipes MAN for connecting locations within a metro area.

In terms of quality-of-service distinctions, Yipes offers four levels of prioritization. The company plans to expand its QoS capabilities, according to Jerry Parrick, Yipes CEO (Martin 2000).

The company is targeting large enterprises. Like many of the carriers mentioned here, it offers promotions. Yipes' most popular promotion to date gives customers two free months of bandwidth at a higher speed; if the bandwidth is not needed, the customer can return to its earlier service level. This giving away of bandwidth seems to be effective; in March 2000, its average customer was using 4.9 Mbps; seven months later, the average usage had increased to 25 Mbps.

Metromedia Fiber Network

Metromedia Fiber Network, based in White Plains, New York, is a provider of both metro services and dark fiber. The company is in the process of a fiber build that will encompass more than 3 million miles of fiber laid in some 67 metro areas both in North America and in Europe. The company leases fiber both to carriers such as GiantLoop, Cogent, and SBC Communications (making it a carrier's carrier) and to end customers directly. In addition to leasing strands of fiber, customers can also lease wavelengths. The usual cost for leasing fiber is $100 per strand per mile for a 17-year contract. With dark fiber, customers have the option of lighting it with whatever technology they choose, whether SONET, ATM, or Gigabit Ethernet. Metromedia has deployed its fiber to make it easily replaceable when needed, designing its concrete conduit so fiber can be pulled and replaced without disturbing the conduit itself.

Paul Vixie is the CTO of Metromedia. Vixie is well-known in the Internet community for his long-time IETF participation and development of important Internet software. He is the primary author for BIND 8, the most widely used implementation of the domain name system (DNS). He founded the Internet Software Consortium and currently chairs its board of directors.

Metromedia is unusual in that it offers both dark fiber and managed network services, both SONET and Gigabit Ethernet.

GiantLoop

Waltham, Massachusetts-based GiantLoop serves a very specific market: large Fortune 500 companies with multiprotocol networks to support. The company doesn't own its own fiber but locates and manages fiber on behalf of its customers. It supports Gigabit Ethernet, SONET, and ATM as well as the major SAN protocols: Fibre Channel, Fiber Connection (FICON), and Enterprise System Connection (ESCON). Rather than building out its network ahead of time, the company lands large customer contracts and builds private networks on the customer's behalf. According to GiantLoop, it takes from 60 to 90 days to serve a customer who is on a fiber ring; to build a network for those who are not takes from 90 to 120 days. For more information and an excellent white paper, visit their Web site listed in Table 6.3.

AT&T Ultravailable Broadband Network

The traditional telcos will not be left out of the new metro market for long. AT&T is the first to offer a metro service, which some companies, including Merrill Lynch, are using for a MAN. Merrill Lynch has linked 11 locations in the New York/New Jersey metropolitan area.

Sites on the network can be up to 25 miles apart; users select the bandwidth amount they need, up to 2.4Gbps. The service features network uptime guarantees (as the name implies). It is not a Gigabit Ethernet service, however; it can carry IP, ATM, and SONET traffic. The DWDM-based service is available in New York, Los Angeles, Chicago, Washington, D.C., and Houston.

Applications Driving Corporate Optical Networking

Optical networking is never done for its own sake. Companies need high-speed bandwidth at reasonable costs to support a variety of applications, including SANs and VoIP.

SANs

Backing up corporate networks has become both time- and cost-prohibitive as storage requirements approach terabit levels. Physically shipping tapes to disaster recovery facilities is also an inefficient means of ensuring that corporate data is safe. Storage area networks are quickly becoming a bulk application, representing a large share of the total data traffic in metro areas, up to 50 percent, compared with an average of 10 percent for IP traffic, according to GiantLoop.

High-speed connections to SANs have replaced older methods of backing up systems. For local backups, the connections might be to SANs in another part of the building or even in the computer room. What makes SANs efficient is the speed of the connection between the network and the storage architecture.

It is just as important to get corporate data away from a particular site to aid in disaster recovery efforts. In this case, data must be shipped long distances over high-speed links. The distance limitations of Fibre Channel make this difficult, however: Fibre Channel can run 30 meters over copper, 300 meters over multimode fiber, or 10 kilometers over single-mode fiber. None of these distances is really far enough to support disaster-recovery SANs, which require substantial physical distance from the corporate network to ensure that natural disasters do not wipe out all copies of the data being stored.

Several IP-based SAN protocols are under consideration. Nishan Systems of San Jose, California, has proposed Storage Over IP (SOIP) to the IETF. The standard basically runs Fibre Channel over IP and includes facilities for a naming service. Cisco, Adaptec, and IBM back another possible standard, SCSI over IP. This approach encapsulates small computer system interface (SCSI) data in an IP packet, tunnels it through the TCP/IP stack, and then unwraps the packet, converting it back to SCSI. A similar approach for Fibre Channel, also endorsed by Cisco as well as by CNT, Gadzoox, Vixel, and Lucent, is Fibre Channel Tunnelling.

Despite the flux in establishing standards, SANs are an important application for corporate networks, both in the short term and the long haul. Only fiber provides the needed bandwidth to move gigabytes and terabytes of data across the enterprise LAN and WAN efficiently.

Voice over IP

As companies invest in high-speed optical networks either connecting remote locations or for their campuses, running voice over this network becomes a practical consideration. Chicago's CivicNet will run all its voice traffic over IP ultimately. While VoIP over the commodity Internet offers lower quality than traditional telephone service, VoIP over private fat optical pipes is an entirely different story. Bandwidth in this environment is nearly unlimited.

VoIP offers some clear advantages. Voice and e-mail can be integrated; Outlook offers the capability to right-click to call the contact in question. Moves, adds, and changes involve simply plugging a phone into a new outlet, very easy by comparison with a PBX, where you have to punch down wiring and reconfigure each time you move a phone. The full range of costs, including maintenance, is comparable, even though IP phones cost much more than traditional phones. And, in organizations such as schools, adding phones to each classroom was not cost-effective, but is now far more reasonable with a VoIP infrastructure.

If an organization is changing infrastructure anyway, deploying VoIP becomes a more serious consideration. For example, when the State of Connecticut's network operations center and data center flooded, cracks in the foundation required the building to be condemned rather than being refurbished. The new facility purchased by the state had an out-of-date PBX that would have been very expensive to upgrade. As a result, the state decided to make this building a pilot deployment of VoIP, which they now plan to roll out to other state offices.

Voice over IP also has some drawbacks. It may lack some features, such as support for conference calling, faxing, emergency 911 services, or analog phones. And it may not reliably interoperate, forcing companies to make a single vendor choice. Currently Cisco leads the VoIP market, with more than a million ports installed and sales of about 1500 IP phones per day.

Other Convergence Solutions

VoIP is not the only choice available for a converged network. Voice traffic can be sent via ATM while other data rides on IP. CivicNet's approach to quality-of-service is to use Diffserv to tag time-sensitive traffic for special handling. In Alberta, MPLS will be used. Since these two standards provide different functionality, with MPLS more analogous to ATM, they could be used complementarily.

While QoS issues often emerge when discussing voice networks, there is controversy about how to approach this problem, if at all. Bandwidth is often so inexpensive that it is cheaper to increase bandwidth than to bother with complex QoS solutions. At Cleveland biotech firm Gliatech, senior IT manager Dave Bujaucius chose to upgrade their T-1 line rather than deploy a QoS system: "We found that the difference between a fractional and full T-1 was less than $100 per month. A QoS product would have taken several years to pay for itself, so we just purchased the extra bandwidth" (Caruso 2001). Certainly, providing nearly unlimited bandwidth is also the approach taken by CA*net3 in Canada, as well as on Cogent's network.

Coarse QoS is another possibility. Rather than supporting many QoS levels, have only two: one for voice and video (time-sensitive applications) and another for all other traffic. This coarse approach greatly simplifies QoS, while efficiently moving traffic across the corporate network.

Case Study: Fiber to the LAN at George Washington University

In 1996, Doug Gale, the CIO for George Washington University, hired Guy Jones as Director of Technology Information. Jones came from the University of Nebraska at Lincoln, where they had just put in a campus-wide copper network, with fiber between buildings and fiber between floors in a number of the buildings. GWU had an initial plan to install a copper infrastructure campus-wide. Until this point, there was no campus-wide network; various departments had built their own networks. Jones proposed scrapping the initial plan for the copper network and building a fiber-based campus-wide LAN instead.

Jones took into account all the costs, not just the cable or wiring itself, but also the maintenance, the space needed for wiring closets, and their associated environmental requirements for air conditioning and physical security, and other installation challenges (in some buildings at Nebraska, the university spent less on electronics than on abating asbestos during the installation). Fiber came out the clear winner. In addition to being much easier to maintain and requiring far less space to install—space is at a premium at GWU with its location in downtown D.C.—fiber would provide an infrastructure for the future as well as for the present.

The Extent of the Network

Deploying the fiber-based campus-wide network was only a small part of the university's Millennium Plan, with about 15 percent of the funding for that initiative going to the network.

The initial deployment of the network involved 8,000 fiber drops and was completed in under three years. Now there are about 10,000 connections, and by 2004, Jones expects the connections to expand to 15,000–16,000.

There are drops to each student living in on-campus housing (a drop per pillow), although some of the buildings GWU has recently acquired cannot be fibered because they are not adjacent to the campus. The university has had difficulty obtaining rights-of-way between on-campus buildings and the nearby (500 yards away) buildings that have just been purchased—probably one of the more frustrating aspects of dealing with this network.

Students, faculty, and staff are each given different default speeds. Students and most staff receive 10Mbps connections while faculty are given an OC-3 (155 Mbps). The fiber infrastructure is based on ATM over SONET. The network includes multimode fiber to the desktop and single-mode fiber between hub sites, most of which is unused or underused at this point.

Jones has integrated some wireless LAN capabilities into the infrastructure and plans to do more: Mobile users in public areas of the campus can access the network via wireless connections. Further, each classroom has a single fiber drop to a desktop; the remaining networking needs in the classroom are met with wireless. When students come to class with their laptops, they are connected via wireless to the campus network.

When GWU started its build in 1996, it was a beta site for 3M's Volition fiber. The installation used both in-house staff and outsourcing. Over time, the university has outsourced more of the installation so in-house staff could focus on maintenance and troubleshooting. Jones' policy has been to outsource any function that did not provide significant benefits to the university. In-house staff members were given an opportunity to gain expertise with fiber. Telecom techs were given the opportunity to train as info techs, which gave them a career path and a salary increase, as well as experience in installing and maintaining a fiber infrastructure. In-house staff also have the expertise to oversee and verify the installation work done by third parties.

Although GWU plans to experiment with Gigabit Ethernet, the SONET infrastructure is working fine. The network handles both voice and data using ATM, which is preferred because it can carry traditional voice and video as well as IP traffic. However, few applications can take advantage of ATM at the desktop; that market appears to be drying up. Media converters are used at the desktop to handle the incoming fiber.

continues

continued

The university is currently in the process of investigating VoIP, but the traditional telephone structure currently offers more features and is slowing the push to VoIP. If all costs are taken into account, including maintenance by personnel and maintenance for PBX equipment, costs for VoIP and traditional telephony were found to be comparable. Current limitations for VoIP, according to Jones, include features and quality of voice services; he states that it seems to be better for workgroups than for larger areas.

Fiber Advantages

In terms of maintenance, Jones has found the fiber optic infrastructure to be much more carefree than a traditional copper infrastructure. The only problems have related to physical destruction of the connectors in the rooms, where connectors have been damaged by, for example, a bookcase being shoved against them.

The space-saving nature of fiber is a prime advantage at GWU, where space is at a premium. Because fiber follows more of a telecom structure than a LAN structure, in that a central office serves many customers, far fewer optical hubs are needed than in a traditional LAN. There are 15 small hubs, as compared with the 160 to 180 that would be needed for a copper infrastructure. In some cases, the hubs were built in a parking space near a building. However, given the growth in the infrastructure, Jones wishes that the hubs were each a bit larger to allow for expansion. With a nearly two-fold growth in drops anticipated by 2004, the hubs are already becoming a bit cramped.

Fiber's flexibility is another advantage. Moves, adds, and changes are easily accomplished. If faculty members move to another floor or another building, their OC-3 moves with them. Further, since all the infrastructure is fiber, any link that needs an upgrade in speed can handle the load. If a particular classroom or lab needs an OC-12, it can be accommodated.

So far Jones finds that the bandwidth is being underused rather than overused. There is no need today to deploy wavelengths when the basic capacity of the fiber is not saturated. Students have at times consumed more bandwidth using such services as Napster (after spring break 2000, bandwidth usage rose 50 percent in a week from Napster and other peer-to-peer applications), but there has been no reason to constrain the usage of the network.

One unintended consequence of having a leading-edge infrastructure has been a rise in hacking attacks that tracks fairly closely to the growth in bandwidth usage. GWU is tightening its security as a result.

The fiber optic infrastructure has made it possible for GWU to participate actively in Internet2 research as well. For example, Dr. Jerry Feinstein teaches a telecommunications class both at Harvard and at GWU simultaneously. When Dr. Feinstein is at Harvard, the class at GWU sees him on a large projection screen.

He can see all the students in the remote classroom through his video link and interact with them just as if he were there in person. Because of the nature of the class, some sessions were up to eight hours long, running video over Internet2's Abilene high-speed network.

Another class is in the works. This time a group of professionals will take a class in São Paulo, Brazil, that is simultaneously offered by Feinstein at GWU. The São Paulo university, IBM EC, is connected to the high-speed research network by way of AmericasPATH (AmPATH), a research network with a fiber optic ring connecting Latin America to a POP on Internet2 in Miami. AmPATH is sponsored by Global Crossing with support from Internet2 and the Science, Technology, And Research Transit Access Point (STAR TAP), the high-speed research network funded by the National Science Foundation that connects high-speed research networks from around the world.

Fiber provides GWU with an infrastructure for today and for the future. Jones, who has recently been appointed Chief Technology Officer, has been a key visionary in developing one of the top infrastructures in the country for GWU.

NOTE

Although the preceding case study focuses on a university deployment, it illustrates fiber to the desktop, an important consideration for all organizations.

Case Study: VantagePoint's Move to Bandwidth on Demand

VantagePoint, an applications service provider for the agriculture industry based in Fort Collins, Colorado, near Boulder, started out as a .com startup, a joint venture of John Deere, Farmland Industries, and Grillmark, a regional cooperative in southern Illinois. Its Web site, which encompasses some 2.5 terabytes of data, provides a variety of services to producers, such as farmers and ranchers, and other professionals, including companies that sell to or purchase from producers. The site offers a mix of subscription and free services, including local weather reports, current market prices, crop record keeping, and satellite images. Companies that sell to producers can rebrand the site's capabilities and offer them to their own customers.

continues

continued

   With its massive site and subscription business model, VantagePoint understandably considers fresh content its first priority. Multiple engineers often wanted to work on the site at once, but the company's T-1 connection to the Internet, through which it would update the site using an Internet VPN to hosting provider EMC2 in Boston, was saturated. In effect, only one engineer at a time could update the site. The site is completely rebuilt once every six weeks, a process which used all the company's bandwidth, keeping other employees offline and taking an inordinate amount of time. The company had clearly outgrown its 1.5 Mbps T-1 connection, but deploying the traditional next step up in bandwidth, a DS-3 (45 Mbps), would entail an enormous jump in price as well as an unacceptably long lead time.

   And the expense of a DS-3 couldn't be justified; it was far more capacity than VantagePoint needed. Jason Wallin, VantagePoint's manager of Network Operations, got a quote from Yipes, a metro Ethernet provider. Yipes could provide bandwidth on demand, starting at 10 Mbps, a more appropriate step up in bandwidth compared to a DS3's 45 Mbps. Further, with Yipes, the bandwidth could be turned up on very short notice if more capacity was needed. Yipes could pull fiber to VantagePoint's offices and have the connection up and running in two weeks after VantagePoint signed a letter of intent. Not surprisingly, Wallin gave his business to Yipes. Wallin did admit that VantagePoint is favorably situated, with its offices just one mile from Yipes' Boulder fiber ring. Installation may have taken longer—or the service may have been unavailable—if this were not the case.

   Initially, management had some misgivings about using a nontraditional provider, Wallin concedes, particularly since VantagePoint was among Yipes' first customers in Colorado. VantagePoint initially kept its T-1 line for redundancy. However, after a month and a half of service with Yipes, VantagePoint dropped its T-1 line. Further, once its bandwidth needs increase to the level of a DS3, the price with Yipes will still be less, and the growth potential greater than traditional telcodata services: The company's connection to Yipes can scale to a gigabit per second without any changes in equipment.

   One unexpected benefit is that latency across the Internet dropped significantly, in part due to never having to change framing protocols. According to Wallin, "the performance is actually better with Yipes than over a traditional frame-relay connection. Using Ethernet all the way out to [our ISP] gets us one step closer to the actual backbone of the Internet, with less latency. And that means our performance times over the Internet are greatly improved, just by changing that one hop" (Wallin 2001).

   VantagePoint is experiencing first-hand the benefits of a high-speed fiber Internet connection. Using Gigabit Ethernet rather than a more traditional SONET architecture enables bandwidth on demand, allowing VantagePoint to purchase the bandwidth it needs as it needs it.

Conclusion

Corporate use of optical networking will increase over the next decade as organizations replace their aging copper infrastructures with far more scalable fiber. In the meantime, Gigabit Ethernet will become an important technology not only for the LAN and the campus, but for the WAN and for flexible, high-speed Internet connectivity.

Fiber to the Home

D epending on how long you have been following optical networking, it may surprise you to find out that fiber to the home (FTTH) was discussed long before alternatives like digital subscriber line (DSL) or cable modems came on the scene. For some, that premature wave of excitement about the technology, followed by its failure to materialize, makes optical networking to the home a moot subject. It's viewed as economically infeasible, impractical, and generally passé.

However, as we will see, DSL and cable modems are stopgap measures at best. Fixed wireless is no better. Especially given the falling costs of deploying fiber and the popularity of high-speed Internet access, FTTH makes sense and is in fact being deployed in numerous places around the United States, Canada, and the world. There are roadblocks to its deployment, however. After all, the existing high-speed access players—cable and telephone companies—are not in most cases going to deploy an infrastructure that could cannibalize their own revenues and their own investments. So if FTTH is to be widely deployed, who will do it?

Background on FTTH

The subject of FTTH is far from new. According to Bruce Kushnik, executive director of the New Networks Institute, in the 1980s and the 1990s, local telcos in the United States promised to build FTTH systems for millions of subscribers. In light of these promises, public utility commissions allowed them to collect fees from customers to support that effort. Because the project was deemed prohibitively expensive when further evaluated, the companies never built the networks. They did keep the fees, however (Oram 2001).

The early wave of excitement surrounding FTTH that so quickly dissipated has left some disillusioned about its long-term prospects. The fact that no applications available today require FTTH further reinforces this negativity. Claude Romans, director for access networks at Ryan Hankin Kent, is pessimistic about prospects for FTTH: "The majority of U.S.-based companies haven't made up their minds as to whether or not they want to invest in FTTH/fiber to the curb [FTTC] networks. The bottom line is that about five years ago, when switched digital video went away as a business case, the FTTH market dried up, and DSL took its place for Internet access. FTTH costs more, and there are no services that require it. I wouldn't rule it out entirely, but I don't think there's going to be an FTTH revolution" (Lindstrom 2000).

Not all experts are pessimistic about the prospects for FTTH. Alastair Glass, photonics research vice president at Lucent, states, "Eventually, fiber will go to the home—sooner than people think" (Hecht 2000). Despite early disillusionment with the concept, falling prices for fiber optic equipment and the lack of long-term, robust, high-speed Internet access solutions for the home are making the industry as a whole reconsider the FTTH market.

The State of Broadband to the Home Today

In the United States today, the exact penetration of broadband is controversial. Estimates vary depending on the methodology used and the types of broadband technologies included. Kinetic Strategies (whose research considers only DSL and cable modem deployment) states that there are some 7.6 million residential broadband subscribers in the United States and 1.7 million in Canada. For Canada, the market penetration is about double that of the United States—15 percent of Canadian households have broadband Internet access, in contrast to 7.5 percent of U.S. households.

NetValue places U.S. broadband penetration at 11.1 percent, slightly higher than Kinetic Strategies' figure of 7.5 percent. Research methodologies may account for these differences. For example, NetValue's figures include satellite broadband access as well as cable and DSL while Kinetic Strategies measures only the latter two broadband technologies. The sampling methodology can also have an impact. If more urban than rural households are sampled, the figure may appear slightly higher. Research from the U.S. Department of Commerce shows that 12 percent of urban households have broadband connections compared with 7.3 percent of all households nationwide, very close to Kinetic Strategies' figure. In fact, the differences between these studies is not that substantial. Drawing conclusions based on all three sources, we can conclude that 90 percent or more of U.S. households do not have broadband.

Why the low penetration rate in the United States? First, government has not made a significant push for broadband. For example, in South Korea, where the government is actively promoting access, the penetration rate for broadband stands at 57 percent (see Figure 7.1). Second, broadband providers have been slow to expand their markets, in part because it requires substantial investment in the infrastructure. Additionally, for telcos offering digital subscriber line (DSL) and cable companies offering cable Internet service, consumer broadband connectivity represents a new market, and it takes time to develop staff to install and support such services.

The two most popular forms of broadband access are DSL and cable modems. Cable modems are the more popular of the two options currently, partly because they have a two-year lead on DSL in terms of adoption. According to Kinetic Strategies, cable currently has about 70 percent of the broadband market, with some 6.4 million subscribers in the United States and Canada, while DSL subscribers stand at 2.9 million. Further, cable adoption continues at a faster rate, with nearly 1 million new subscribers added in North America in the first quarter of 2001 while DSL had about half that many during the same period at 560,148.

% of Internet households connecting via broadband. February 2001

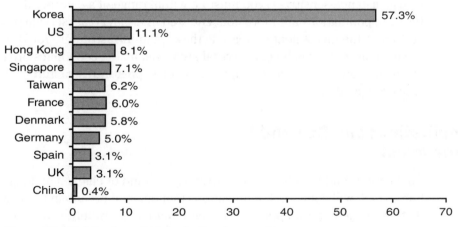

Figure 7.1 Relative broadband adoption by country.

Copyright February 2001. Courtesy of NetValue.

Demand for Broadband to the Home

What is the problem with adopting broadband to the home technologies? Does the relatively low adoption rate indicate a lack of demand? On the contrary, there is good indication of a pent-up demand for broadband services that is not currently being met and which cannot be met long-term by existing technologies.

Telework Requires Home Broadband

In addition to recreational and home use, the growing numbers of teleworkers are fueling the demand for broadband access to the Internet, something that can happen only through broadband access to the Internet from home. Whether the work from home is full-time, part-time, or supplementary, a dial-up connection makes such work nearly untenable.

Second Class Access in Rural Areas

Although demand for broadband to the home is widespread, rural areas have far less hope of gaining broadband access. Home broadband alternatives tend to be few and far between in rural areas.

Simply put, it costs service providers more to provide broadband to rural areas than it does in urban areas. Cable laid for television is a receive-only medium, and upgrades for two-way transmission are costly and time consuming. There is little economic incentive for service providers to bring cable Internet access to rural areas.

DSL is distance-sensitive—you must be within range of a central office. Because populations are more concentrated in urban areas, service providers may make the investment to upgrade the copper infrastructure for DSL in urban areas, but virtually ignore rural areas. Again, the economics break down when you consider the cost of upgrading the copper infrastructure in rural areas versus ROI.

Applications and Demand for Broadband

Applications and broadband are currently in a kind of chicken-and-egg situation. Which will come first, applications that demand broadband or broadband that paves the way for applications that require it? Certainly, using the Internet over dial-up lines is frustrating. Even Web page downloads are painfully slow. Add a multimedia element—streaming video or audio, large files such as music or other multimedia files—and the pain outweighs the advantages of the service, causing all but the most determined and patient users to simply eschew the applications until they have better connectivity. Further, content providers can't target broadband users when the ratio of dial-up to broadband users stands at 50 to 1.

Bill St. Arnaud at CANARIE believes that bandwidth will pave the way for advanced applications:

> The advent of low-cost, high-bandwidth to the home may usher in a new world of applications where the network, in effect, becomes the computer. Currently there are few traditional applications that require bandwidth to the home in excess of a few megabits per second. But the same story was true for the personal computer, where 15 years ago there were few applications that required more than kilobytes of memory and all the data could be easily stored on a single floppy disk. It is now difficult to conceive of operating a PC with anything less than 32 Mbytes of memory and a 2 gigabyte drive (St. Arnaud 2001).

Consider the bandwidth requirements of a video-on-demand application deployed to 250,000 homes. If there were a peak demand of 25 percent of those customers using the service at once, it would result in 37,500 simultaneous video streams. With 3.2 Mbps per stream, a throughput of 120 Gbps would be needed during peak periods, according to calculations by Gall and Shapiro (2001). Were this application rolled out nationwide to the 108 million households in the United States, the infrastructure would be taxed. These streams are smaller than those needed for real-time interactive video, which requires 13 to 40 Mbps per stream. Neither cable modems nor DSL can provide that throughput.

Home Broadband Options

Today's broadband to the home options include cable modems, DSL, and to a far lesser extent, fixed wireless and satellite. In the case of cable and DSL, both represent options that exploit the providers' existing infrastructure. Some coaxial cable systems have been upgraded to allow for cable modem access; copper plants are being reworked to provide DSL access. Let's look at these options in a bit more detail.

Cable Modems

Cable modems range in speed from 1.5 Mbps (the most typical throughput) all the way to 10 Mbps. Some companies are testing speeds of up to 40 Mbps, but this is currently experimental. Advent Networks' Ultraband technology can produce 40 Mbps, but it is currently in testing. In part, cable was a natural for home broadband because the wide downstream pipe provided by coaxial cable for broadcast meant that a one-way broadband medium was already in place; cable companies needed only to add the upstream portion. It is still not a trivial upgrade, however. To provide a neighborhood with cable modem service, the cable company must upgrade infrastructure to 500 or more homes before any receive the new service.

Early cable modems used a dial-up connection for upstream, but newer cable connections provide an upstream without use of telephone lines. However, like most home broadband solutions, the downstream throughput far exceeds the upstream throughput, with typical speeds of 500–1500 Kbps downstream and 128–500 Kbps upstream. The average customer pays about $40 a month for cable Internet.

Cable modem deployment entails fiber optic deployment as well. Cable companies are putting fiber further and further into the neighborhood as demand accelerates. This is why such deployments are often referred to as hybrid-fiber coax or HFC. The proverbial "last mile," however, is coax.

Cable modems present security concerns. Not only are they *always-on* connections, in effect exposing the home user to attacks from the Internet, but cable is a shared medium. All information is delivered to all users, like a LAN. If the home system is set up to share its disk with other LAN-based systems, users in the neighborhood can access one another's hard drives. Because it is like a LAN, speed degrades as more users come online. For cable providers to maintain network performance, they then have to install fiber farther into the neighborhood.

DSL

Like cable modems, DSL also requires fiber deployment. Fiber is deployed just far enough into the neighborhood to ensure service. The last three to nine thousand feet are copper.

DSL is highly distance-sensitive. Users can get DSL service only if they are near enough to the telephone company's central office (CO). Copper phone lines are subject to cross-talk. Even if a residence appears to be close enough to the CO, a technician may have problems installing DSL because of the need for a clean circuit that will not experience substantial electrical interference.

Prices for DSL have been rising along with cable modem prices. Other challenges include the tendency of providers to disappear in a volatile economy. Northpoint, which wholesaled DSL service to ISPs (including MSN, Telocity, and Verio) which could then resell it, sold its assets to AT&T in March 2001 and immediately shut down its network. The outage further undermined consumer confidence in DSL and left a hundred thousand primarily business customers stranded without service (AT&T bought the company, but not its customer base). This has created further bad press for DSL, which was already plagued with installation problems, sometimes stretching on for months. Part of the reason for instability in the DSL market is that ISPs and wholesalers barely make enough from providing the service to cover their costs; ISPs providing DSL services have stated that after paying the RBOC's charges, they in fact make more money on dial-up accounts than they do reselling DSL.

DSL is typically asymmetrical in speed, at least in its consumer incarnation, ADSL. A typical consumer offering is 128 Kbps upstream and 768 Kbps downstream for about $50 per month, but faster speeds may be available at a higher price. More expensive symmetrical connections are available but are generally priced out of the range of most consumers ($150–160 per month or more).

Although the price for DSL is higher than dial-up, it obviates the need for a second phone line, an expense that many Internet users have incurred. Another DSL positive—it is not a shared medium and, therefore, doesn't suffer from some of the security risks that cable modems do. However, DSL is still an always-on connection and as such, requires some kind of firewall to prevent Internet attacks from compromising the user's computer.

Fixed Wireless

Although there are currently fewer deployments, fixed wireless, also known as multipoint multichannel distribution system (MMDS), is another alternative for home broadband, especially for those beyond the reach of cable modems and DSL service. It provides a downstream throughput of 385 Kbps to 1 Mbps and an upstream throughput of 384 to 512 Kbps. The typical downstream is 512 Kbps; typical upstream is 256 Kbps. It has the advantage of being able to serve thousands of residential customers from a single antenna on a high point.

Some of the first prominent names in fixed wireless have gone out of business, however. Advanced Radio Telecom, Teligent, and WinStar all filed bankruptcy in the first half of 2001. Sprint, AT&T, and MCI WorldCom have entered the market, an indication that IXCs may dominate this nascent market at least for the near-term. There are other players, however, including WaveRider, which has a fixed wireless system installed in Roseville, Minnesota, and Prime Companies, which is establishing service in rural areas of western Pennsylvania. Much like DSL, pricing varies on fixed wireless connections. Sprint's data only service, aimed at home users, costs about $50 per month while AT&T's service, which includes two phone lines, costs $80 per month. Some ISPs, including Gecko Internet, sell the service for varying prices depending on the speed of the connection: 128 Kbps costs $250 per month while 512 Kbps costs $600 per month. Although fixed wireless has yet to gain much ground, given the fact that many subscribers across the U.S. have no form of broadband available to date, fixed wireless may fill the bill. Fixed wireless also holds promise for international deployments where there is no existing infrastructure in place, such as southeast Asia and Latin America. According to research from Allied Business Intelligence, the world market for fixed wireless subscribers is set to grow from 644,000 in 2001 to 15.5 million by 2006 (Stokes 2001).

Satellite

Satellite systems are another alternative for broadband consumer access, particularly for rural areas. Dataquest predicts that the satellite broadband market will surge by 2005, according to a February 2001 study.

Satellite broadband adoption is likely to parallel adoption for digital satellite television. In some areas it is likely to be the only choice other than dial-up. DirecPC from Hughes offers downstream speeds of 400 Kbps while StarBand Communications offers 500 Kbps downstream. Upstream ranges from 125 Kbps (Direcway) to 150 Kbps (StarBand). Both Starband and Direcway service costs $70 per month. Like satellite television, these services require the purchase and installation of a satellite dish at an additional cost. It is likely that most customers who subscribe to satellite data services will also have satellite television.

Fiber to the Home

We have discussed some home broadband options that have seen relatively slow adoption. Is there a need for fiber to the home that would provide an incredible amount of long-term bandwidth? Jim Bauer, a network manager, says yes. Bandwidth requirements for homes will grow just as his campus network has.

Further, current broadband alternatives restrict teleworkers, who represent the most hungry market for bandwidth to the home. These technologies often prevent the very activities that teleworkers need to perform. Some cable modem services restrict the use of *virtual private networks* (VPNs) that encrypt data as it transverses the public network, a requirement for remote access for many businesses. Cable modems rely on caching popular data in order to provide adequate bandwidth to all subscribers. VPNs make that impossible. Other services also restrict the use of VPNs, stating that they require too much bandwidth.

Another forbidden activity is running a server from home. And, even if it isn't expressly forbidden, it is essentially impossible because bandwidth is so asymmetrical, with the downstream pipe far wider than the upstream pipe. As St. Arnaud (2000) states, "More importantly because of the highly asymmetrical nature of cable modem or xDSL service it will be difficult for a home, school or small business to be a data exporter rather than a data consumer."

Cable and DSL are interim technologies at best. The coaxial infrastructure is 30 years old and has been upgraded only with difficulty. Further, it creates a shared medium whose speed degrades as more users come online. In the case of DSL, it is highly distance-sensitive and subject to interference. With fiber prices falling faster than copper prices, it makes sense to consider FTTH solutions, particularly for new developments, rather than making these ill-equipped, aging infrastructures bear the weight of the coming broadband revolution.

Compare these interim technologies to a long-term investment in fiber. The peak hour of all U.S. telephone traffic could fit on a single fiber. It is a future-proof technology. Unlike copper's crosstalk problems, fiber is not subject to electrical interference or eavesdropping.

Further, the additional cost for fiber is marginal when you consider it as a long-term investment. As Jeff Starcer, plant manager for Rye Telephone points out, "Using FTTH will cost us about an additional $600 per subscriber—but unlike copper, we won't have to replace it within seven years" (Lindstrom 2000). Rye has deployed FTTH to a subdivision of Denver known as Hatchet Ranch. Distance from the CO was also a consideration in choosing fiber over DSL.

Vint Cerf, Senior Vice President for Internet Architecture and Technology at WorldCom and one of the Internet's chief designers, also sees FTTH as a decision based on economics as well as throughput. He suggests that power companies might be the ones to deploy it, given their existing infrastructure:

> DSL may eventually turn out to be more expensive to maintain as a physical plant than optical fiber. So economics may drive us in the direction of fiber to the home. Very few people have been building fiber to residences, but when you look at the power companies, especially in California, you have to wonder if they need another business line. In addition to supplying electricity, they might permit the use or right of way to carry photons as well as electrons. Optical fiber is relatively immune to interference, as

is typical power cable, because they operate in the same regime. It might be that power companies could become the dark horses of the fiber business (Luzadder 2001).

Deploying interim broadband measures like DSL requires laying fiber farther and farther into the neighborhood, particularly as the number of subscribers increases. At a certain point, it makes sense to take fiber to the curb and then to the home. Certainly, applications will be bootstrapped without adequate bandwidth. According to Cerf, "There are a lot of applications that just won't work without enough bandwidth. If we can get a Gigabit Ethernet up and running at the end of the Net . . . it would allow us to deliver an enormous amount of information in a short amount of time. But the only way to do that is to get fiber closer and closer to the destination."

All of these pseudo-broadband solutions share common problems. First, they provide little to no room for growth in broadband traffic over time, providing only a meager, short-term solution to home broadband requirements. Second, the current options lock users into a single provider.

Common applications such as video require a far greater throughput than is currently available with today's broadband alternatives. DVDs require a throughput of 40 Mbps and full-motion JPEG with improved compression requires more than 20 Mbps per stream. Without even considering what other bandwidth-hungry applications are on the horizon, there are applications that people would like to use today, but can't, because of bandwidth constraints.

These same bandwidth constraints make convergence almost impossible. Apollo Guy, Vice President of Marketing and Business at Toronto-based Futureway Communications, recognizes fiber as the only long-term choice for broadband to the home: "There isn't a platform besides fiber that can deliver all those services [switched voice, NTSC video, high-speed data, CATV] on the same pipe" (Ploskina and Williamson 2001). With fiber, convergence is possible, though as we will see, convergence is not necessarily the best approach.

DSL, cable, satellite, and fixed wireless are at best interim solutions to providing broadband to the home. Fiber prices are falling, making FTTH an attractive, future-proof, long-term investment.

Costs and Profitability of Deploying FTTH

What are the per-household costs for deploying FTTH? Depending on the technology used, the cost ranges from $1700 to $3500 per subscriber. Optical Solutions, a firm that specializes in passive optical networking (PON) to the home, states that a hybrid-fiber coax connection to the home costs $1907 and a DSL solution costs $2484. The pure fiber solution falls slightly below DSL costs, at $2385 per home for a PON solution. In the Swedish case study later in this chapter, subscribers paid for the fiber to their homes based on the speed of their connections. For a 10-Mbps connection, the cost was $1700 while for a 100-Mbps connection, the cost was $2000. In Grant County, Washington, the cost for FTTH was about $3500 per subscriber, expected to decrease to $2600 as equipment prices drop. Both Sweden and Grant County implementations were Ethernet FTTH. The pricing variations reflect differences in equipment used, business models, and the availability of existing dark fiber to lease.

Fiber makes sense for new developments in particular. Further, it has a far longer depreciation cycle, 10 to 20 years compared to less than 10 for cable or DSL.

But is FTTH profitable? That greatly depends on the deployment and its purposes. In Glasgow, Kentucky, FTTH provides residents with both high bandwidth and considerable cost avoidance.

In the Swedish FTTH case study, residents pay only $8 per month for the highest-speed residential Internet access available because they themselves own the underlying infrastructure.

When cities own the infrastructure for fiber to the home, there are further economic considerations. According to research from the city of Winnipeg: "Cities that have done fibre to home installations have, as a rule, not made money but they are breaking even. However, surplus revenues are realized from the leasing of fibre to carriers, service providers (ISPs), and institutions" (Smart Winnipeg 2000). In part, the profitability of FTTH is a long-term proposition, depending on how the bandwidth is used and the applications for which it is deployed.

Approaches to FTTH

There are several considerations for FTTH deployment. Where does it make the most economic sense? Who should own the infrastructure? Should we focus on convergence when deploying FTTH today?

FTTH for New Builds

Existing homes typically have copper and coaxial infrastructure in place. Deploying fiber in these areas takes special effort and involves disruption to streets and yards, in most cases. However, new developments offer an opportunity to include fiber from the ground up at a marginal additional cost. Some analysts predict that by 2004, fiber to new homes will be a standard feature. Aliunde is a UK company that works on this model, installing fiber in new apartment buildings and planned communities. In this case, the developer pays for the in-home wiring.

Municipalities can put policies in place that encourage deployment of FTTH. The Greater London Authority calls for all new buildings in London to be broadband ready. Developers must at least install ducting through which fiber can be deployed at a later time.

Who Will Own the Infrastructure?

When we consider fiber as a future-proof technology that could ultimately handle a host of converged services to the home, the ownership of this critical infrastructure becomes crucial. The owner of this ultimately converged network would hold many cards that today are held by different private interests. For this reason, the question of infrastructure ownership bears serious examination. As you will see, many of the ownership principles from our discussion of municipalities apply to FTTH as well.

Carrier-Owned Infrastructure

In the United States, typically carriers own the infrastructure that provides services to our homes. The electric utility owns the power lines; the cable company owns the coaxial cable; and the local telephone company owns the local loop. As a result, third-party providers who want to offer competitive services over these wires must pay a premium to the dominant carriers who own the infrastructure. In many cases, it is not even possible to offer competitive services, creating an effective monopoly.

Some FTTH projects in the United States are examples of carrier-owned infrastructure (see Table 7.1). SBC Communications' Project Pronto is among these. Pronto is to be admired because it represents a true upgrading of infrastructure to serve its constituency. The company is investing $6 billion so that it can provide high-speed Internet access to 80 percent of its customers. Although the broadband being offered to consumers is DSL, the company is also installing fiber deeper into neighborhoods and plans to offer PON connections to businesses, as described later in this chapter.

Rye Telecommunications, mentioned earlier, and Hatchet Ranch are other examples of carrier-owned infrastructure. Additionally, BellSouth has an FTTH trial in the Atlanta suburb of Dunwoody, in partnership with optical networking vendors Lucent and Okidata. This FTTH solution is also based on PON. The cost for this effort is comparable to deploying DSL to an area.

Carriers are to be commended for taking an active role in upgrading infrastructure for their customers. However, some other approaches to infrastructure ownership should also be evaluated.

Table 7.1   Where Is Fiber to the Home Being Deployed?

CITY	DEPLOYMENT DETAILS
Blair, Nebraska	Carrier-owned; Blair Telephone Company deploying ATM PON for 200 homes in new subdivision
Brossard, Quebec	City and utility owned; 3000 new homes to receive FTTH via open access fiber; Gigabit Ethernet
Dunwoody, Georgia	Carrier owned ATM PON to 400 homes
Grant County, Washington	Public utility owned; Gigabit Ethernet to the home; existing homes
Guthrie Center, Iowa	Carrier-owned ATM PON to existing homes
Hatchet Ranch, Colorado	Carrier-owned ATM PON to new homes
Palo Alto, California	City-owned Ethernet to the home; existing homes
Red Creek Ranch, Colorado	Carrier-owned ATM PON
Rosemount, Minnesota	Vendor and developer owned; ATM PON to new construction in Evermoor subdivision
Umeå, Sweden	Customer-owned; Ethernet over fiber; existing homes
American Canyon, California	Private utility owned; Ethernet over fiber; new construction in Poppy Meadows development

Because a carrier-owned infrastructure inherently limits competition, a different approach is in order. Open-access fiber promotes competition and can be accomplished in two ways: customers own the infrastructure or neutral third-parties own it.

Cooperative or Condominium Owned Infrastructure

A *Neighborhood Competitive Access Interconnection Point* is similar to a carrier-neutral co-location facility but designed for a neighborhood instead. The infrastructure to a carrier-neutral location is either owned by the neighborhood or a neutral third-party.

Service providers would have equal access to this facility and different entities could provide service to any home in the neighborhood, as desired by the occupant. The carrier-neutral facility can be owned by the neighborhood that owns the fiber, as in the case in the Swedish neighborhood profiled in a case study later in this chapter.

Third-Party Owned Infrastructure

Neutral third-parties can also own the infrastructure, but not provide the service. Instead, they offer open access to all carriers. This is the model that some companies and municipalities follow in providing FTTH.

Municipalities may select a single ISP or offer open access. In the public sector, Palo Alto, California, is offering Ethernet-based FTTH through its public fiber utility (Figure 7.2). A 70-home trial began August 1, 2001. However, although a neutral third-party (the city) owns the infrastructure, they also select a single ISP to service the area. Costs to participants living in the area of the FTTH trial are about $90 per month for a 10-Mbps connection and about $170 for a 100-Mbps connection.

Municipal selection of the ISP is also the practice in Glasgow, Kentucky. However, Chicago's CivicNet provides for open-access fiber, allowing users to select their own service providers. While this is true for CivicNet as a whole, the dream will not be realized if, for example, businesses and neighborhoods do not build their own third-party infrastructure to CivicNet POPs. If instead they accept the offer of a carrier to build the last-mile infrastructure to reach their facility or neighborhood, it is likely that they will be locked into that provider, even though open-access fiber is available throughout the city.

Developers or homeowner associations could also play the role of neutral third parties initiating fiber builds to their areas. For developers, it could be a

Aliunde's Fiber Model

Aliunde in the UK takes the third-party approach. Aliunde installs the open-access fiber and then creates facilities where service providers can offer services to end customers.

Aliunde's founder and managing director, Stewart Jones, refers to this as community-empowered networking: "Apart from creating Customer emPowered Networks at a building level, it has been my vision for some time to eventually drop back from each community to a centralised city node running 'neutral' fibre to each Neighbourhood node and ourselves effectively acting as a clearing house for service providers who 'rent' strands of fibre to deliver their services. I call this the 'Community emPowered Network.' This would be paid for by charging service providers access fees to utilise the fibre connectivity to each community. This offers tremendous value for residents as they get all the benefits of competitive services (better pricing), and uncluttered environments in terms of equipment (antennas etc)" (Jones 2001).

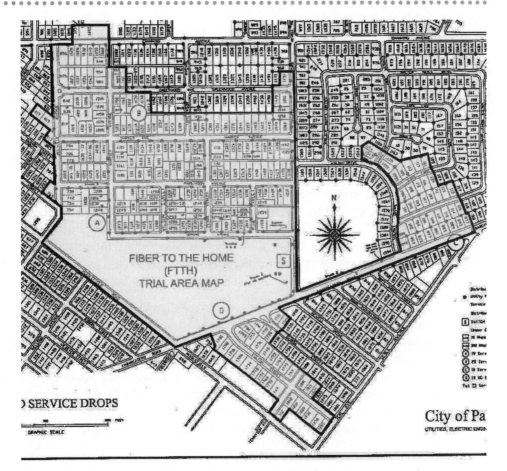

FIBER TO THE HOME
(FTTH)
TRIAL AREA MAP

> SERVICE DROPS

City of Pa

Figure 7.2 Ethernet-based fiber to the home in Palo Alto, California.

Copyright 2001. Courtesy of Bennett Smith and City of Palo Alto Utilities.

selling point and for homeowner associations, it could help to raise all the property values in an area and encourage telecommuting, which ensures that a neighborhood does not become an unoccupied bedroom community during office hours.

Open-access FTTH seems like a radical concept to those in the United States and elsewhere who are used to having service providers own the infrastructure. But Bill St. Arnaud, Stewart Jones, David Isenberg, and World Wide Packets CEO Bernard Daines, among others, are not alone in their support for this idea. Gartner Dataquest recently published research that recommends open access, separating infrastructure ownership from service provision, and allowing all operators to have equal access to the infrastructure (Gartner Dataquest 2001).

The Issue of Convergence

Today FTTH services are not converged, for the most part. Aliunde runs three kinds of cable: Category 5 enhanced copper for voice, Digital 799 for video (a UK video standard), and fiber for data. The company anticipates that in the future all services will run over fiber, but for now installs all three types of cable. The flexibility of fiber allows it to carry all services over a single connection. However, initially, fiber may carry only high-speed data services. A network of divergence rather than convergence has regulatory advantages: "More importantly an independent residential Internet network would not be encumbered with delivery of legacy services particularly in dealing with complex regulatory and technical issues such as 911 services, number portability, voice splitters, battery backup, digital to analog conversion, etc. Such a green field deployment would also allow for new network architectures and regulatory environments that support competitive equal access as a first principle rather than as a retroactive service requirement" (St. Arnaud 2001).

Network divergence allows time for service providers to begin to offer converged services to home users, such as VoIP or video-on-demand, while creating an immediate viable, long-term broadband solution for data transport. Further, it is possible that services currently offered by telephone companies will move increasingly to wireless, and broadcast satellite services may gain more of a market share than traditional coaxial cable TV. Converging traditional voice and traditional cable services onto FTTH may indeed be premature until we see how the voice and video markets develop.

Technologies for FTTH

There are several approaches to deploying FTTH, including two flavors of PON (ATM/SONET and Ethernet) and Ethernet to the home.

PON

Passive optical networking is a particularly attractive solution for FTTH deployment. For one thing, it eliminates active components, replacing them with passive versions that are less likely to break. The electronic components requiring power are placed at the home and thus draw power from the end-customer rather than the networking provider.

A passive optical network consists of three components. At the carrier, service provider, or carrier-neutral facility, an optical line terminal (OLT) is deployed. At or near the premises of the subscriber, an optical network terminal (ONT) is installed. Optical network terminals are also referred to as network interface devices (NIDs). Note: The economics of NIDs will have a strong impact on PON adoption. In between the OLT and the connected ONTs is a passive optical coupler, which divides the light into as many streams as needed, either evenly or unevenly depending on customer demand (and the type of coupler used). For upstream data, the coupler device combines the light into a single feed to deliver it back to the OLT.

The long-term bandwidth prognosis for PON is good as well. In addition to the inherent capacity of fiber, wavelengths can be deployed for individual users. (Wavelengths are not currently used in PON deployments, but could be, particularly as prices for DWDM equipment fall and the demand for bandwidth increases.) In addition, bandwidth can be split unevenly, with one customer receiving a faster connection than others on the same network if desired.

Passive optical networks also have disadvantages. Since they typically split the bandwidth of a fiber among 32 residences as PONs are currently deployed, each home typically would receive less than 30 Mbps, and there must be a form of arbitrage in order to keep collisions from occurring. In fact, PON can be compared to the old, collision-based Ethernet (Ethernet has evolved beyond that architecture today). Because PONs share bandwidth much as cable modems do, there is the potential in the long-term for degraded performance and competition for bandwidth among users.

As mentioned earlier, there are two varieties of PONs: ATM/SONET and Ethernet. PONs themselves are agnostic in terms of protocol, making either solution possible and practical. Although optical technologies based on traditional SONET architectures require installation of expensive equipment and changing that equipment as speeds change, PONs do not have these restrictions.

Ethernet is certainly the newer of the two PON architectures and, as a result, there is little experience with it in practical terms. However, like most Ethernet-based solutions, it is likely to be far cheaper than SONET.

ATM/SONET PON

Several companies specialize in ATM/SONET PONs, notably Optical Solutions, based in Minneapolis. BellSouth is using ATM PONs for the company's FTTH trial in Atlanta. SBC Communications is also using PON for Project Pronto deployments.

Initially, SBC will use PON not for home connections, but for high-speed connections to small businesses. Small businesses typically have heavier data communication needs than home users so they can be served by fiber while the existing copper infrastructure is used exclusively to handle DSL connections for residential users. The company plans to bring PON to 1,000 business customers in 2001 and 9,000 more in 2002.

Using ATM over PON enables multiple types of services to flow over the fiber. Asynchronous transfer mode is particularly advantageous for running different data streams over a single connection; Project Pronto uses ATM over PON.

Incumbent local exchange carriers are likely to favor ATM PONs over other FTTH solutions because it is both relatively inexpensive and allows the carrier to maintain control over the connection to the home. In this way, it does not cannibalize their existing business but makes it future-proof. Companies like Optical Solutions partner with carriers such as Rye Telephone, Qwest, and many others to install PON solutions for FTTH. The company has been installing its product, FiberPath, since 1996; 17 communities have installed FTTH through this method. Further, Optical Solutions latest product, Fiber-Path 400, allows for 100-Mbps connections to up to 32 users over a single fiber by running fiber deep into the neighborhood but not all the way to the home. Optical Solutions products are also converged and are particularly known for their ability to carry cable television in addition to other data streams.

The standards for *ATM PONs (APONs)* are the Full Service Access Network (FSAN) standards, created over a 10-year period and published by the ITU. Optical Solutions modifies the standard somewhat to achieve its price-performance ratio. (The company is also interested in exploring Ethernet PONs, discussed next.)

Ethernet PONs

Ethernet PONs are just emerging and are one of two technologies for Ethernet-based FTTH. The IEEE established an Ethernet in the First Mile study group in November 2000, which includes Alloptic Inc., OnePath Networks, and Cisco.

AllOptic's GigaForce technology can move data at 1.25 Gbps to up to 32 home users, delivering a converged service of Ethernet, telephone service, and cable TV, showing that Ethernet-based solutions can also be converged. Some 23 carriers are doing field trials with GigaForce, including Shaw-Big Pipe, IP Networks, Fiberhood, Aexis Telecom, Changzhou Broadcast and TV Information Networks, and Dynamic Systems Integration.

Ethernet is an advantageous technology for home access in general because it works so well with IP and users who have Ethernet-compatible PCs. This is true for Ethernet PONs as well as Ethernet to the home, discussed next.

Ethernet to the Home

In addition to Ethernet PONs, there is the possibility of running Ethernet directly to the home over fiber. Bernard Daines, founder and CEO of World Wide Packets, calls this approach home-run fiber.

Running fiber to the home rather than deploying a PON provides greater dedicated bandwidth. Passive optical networks ultimately split bandwidth among typically 32 subscribers, creating contention and limiting the speed of the connection to about 30 Mbps. Further, any number of services, from video to traditional telephone service, can be run over Ethernet along with high-speed data services using virtual LANs (vLANs); many mistakenly suppose that only ATM can provide such a diversity of services.

World Wide Packets' product allows eight connections per subscriber running at 10 Mbps or 100 Mbps. The architecture is designed for gigabit service to each home (although it is possible to get 100 Mbps to the home for a lower cost). Offering a full 1-Gbps connection to each home is a solid strategy for the long-term, ensuring that bandwidth upgrades to the subscriber will not be needed for a long time to come. Particularly compared with stopgap broadband measures, this foresight is commendable.

The company sees utilities, especially publicly owned utilities, as logical access providers; after all, these entities have rights-of-way to each home and business, repair crews, and access to poles for aerial fiber, where desired. Many utility companies have an existing fiber infrastructure used to support their own business. World Wide Packets makes an important distinction between access providers, who create the infrastructure, and service providers, who offer a range of services over that infrastructure. World Wide Packets adheres to the open access model for fiber deployment that allows for true competition to keep prices low.

Case Study: A Grassroots FTTH Project in Northern Sweden

Although FTTH projects are often undertaken by developers, city governments, or telecom providers, this isn't always the case. On Måttgränd St. in Umeå, a large city in northern Sweden, a group of residents decided that their high-speed options paled in comparison to the city's own network capabilities. It began with a group of citizens, including Torgils Toral and Lars Bjornerback, who wanted to investigate high-speed access for their 62-home neighborhood on Måttgränd Street. They began initial negotiations with the local utility, Umeå Energi, and Telia, the phone company.

continues

Ultimately, the first round of negotiations fell through, but the group persisted, this time aided by Bjornerback's two sons, Tomas and Robert. A nonprofit neighborhood organization was formed and the ultimate result is reliable, cheap high-speed access that is the envy of neighbors with cable modems.

One of the drivers for this effort was the city's high-speed network. After one connects to Umeå's network, run by Norrnod, traffic is free and unmetered throughout the city (see Figure 7.3). The network peers with a few other large networks, including Umeå University's network and SUNET, the Swedish University Network. In effect, all traffic throughout Sweden is unmetered, given this connectivity. The city's network runs Gigabit Ethernet in its backbone, with some portions running 10-Gigabit Ethernet.

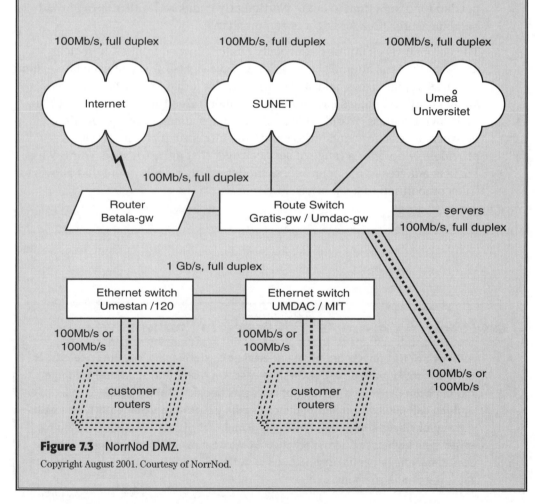

Figure 7.3   NorrNod DMZ.

Copyright August 2001. Courtesy of NorrNod.

Once traffic passes through NorrNod's network to the Internet, it is metered, and users must pay for the level of traffic they generate if it exceeds an agreed-upon level. In the case of the Måttgränd network, each household is not supposed to generate more than 550 Mbps of metered Internet traffic per day. For most folks, this is an easy limit to stay within, but some of the teenagers engaged in online gaming over the Internet were exceeding the limit. Tomas Bjornerback pointed them to other gamers within Sweden, allowing them to play all they wanted without generating additional traffic.

The Måttgränd neighborhood network is a wonder. True FTTH, the 62 houses connected to the network had a choice of connecting at either 100 Mbps or 10 Mbps. The network consists of two kinds of fiber in a star configuration, multimode (currently in use) and single mode (reserved for future use). Copper and coaxial cable are also configured in a star; the copper is currently not being used (it was put in place for home automation, burglar alarms, and the like) and cable television is available over the coax.

The utility company owns dark fiber, which the Måttgränd neighborhood leased. Umeå Energi began putting in dark fiber as they replaced aging underground pipes; now their fiber infrastructure is so widespread that the city council has barred further trenching, preventing a repeat of what happened in southern Sweden, where streets were trenched and retrenched repeatedly by various providers. Competitive access to the Umeå fiber is guaranteed.

The Måttgränd IT association, as the nonprofit was called, worked with Bonet, a company that subcontracted the installation of the fiber and connected the network to Norrnod at an initial cost of $6000. Households pay $8 per month for their connections to the network.

Because of their technical expertise, Toral and Bjornerback and his sons were able to do far more supervision of the subcontractors installing the fiber. Their expertise came in handy and the network, which was completed in March 2000, includes gigabit access to Norrnod.

Lars Bjornerback was instrumental in getting neighborhood support for the project. Within a few evenings, 60 of the 62 houses in the area had committed to being involved with the network. The cost for each house depended somewhat on the type of access desired; if someone wanted a connection eventually but was not hooked up at the moment, it would cost about $1400 (only one of the households fell into this category). To connect to the network at 10 Mbps cost $1700; some 35 households chose this option. A 100 Mbps connection cost $2000. Most households financed the one-time expense by adding it onto their home mortgages. Each household has between two and seven IP addresses allocated for home networks, and there is an IP address per household reserved for IP telephony, in the event that it is ever implemented.

continues

continued

The Måttgränd network provides its lucky residents with the fastest form of home access in Sweden. It also illustrates clearly that FTTH need not be deployed by a provider or even a government. Frustrated users who are near a high-speed network can lead the charge to innovation. For more information, see Tomas Bjornerback's Web page about the project, which includes a number of pictures of the network being built and the equipment deployed, at www.acc.umu.se/~tfytbk/Mattgrand.

Case Study: Grant County, Washington's Ethernet-based FTTH Revolution

Grant County, Washington, is a sparsely populated, mostly rural area. With an average of 12 people per square mile, it is not exactly the hottest prospect for broadband rollouts by telcos and other mainstream firms. In fact, telephone service itself suffers there; the main switches are technically listed as "for sale" by US West, and the company doesn't upgrade the switches to handle modern services such as call waiting or caller ID, let alone deploying high-speed Internet service such as DSL. Some residents can't even get basic telephone service, and those that do use the Internet can get only 28.8 Kbps dial-up service.

Cable television has a similarly limited reach, being offered only in the city limits and with a maximum of 32 channels of analog video. Alternative television access methods, such as satellite dishes, are the only way to receive more channels in much of the county.

In addition to an underserved public, the Grant County Public Utility District (PUD) itself found that it was having trouble meeting its internal bandwidth needs. The telco stated that to run a T-1 line between the utility's buildings would take six to nine months. As a stopgap measure, the district deployed microwave links, but the spectrum for such links is becoming rapidly unavailable. Clearly, the utility district needed its own fiber infrastructure as well; it began installing fiber between its electric substations. By definition, then, the utility had fiber in place within two to three miles of every house, prepositioning it to offer residential services.

Frustration with the incumbents led the Grant County Public Utility District to do something about the current state of affairs in the county. A law passed in 2000 allows the utility to offer other services—besides electricity—for the first time. And they are doing so with a vengeance.

Using World Wide Packets' Ethernet-to-the-subscriber technology, the Grant County PUD has run fiber over its existing poles and rights-of-way to a cross-section of 170 homes and businesses. Referred to as the Zipp project, this open-access fiber network allows any number of companies to be providers of services such as video, plain old telephone service (POTS), and high-speed Internet access over the utility district's fiber infrastructure. Ultimately, the service can reach 40,000 residential customers and 1500 businesses.

World Wide Packets' product creates Gigabit Ethernet connections to homes and businesses. It is not a PON, but a direct Ethernet connection. The bandwidth is symmetrical, allowing servers to be placed in homes. For this reason, the Grant County PUD doesn't charge home subscribers any more than business subscribers. After all, a web server farm in a basement could take more bandwidth than the local barbershop uses, making home and business a rather futile distinction from a pricing standpoint, according to Jon Moore, senior telecom engineer at Grant County PUD.

Putting in this infrastructure is costing the PUD about $3500 per subscriber as an early adopter, a cost expected to decrease to $2600 as equipment prices continue to drop. Considering that this is true fiber, not hybrid-fiber coax, which can be depreciated over many years, the investment is reasonable. The utility expects that it will take about 15 years to recover its costs.

The economic benefits to the area, however, are substantial and far more immediate. For example, a house with a fiber connection wound up on the market next door to a house that wasn't connected. A bidding war ensued for the house with FTTH, driving up the asking price.

A bed-and-breakfast in the trial area offers lovely rooms and 100-Mbps Internet access for $60 per night. It is fully booked at all times. Moore envisions companies coming to area hotels to gain access to the high-speed infrastructure, running servers out of their hotel rooms for a period of weeks while they do a trial broadband deployment of a new Internet service for the price of a hotel room.

Several new businesses have located in the area since the trial began, and these businesses are attracting substantial venture capital, even in a tight market. In addition to new businesses locating in the area, however (and given the bandwidth availability across the county, they could just as easily locate in a barn as in a downtown building), the high-speed data services are helping farmers with strategic planning. Moore envisions them being able to sell directly to consumers or roadside vendors over the Internet, further increasing their efficiency. Distance learning can also bring economic benefits to those who are unable to attend traditional universities.

continues

continued

Although it is too early to quantify the economic benefits to the area, Grant PUD projects that for every dollar spent, the benefit to the local economy is six dollars. Further, local workers have deployed the fiber infrastructure, creating new jobs in the area.

Pricing for subscribers varies depending on the services they select. First, the home or business must be prepared to receive the service, including installing wiring for Ethernet and a possible set-top box for video services. Some of the service providers offer free installation (with a year's contract) in an attempt to differentiate themselves from others. A sample offering includes 50 cable channels, high-speed Internet service, and two rooms with Category 5 wiring with no installation charge for $39 per month. This is about half the price that cable companies charge for these services if cable television and cable modems are installed.

Customers can choose from a range of speeds. World Wide Packets' product is designed to provide up to eight connections per location at 10 Mbps or 100 Mbps, making the maximum speed for any given appliance 100 Mbps. All eight connections can run simultaneously with no congestion. However, if subscribers need full Gigabit Ethernet access, they can install a different end unit to achieve it.

The take rate for high-speed data services has been especially high. For those who chose to become part of the trial, 100 percent of businesses took Internet service and 80 percent of homes did as well. Video is a relatively new addition, with the take rate expected to run at about 60 percent. Video service includes nearly 270 channels of IP multicast, video on demand, and pay-per-view, in addition to interactive games. The telephone service take rate is substantially lower for now, primarily because only homes or organizations that need a second line will subscribe. The FTTH-based telephone services, which include offers such as unlimited long distance for $20 per month, entails getting a new phone number, which few single-line subscribers are willing to do. To gain access to 911-type services, customers must currently maintain a phone with the telco.

Grant County PUD is to be commended for its forethought in deploying this type of service. It is revolutionary on several levels, offering symmetrical bandwidth running over fiber with nearly unlimited potential for future growth. Further, by opening its infrastructure to numerous service providers, it offers consumers and businesses real choices and fosters competition that will keep prices for subscribers low.

Case Study: BellSouth: A PON in an Atlanta Suburb

BellSouth has been exploring FTTH for some time. The company began examining FTTH around 1985 with some early trials but decided at that point that the technology was too expensive. In 1995, when PONs came on the scene, the company began reexamining the technology. BellSouth has actively participated in the FSAN standards group specifying APONs. The company sees PONs as particularly advantageous because the electronics are powered by the home user rather than by the telco, generating a substantial cost savings.

The trial in Dunwoody, Georgia, a suburb of Atlanta, covered about 400 homes in two large neighborhoods and two to three smaller ones. The fiber to the Dunwoody area is 85 percent aerial and 15 percent trenched. There are two fibers to each home: one for video and one for data.

To keep from biasing customers toward taking the service, all services were priced identically to existing alternatives and kept comparable as much as possible. The high-speed data service is identical in speed and price to the local DSL offering (1.5 Mbps downstream and 56 Kbps upstream); the video offerings are comparable to area cable offerings. BellSouth was interested in seeing whether customers perceived that the video offerings over fiber were better than cable, and in fact they did. Additionally, it is interesting to note that BellSouth didn't market the trial; requests largely came by word of mouth.

Dunwoody is called a *first office* application. In other words, rather than a trial with a beginning and end date, the Dunwoody deployment continues to function. Currently, BellSouth does not plan to include video in its offerings when it rolls out FTTH in other areas within the next several years, according to Brian Ford, a senior member of the technical staff in BellSouth's Exploratory Development Group.

Conclusion

Currently, FTTH is not widely deployed. The falling cost of fiber and technologies that enable FTTH may change the pace of deployment. To avoid service monopolies, there should be a clear separation between infrastructure providers and service providers—currently not the case in the United States nor in many other markets where telcos have a dominant hold on data and voice services. After all, because incumbent cable and telephone providers have so much riding on the existing infrastructure, providing a different, high-speed alternative at a competitive price could cannibalize their existing markets.

Certainly, FTTH is easiest to deploy in areas of new construction. High-speed data is clearly an important service for the future, and deploying fiber as a broadband alternative helps ensure that the new housing developments are future-proof.

Telework benefits cities in multiple ways. It takes cars off the highway and keeps business in the community rather than moving it to the cities. However, teleworkers cannot be effective without true broadband access to the Internet. Cities interested in encouraging telecommuting should take specific measures to ensure that broadband deployment occurs in a timely fashion.

Governments play an important role in encouraging the deployment of FTTH. Government permitting policies can help encourage the deployment of fiber or hold it back. New builds should be required to have ducting for fiber installation. If streets are being torn up, municipalities can insist that conduit be laid for fiber. Government policies can help evolve the infrastructure that supports FTTH.

Further, FTTH is most likely to be deployed where a high-speed city network is already in place. This is certainly the case in Glasgow, Kentucky; Umeå, Sweden; and in Chicago, as CivicNet is deployed.

Fiber to the home is certainly the ultimate solution for the last mile. Digital subscriber lines, wireless, and cable modems cannot begin to match the speed offered by fiber, nor can they provide the same type of long-term benefits that fiber can. However, the lack of FTTH must not be bemoaned only in the last mile. Current network backbones are not adequate to handle the traffic that would be generated by fiber connections to millions of homes. The infrastructure must not be built only in the last mile, but in the backbones. According to Daniel Lewin, CTO of Akamai, if everyone had even interim broadband such as cable modems, "the Internet would burn down immediately, and all the routers would just catch on fire" (Weinberg 2001). Surely Lewin makes this dramatic statement figuratively, but it does illustrate that the Internet infrastructure is unprepared for widespread adoption of any broadband, even limited broadband, at this time.

Fiber to the home is the wave of the future, far surpassing interim measures such as DSL and cable modems. If you consider Canadians, with their goal of FTTH by 2005, the United States and other countries would do well to emulate their vision and ambition. Further, because so many services can ride over fiber, it is critical that the service providers not own the infrastructure, enabling customers freedom to choose the providers—and services—that they want rather than locking them into a single, monopoly provider.

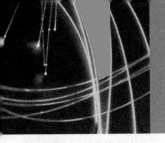

CHAPTER 8

The Outlook for Optical Networking

O rganizations considering adoption of optical networks face a range of issues that will affect the future of their technology needs and capabilities. They must separate hype from fact so they can reasonably assess what fiber can do for them. Throughout this book we have touched on a number of issues that affect deployment of optical networks, from competing technologies to infrastructure ownership. In this chapter, we will recap macro-considerations and look to the future of optical networks.

Deployment Issues

When deploying an optical network, whether it is a LAN, a WAN, or an optical connection to a carrier, you face some basic questions: How should the fiber be deployed? What are the costs involved? What are the alternatives to traditional trenching, which is both expensive and difficult? Where can you find qualified people to help with the project? This section addresses these deployment issues.

Dealing with Rights-of-Way

No matter what installation method you choose, it's likely that you don't own the rights-of-way on all the areas where you want to deploy fiber. Sometimes obtaining right-of-way permission is as easy as talking to the person in charge of the area. That was the case when Frank Miller decided that he wanted a fiber optic connection to the local phone company, Beehive Telephone Co. in Wendover, Utah. The phone company was glad to oblige, but to reach Miller's property, which was three miles from the company's fiber drop, meant that the fiber would have to be plowed into land owned by the Bureau of Land Management. After half an hour, the permission to lay fiber through the government land was procured.

Frank's experience is far from typical, however. Cities deploying networks typically have the rights-of-way needed. But telcos deploying long-haul networks spend a major amount of time and money negotiating rights-of-way from potentially hundreds of parties. According to Gerwig, "The rule of thumb these days is that building a network requires about one permit per mile— from a private landowner or a government body—before the backhoes dig in" (2001). Right-of-way permits now represent 20 percent of the cost of new network projects, up from 10 percent earlier. Williams Communications completed a 33,000-mile optical network at the end of 2000; at one point the company had 400 agents in the field negotiating 31,000 agreements. It had to apply for 10,000 licenses and permits over the course of the project. Particularly for long-haul networks, rights-of-way have become a major issue.

For cities, they are also a source of income. Washington, D.C., expects to generate some $30 million in annual revenue from right-of-way permits. The capitol charges 88 cents per linear foot for trenching fiber and $1.32 per linear foot for aerial fiber.

Negotiating rights of way can be straightforward or complex. Depending on the extent of the optical network you are deploying, it may make sense to hire a consultant to help with right of way issues. Local government offices often have information about obtaining rights-of-way. The Internet can be a source of information and help when needed; one helpful site is www.rightofway.com.

Options for Deploying Fiber

How you choose to install fiber, whether trenched, using some variation on trenching, or aerial, impacts the cost and the speed of the deployment. There are far more options for deploying fiber today than there were even five years ago, and many of the newer methods allow fiber to be placed underground without disrupting roads as much as traditional trenching does.

Trenching

Trenching is still a common method of installation for fiber. In metropolitan areas, trenching involves digging up streets and then repaving, which is one reason that alternatives are being sought. Since the Telecommunications Act of 1996 was passed in the United States, the percentage of companies applying for permits to lay fiber in urban areas has skyrocketed; of the 85 million miles of fiber laid from 1980 through 2000, more than two-thirds were laid since 1996. Some cities, as described in Chapter 5, *Optical Networking and Urban Planning*, have placed a moratorium on new fiber deployments because of it.

Wherever fiber is being trenched, it's important to check with local authorities about guidelines for depth and other environmental considerations, even if you own the land that is being disrupted. Different types of fiber optic cable and conduit are recommended for different areas, and depending on weather and other factors, the depth at which conduit is laid may be affected.

Alternatives to Trenching

Emerging methods that circumvent the need for trenching include fiber plows, *in-the-groove* or *in-the-road* systems, and robotic installation in sewers.

Fiber plows are generally used where fiber is installed in dirt. Some fiber plows bury shielded fiber directly into the ground; there is no conduit involved. Henkels & McCoy, based in Bluebell, Pennsylvania, is one company that installs fiber optic cable along railroad rights-of-way using a fiber plow.

In-the-groove systems cut a narrow groove into the roadbed. The Corning Micro Cabling System installs 144 fibers in a 7-mm cable. The system cuts an 8-cm slit in the roadway using a circular saw, puts in the cable, adds a rubber strip, then seals it all with sealant. According to Corning, this is eight times faster and five times cheaper than trenching. Alcatel also takes an in-the-groove approach. Its in-the-groove system lays fiber in a ring architecture on both sides of a highway; the company can lay 12 kilometers of fiber per day in this fashion. It also lays fiber in gas and sewer pipelines. In France, it laid some 200 kilometers of fiber in the River Seine, with 60 kilometers in Paris alone.

Deploying Fiber Optic Cable in Sewers

Probably the most innovative of the alternatives to trenching is the deployment of fiber optic cable in sewers. The installation is handled by specially designed robots. In the late 1980s, Japan wanted to start laying fiber optic cable in many areas of the city but recognized how disruptive that would be to already crowded and high-traffic cities such as Tokyo. Robots had already been used to clean and inspect sewers; why couldn't they also be used to deploy fiber optic cable in them?

The sewer infrastructure, although an unusual location for high-speed telecom equipment, is ideal for it. Using sewers, some 900 kilometers of fiber have been laid across Japan. While it may seem unsanitary and high-risk, in fact, special stainless-steel pipe protects the fiber from its surroundings. Fiber can be deployed in either storm sewers or sanitary sewers using this method.

Deploying fiber optic cable in sewers solves the last-mile problem: sewers run into every building. There is no need to tear up the streets to install the fiber, making this method far less disruptive than traditional trenching. Additionally, some companies use their robots to maintain city sewers as well as installing and maintaining the cable there.

In addition to the convenience of sewer-based deployment, it is faster and cheaper than other methods. Toronto-based Stream Communications estimates that this method is eight times faster than trenching. The company states that it can lay 800 meters of cable per day using robots versus 100 meters per day with trenching. CityNet states that robots make the process about 60 percent faster and cheaper than trenching.

Sewer deployment of fiber optic cable originated in Japan and began in Europe in 1998. North American deployments are more recent, with the first installations occurring in 2000. The companies that sell the robots are primarily located in Europe: Robotics Cabling Company GmbH of Berlin, Germany, and KA-TE in Zurich, Switzerland.

CityNet, in Silver Spring, Maryland, was founded in October 1999. The company uses its Sewer Access Module (SAM) to deploy up to nine conduits in a sewer with 144-strand cable in each conduit. SAM is 6 inches wide and 3 feet long (see Figure 8.1). Before deploying cable, SAM does a photographic inspection of the sewers and then maps them. The robot puts rings in the sewer pipe walls with up to nine clamps for conduit. Conduit tubes are then fed through the rings. Finally, high-pressure air threads fiber through the ducts.

CityNet has contracts to deploy cable in Indianapolis, Albuquerque, Omaha, Scottsdale, St. Paul, and Fort Worth, as well as in Vienna, Austria. Some 25

Figure 8.1   CityNet's Sewer Access Module (SAM) robot.

more cities are in the process of negotiations with CityNet. Alcatel, which has also deployed networks in wastewater pipes in Hanau, Germany, and elsewhere, is the company's technology partner.

Usually, the company arranges for the city in question to receive a small percentage of the revenue from the network it installs, in exchange for use of the right-of-way. CityNet also cleans and maintains the city sewers.

Stream Intelligent Networks works with Robotics Cabling Company GmbH of Berlin to install fiber optic cable in Canada, and they have installed a five-kilometer network connecting 14 buildings in Mississauga, Ontario. The network took just 21 days to deploy using the Robotics Cabling's Sewage Telecom Access by Robot (STAR) system. STAR has also been used in Berlin and Tokyo. The 1.8-meter robot is equipped with five television cameras so that it can be closely monitored and can work in pipes from 8 to 47 inches in diameter. A large-scale deployment is planned for Toronto.

Jet Fiber

An alternative to trenching for FTTH deployments is jet fiber. In this scenario, developers deploy micro-conduit to the home or building and then blow in fiber later when it is required. The micro-conduit requires no splicing and is easier to install than fiber optic cable. Homes built with jet fiber conduit installed are called *fiber-ready*.

Although the jet fiber is more expensive (four times more expensive than standard fiber), the difference is made up in installation costs. Ericsson's Ribbonet takes 2–12 strands of fiber and bonds them flat to each other, using Kevlar yarn for support. Compressed air then shoots the fiber into the micro-duct. For more information on Ribbonet, see www.ericsson.com/infocenter/news/Ribbonet.html. LinaNet, an ISP in Iceland and a subsidiary of Reykjavik Energy Company, is deploying jet fiber to 18,000 homes in a trial.

Aerial Fiber

Aerial fiber is deployed on existing utility poles. It is the cheapest to install and is very strong, in that fiber has greater tensile strength than steel. However, depending on where the fiber is being deployed, regulatory bodies govern whether it is possible to gain access to existing utility poles and add fiber to them. Alcatel is one company that deploys aerial fiber; it can do so over live lines, obviating the need for taking utilities offline during fiber installation.

Costs for Deploying Fiber

Certainly, everyone considering fiber deployment is interested in the cost of deploying fiber. The cost, as mentioned, depends on the method of installation.

One very important factor to keep in mind is that the cost is marginal to install more strands of fiber. To future-proof the network, it is a good idea to install more fiber strands than you anticipate the need for. There is very little difference in cost between installing a 144-strand fiber bundle compared with installing a 96-strand fiber bundle. The more strands, the lower the cost per strand is.

Aerial fiber is the least expensive, costing about $3 to $6 per meter. To bury cable in existing conduit costs $7 to $10 per meter, while trenching, laying new conduit, and installing fiber costs from $35 to $200 per meter. Jet fiber costs from $3 to $15 per meter.

Another cost that must be considered is annual maintenance. Usually, maintenance fees run about 5 percent of the initial installation costs. Right-of-way costs and annual maintenance are charged against the entire bundle of fiber. In a condominium fiber arrangement, where many different organizations will be leasing the fiber, these costs can be distributed accordingly.

Keep in mind, when considering cost per meter for fiber installation, that these costs represent a one-time investment in a 20-year indefeasible right of use (IRU). Fiber is an asset that can be depreciated for tax purposes over the long term. As an asset, it can also be traded or sold.

An important resource for the topic of deployment and costs is Bill St. Arnaud's "Frequently Asked Questions about Customer Owned Dark Fiber, Condominium Fiber, Community and Municipal Fiber Networks," listed in Appendix A. Much of the pricing information in this chapter has been derived from Bill St. Arnaud's FAQ.

Finding Optical Networking Expertise

Prices for fiber and optical networking equipment have been falling, but one cost that is not dropping is the cost of optical networking expertise. Although telcos have traditionally deployed optical networks, more and more organizations are doing it themselves. In many cases, the market hasn't caught up with this development. Companies that install fiber for telcos are typically good candidates to do dark-fiber installs for other organizations, including corporations, municipalities, and coalitions of organizations banding together to install condominium fiber.

If the organization doesn't have in-house optical networking expertise, it is a good idea to hire a consultant to oversee the effort and verify the work done by professional installers. If the network will be maintained by in-house staff, staff must be developed to handle the task. In-house maintenance was the approach that George Washington University took, training in-house staff to handle all aspects of network maintenance. In other cases, particularly when looking at MANs, maintenance of the network (including a number of adds, moves, and changes) is agreed-upon as part of the total network cost. Professional installers often certify fiber and offer long-term warranties as long as 15 to 20 years. Partly, such warranties are offered because fiber, once installed, is typically trouble-free apart from accidental cuts.

The Future of Optical Networking

Even though fiber optics have been in use for years, optical networking for many applications is just coming into its own. Recent developments with optical Ethernet, DWDM, and falling fiber costs are changing the way optical networks are deployed at all levels.

What is ahead for optical networking? Next, we will explore the market dynamics as well as future technologies that are going to impact optical networking implementations in the near-term.

Paradigm Shift: What Happens When Users Own the Infrastructure

In terms of social forces, customer-empowered networking is a very important trend that is emphasized throughout this book. When users of the network own the network, new dynamics come into play. For one, owning the infrastructure ensures that access is separated from service, which is particularly important for optical networking. However, there are access providers who are also willing to ensure open access to fiber networks, so that true competition for services takes place.

Owning the infrastructure moves networks out of the realm of service into the realm of assets. Since fiber is a long-term investment that can be depreciated over 20 years, accounting for fiber infrastructures as assets makes great economic sense.

Customer-owned infrastructure, although not unheard of, is a fundamental paradigm shift whose effects are largely unknown. CANARIE's Bill St. Arnaud (2000) asks, "Will 'empowering' customers to control and manage their own networks result in new applications and services similar to how the PC empowered users to develop new computing applications?"

Moving from Owning Fiber to Owning Wavelengths

Another important trend that is coming into play is ownership of wavelengths versus fibers. Rather than condominium fiber, there is no reason organizations cannot own (and control) their own wavelengths or lambdas. These wavelengths can be traded or swapped as assets as well. A prospective Internet standard, Optical Border Gateway Protocol, is in part designed to allow customers to set up and tear down their own wavelengths as needed. Further, running one's traffic over a wavelength keeps it physically separate from other traffic. While there is no encryption, this physical separation has caused some, including Desh Deshpande, cofounder and chairman of Sycamore Networks, to refer to it as an optical VPN.

Carriers are beginning to offer their customers dedicated wavelengths, expanding the use of their existing fiber using DWDM. Metromedia Fiber Network and Yipes are two such providers. Because wavelengths can carry any type of protocol, protocols can be mixed freely even over a single fiber, depending on the protocol needs of the end customer. Long-haul carriers are also deploying DWDM to squeeze as much bandwidth as possible from their existing lit fibers, which is cheaper than deploying equipment to light other dark fiber that they own.

Movement to the Edge

The movement toward customer-empowered networking also means that more and more is happening at the edge of the network, from peering to applications. In fact, for Internet applications, the real action has always been at the edge: E-mail comes to mind.

Now higher-bandwidth applications, including peer-to-peer services such as Napster, Gnutella, and others, are also finding a place at the edge. Although networks traditionally provide a service, such as telephone service, high-speed data services provide just a pipe. The Internet is, in essence, a "stupid" network, as telecom guru David Isenberg calls it.

Calling a network stupid "means that the network is just an empty pipe, it's a utility, and that the value is created where the pipe comes out of the ground at the edge of the network" (Moritz 2000b). The fact that innovation is at the edge, in the hands of users, has a democratizing effect: "It lets people have control over their own network services. It lets people decide how their networks are going to create value for them, rather than letting companies decide how the network creates value" (Moritz 2000b).

All of the most important applications are at the edge: "[T]he e-mail is at the edge, the Web browser is at the edge, MP3 is at the edge, peer-to-peer is at the edge, all the killer apps. TV over IP is at the edge; Voice over IP is at the edge; all the killer apps of the last five years that . . . let's face it, that's the history of the Internet that we know; all of these killer apps are edge-based applications. They weren't invented or sold by the owners of the wires and the switches" (Moritz 2000b).

Bandwidth on Demand

Another important trend is the availability of bandwidth on demand from carriers. Rather than being locked into a long-term contract, look for shorter and shorter contracts with flexible provisioning, typically through Web-based interfaces. Given the changes in bandwidth needs from day to day, this ability to provision bandwidth dynamically is important to agile corporations.

Peering at the Edge

A large portion of an ISP's charges for connectivity go to larger backbone providers. Peering allows carriers to exchange traffic for free. Swedish telco Telia states that it saves up to 75 percent off Internet transit fees by peering with other networks. Peering has other advantages, too. In addition to reducing Internet transit fees, peering with multiple entities makes connections more reliable. Rather than having one route, there are at least two ways to reach given providers. Carrier-neutral exchanges reduce costs and foster competition. The facilities have meet-me rooms where various carriers can provide service over public networks and exchange traffic with each other. The need for such pooling points is particularly critical in metropolitan areas. Analyst Peter Sevcik sees this need growing. He estimates the current requirements at 1500 interconnections in each city, a need that will only increase: "It is reasonable to expect the need to interconnect 40 long-haul networks, 20 local networks, five hosting sites, and five acceleration services within a single metropolitan area today, with each group growing in number. That would increase the number of interconnections for various types of services in each major metropolitan area to over 8000, something I predict will happen in the next four years or so" (Wetzel 2001). While there is not a tremendous market for pooling point providers (there may in fact be a market shakeout of those that exist), there is still a need among carriers, ISPs, and other network own-ers for this type of interconnect facility. Not all peering/collocation facilities are privately owned. Hayward, California, will have a carrier-neutral facility on the California State Hayward campus. It will enable peering between the col-lege, the municipality, and business interests.

Content providers such as Yahoo have also begun to do peering to help spread their content around. Yahoo is using Equinix facilities in the Silicon Valley, Dallas, and Washington, D.C., areas to allow peering of its streaming media service, Yahoo Broadcast. Tier 2 ISPs can use peering to avoid paying to reach broadcasts at a remote facility.

The decision for ISPs to peer with others is not always straightforward. One resource for deciding whether to peer is William Norton's paper, "Internet Ser-vice Providers and Peering" (see Appendix A, *Recommended Resources*). This paper examines many factors that go into the decision-making process.

Bandwidth Trading

Peering is one aspect of what is happening in the market for bandwidth. Another emerging practice is bandwidth trading. Those with excess capacity along a route can sell or trade it for bandwidth on another route. Without pooling points to interconnect the routes, such arrangements cannot be con-summated, however.

Enron Communications, a subsidiary of the energy company, came up with the idea of an online market for trading bandwidth as a commodity. Before this, negotiating bandwidth contracts took months and getting the capacity took another period of months. Further, the contracts were long-term, so while bandwidth prices dropped, the contracts locked companies in at partic-ular rates. If delivery on a particular order was late, there was no compensa-tion for the delay.

Enron's idea was to have a master contract with agreed-upon service levels and damages for late delivery. With details in place in the standard contract, trades could happen quickly rather than taking a period of months. All compa-nies needed to agree upon was the price and the date.

Of course, for the market to become really effective, capacity must be avail-able along a variety of routes. It will take time for the market to mature to that level.

Enron is not the only company in the bandwidth trading business. Online bandwidth exchanges such as Band-X, Arbinet-thexchange, Dynegy, and The

Williams Co., are also actively pursuing this market, which research firm Ovum predicts will facilitate $20 billion in contracts in 2006 (Bryce 2001).

The process works like this: Sellers list bandwidth for sale along a particular route, and buyers list routes in which they are interested. After details of the deal are settled, the identities of the two parties are revealed, and the exchange charges a commission. Enron states that it conducted 321 bandwidth trades in 2000 and that in the first quarter of 2001, it conducted more trades than in all of 2000. So the market is growing, particularly as carriers try to be more conservative with build-outs during times when the availability of venture capital is restricted.

Reality Check: The Internet Infrastructure

Although optical networking is an important innovation and high bandwidth helps companies and individuals achieve important goals, it must be clarified that it is not the cure-all for the Internet. Although fast connections open the possibility for new Internet applications, there are also weaknesses in the Internet infrastructure itself that must not be ignored.

The truth is that the end-to-end bandwidth of the Internet is less than the sum of its parts. Even researchers with 100-Mbps connections find that their actual end-to-end throughput is often less than 3 Mbps. What gives? The Web100 Project, jointly sponsored by the National Center for Supercomputing Applications, the Pittsburgh Supercomputing Center, and the National Center for Atmospheric Research, is investigating this problem and providing software (also called Web100), that can help pinpoint infrastructure problems. Another effort focused on this problem is the Internet2 End-to-End Performance Initiative.

The Web100 project is focused on fine-tuning the TCP stack for Linux since problems in the stack are often responsible for bottlenecks in end-to-end transmission. Some 21 researchers are testing the software.

What kinds of problems contribute to the slowdown in end-to-end performance? In addition to TCP problems, configuration problems across the network contribute, including configuration problems in backbone routers, LANs, computers, and the Domain Name System. There are also problems at peering points.

These infrastructure problems also slow Web server performance. Mercury Interactive (2001) conducted a study of some 2,000 Web sites of 600 corporate customers. Of these, 98 percent had significant performance problems. The company was surprised to find that 35 percent of the performance problems came from outside the corporate firewall, attributable to problems in ISP routers, gateways, switches, and peering points. In another 25 percent of the cases, companies did not have adequate bandwidth to their sites, either because the requirements were higher than anticipated or because they were not receiving the amount of bandwidth they were paying for from their ISP or hosting service. Some 27 percent experienced database tuning problems and 23 percent had misconfigured application servers. Other problems included firewall incompatibilities, overly restrictive security settings, and badly installed load balancing equipment. While all these findings are relevant to corporations, it is particularly important to note that 35 percent of the problems were outside the company's own configuration and in some cases beyond their control.

Another burgeoning problem for the Internet is in the backbone routers. Massive peering, endorsed throughout this book, will in fact aggravate this problem. According to the IETF, the problem is not the number of entries in a backbone routing table but the number of updates it undergoes. More and more corporations are multihoming their hosts, connecting them to different ISPs to ensure uptime. Some 70 percent of new entries to the routing tables, which then have to be propagated across the Internet, come from multihomed hosts. The IETF is upgrading Border Gateway Protocol to help handle this routing table update problem (Marsan 2001).

Optical networking offers unprecedented speed. But unless problems in the Internet infrastructure itself are resolved, the fastest data connections will mean very little improvement in end-to-end performance.

Reality Check: The Last-Mile Problem

As fast and efficient as optical networks are, they are not to be found everywhere. Particularly frustrating is the last-mile problem. Certainly, *last-mile* is a metaphor. Sometimes, as at George Washington University, all that is needed is permission to take a fiber optic line across the street. Sometimes it could be several miles. But in general, the last mile denotes the gap in speed between fast corporate LANs and fast optical backbones. For homes, it represents the distance between the high-speed connection and the home itself.

It is important to note that even in countries such as Sweden where the optical infrastructure is highly developed, the last mile can still be a problem. In February 2000, Swedbank officials stated that of their 1000 branches, only 50 to 60 could be connected using the initial offerings of startup carriers (Saunders and Heywood 2000). For its part, the bank hoped to pressure the incumbent telephone company Telia into providing optical connectivity to as many branches as possible.

The last-mile problem will be addressed in part as networks are built out to businesses and customer premises. In the meantime, organizations should consider integrating wireless and optical networks to address the last-mile problem.

Technology Trends in Optical Networking

For technologists, optical networking is an exciting field. New developments that improve the inherent capacity of fiber arrive on a regular basis. However, it is also a field where it is difficult to separate hype from true innovation. Reading a company's press release about a new breakthrough product may give the impression that the technology in question is real and available. In the vast majority of cases, it takes time to integrate these new technologies, and the latest trade press articles about optical networking should be taken with a grain of salt. The time from innovation to widespread implementation is always longer than anyone anticipates.

With this caveat, it is important to take a look at upcoming trends in optical networking technology and consider how they will impact your use of the technology in the short-term and in the long-term.

The DWDM Revolution Continues

Dense wavelength division multiplexing is clearly one of the most important developments that optical networks have seen. In addition to the inherent high capacity of fiber to carry data, dividing light into wavelengths expands the capacity of the fiber even further. Dense wavelength division multiplexing continues to be important for the following reasons:

➤ As optical networking providers saturate their existing fiber, adding DWDM equipment multiplies capacity less expensively than lighting additional dark fiber.

➤ Corporations can enjoy the same advantages, adding wavelengths to handle dedicated streams of data between two points as fiber becomes saturated. Since Coarse WDM equipment is less expensive, it is often a viable alternative to DWDM for implementing wavelengths and hence multiplying bandwidth.

➤ Dense wavelength division multiplexing equipment prices are dropping, encouraging organizations to implement wavelengths.

➤ As more providers implement wavelengths, it becomes possible to purchase a wavelength rather than an entire fiber, making optical networking more affordable for enterprises and other organizations.

➤ Protocols that allow users to manage their own wavelengths, such as Optical Border Gateway Protocol, are under development.

➤ Dense wavelength division multiplexing is inherently protocol agnostic. Any type of data can be run over a wavelength, whether IP, ATM, voice, or something else. This allows a single fiber to carry multiple traffic types, if desired.

Dense wavelength division multiplexing remains a very important technology with continued applications and impact on this entire market segment. Gaining experience with DWDM is critical to organizations that want to expand the capacity of existing fiber and exploit new fiber to the greatest degree possible. Such experience is rare at this point, making DWDM a critical training area for those involved in designing, deploying, and maintaining optical networks.

Tunable Lasers

Tunable lasers are a technology under development related to WDM. Today, WDM networks require that a laser be deployed for each wavelength. Since wavelengths carry important data, it is important to have a backup for each of these lasers. So, if you are running 64 wavelengths, you need 64 lasers *and* 64 backup lasers for each end of the connection.

Tunable lasers allow a single laser to be tuned to a range of frequencies, so that companies can have a few tunable laser systems for backups rather than a laser per frequency. In addition to making DWDM cheaper to deploy in the long term (since the one-laser-per-frequency requirement is eliminated), the benefits of tunable lasers could be even more significant. Tunable lasers could be configured to search for an available wavelength, allowing wavelengths to be changed using software rather than a visit to the site. Further, after a wavelength is dropped, it could be reused without fear of contention by using tunable lasers. The features mentioned here are more potential than currently deployed, but the technology to create them exists, making tunable lasers another important trend in optical networking.

All-Optical Networking

Perhaps the most talked-about innovation in optical networking is *all-optical* networking. Today, optical signals lose their strength over distance, requiring electronic switches to translate the lightwave back to electrical signals and then back into light periodically along the optical network's path. This electronic switch model is referred to as *OEO (optical-electronic-optical)*, and it has many disadvantages.

First of all, OEO impacts speed. Data speeds along on light waves and then slams into a brick wall when it must be translated into electrical pulses and then back into light waves. The translation is inefficient and wasteful. Paul Johnson of investment bank Robertson Stephens came up with this colorful analogy: "It is like forcing a 747 en route from New York to San Francisco to stop at Chicago and Denver along the way (and unload all the luggage and passengers)" (Hughes 2000).

Another negative impact of OEO is cost. Optical-electronic-optical conversion is now the most expensive aspect of optical networking, but not because it slows down the network: In an optical network, costs are shifting towards electronics. Some 75 percent of the investment is in OEO equipment and 25 percent is on transmission. Additionally, all-optical networks would require less power to operate.

Without OEO, optical networking wouldn't exist today; however, it is clearly a transitional technology. As all-optical solutions become more stable and more widely deployed, networks will shift away from OEO and towards all-optical networking. At first, OEO will not be eliminated; it will simply be reduced. Vendors often boast that their product allows a signal to be sent a certain number of kilometers without regeneration. This points to a reduction in the need for OEO, not its complete elimination.

Today, all-optical networking has disadvantages as well. To start with, it's an immature technology that is applicable only to certain markets. Clearly, if your network is designed with distances too short to require regeneration, there is no need for all-optical networking. Some networks, like the emerging Gigabit Ethernet networks for metropolitan areas, are designed to maximize cost savings. It is so much cheaper to use OEO than all-optical components that it makes all-optical impractical. All-optical networks make the most sense for long-haul networks deployed by carriers.

There are other all-optical disadvantages, too. You can't monitor all-optical networks as you can optical networks with electronic regeneration. Electronic switches react to failure; light isn't conducive to failure reaction. John Adler, director of marketing for Cisco's optical transport group, says, "You can't take a sample of that light and really find out the detailed kind of analysis you could for a telephone. Most carriers today are pragmatists. They want to build networks today that they can scale and make fault-tolerant. So they are still keeping regeneration in their networks" (Matsumoto 2000).

Another important problem is that all-optical networking works only for switched routes. You can't do conventional routing with an optical signal. For

IP-based networks, which need to have their packets routed, this lack of conventional routing is a serious drawback. And optical routing isn't on the near horizon: Fred Harris, director of network planning for Sprint, states that "True photonic routing is so far in the future that I don't have a clue when it will happen"(Neel and Moore 2000). Interpreting traffic is, to date, the province of electronics. All-optical networking depends on eliminating electronics—a goal not yet possible for routers.

Additionally, when more data comes in than systems can handle, all-optical networks are incapable of buffering data. There is no efficient way to store light data yet, so buffering cannot occur (Newman 2001).

Optical Switches

How do all-optical switches work? For the most part, all-optical switching is achieved through passive technologies, including arrays of tiny mirrors, bubbles, heaters, and liquid crystals similar to those in a cell phone display. The systems using arrays of mirrors are referred to as *micro-electro-mechanical systems (MEMS)*. These devices are tiny, with as many as 256 mirrors on a few square centimeters of silica. A second technique for optical switching uses bubbles produced by heating a liquid into a gas. As a liquid, light passes through; as a bubble, the refractive index changes and the light jumps to an intersecting waveguide, redirecting it. Still other vendors use tiny heaters and silica wafers to perform optical switching. Corning uses liquid crystals (such as those found in cell phone displays) to redirect the beams of light in its optical switches.

No matter what, it's important to realize that for now, no one is running an all-optical network. The current goal for most carriers is to reduce regeneration, not eliminate it. Despite this, vendors bandy about terms such as all-optical switches in a way that is confusing, to say the least. Nevertheless, as these developments become solidified, all-optical, or perhaps we should say *more* optical, networks will significantly enhance throughput on long-haul networks.

Software-based Provisioning

Another enhancement to today's optical networks is how they are provisioned or controlled. Older networks require that engineers map out circuitry on whiteboards and then physically go to the network switches and reconfigure them. No wonder it takes time to provision services in this way. Newer optical Ethernet-based networks are more flexible about provisioning, handling it through software. Software-based provisioning will become a baseline for all types of networks over time, eliminating the need for costly and time-consuming physical configuration of switches.

The Role of Governments in Optical Networking

Commercial optical networks are unlikely to provide service to every area of any country. The economic reality means that some areas are considered more profitable than others. We hear of a glut of fiber and then discover that there's no fiber where we need it or want it to be. Commercial interests won't take fiber to an abandoned warehouse in the low-rent districts of our cities, and they won't serve rural areas. Governments must take an active interest in encouraging the building of this important infrastructure, just as they have many other infrastructures.

NOTE

A need for government involvement does not imply that governments should become network service providers or get into the telecom business. Nor does it mean governments should actively build fiber optic networks. However it may be optimal if they—or another impartial entity—undertake deployment of the fiber infrastructure rather than leaving the task to carriers.

There are several levels of government and various ways of encouraging the development of a full-orbed optical infrastructure. At the federal level, governments should fund long-term research. They should ensure that laws and precedents encourage an open market, open to all players, not just incumbent carriers or telcos. There is no reason that publicly owned utilities should be prohibited from bringing fiber to their subscribers and expanding their range of services. State governments are also subject to pressure in this area from lobbying interests. Local governments can become more intimately engaged in ensuring that their populations have the infrastructure they need, and at the very least create conditions that encourage the development of an optical networking infrastructure rather than hindering it.

Funding for Advanced Networking Research

Canada currently has a strategic advantage over the United States in terms of its advanced networks, both for research and at all levels of government. The Canadian government has been extremely supportive of efforts to build a long-term infrastructure and to support networking as a whole.

In the United States funds for network research are more scarce. The nation spent $1.76 billion on technical research as a whole in 2001 and plans to increase it only 1 percent for 2002.

Although corporations do have research and development efforts, these efforts are typically restricted to short-term research that can result in product development and revenue fairly quickly. The research that needs to be funded at the university level is more long-term. Indeed, if it weren't for the U.S. government funding research into a certain network called the ARPANET, we wouldn't have the Internet today. At the time, the very design of the Internet, with its peer (versus hierarchical) structure, seemed absurd. No corporation would have created it.

Low funding levels will affect the quality of research at U.S. universities and place the United States at a competitive disadvantage. Examining Canada's infrastructure and that of other countries where there is more government support for advanced networking, one could say it is already at such a disadvantage, and this will only become more evident over time.

Broadband for Citizens: A Government Concern?

The federal government can also support the spread of advanced networking in other ways. Providing businesses with low-cost loans to deploy broadband to rural areas is another important way for the government to encourage the development of an infrastructure that serves all its citizens.

Other countries are engaged in such efforts: France is funding an effort to bring broadband to everyone in that nation by 2005. The French government was skeptical that this would happen through the efforts of the private sector alone. A French government spokesman told Reuters that "If we bowed to the logic of the market, in five years time a quarter of the French population and 70–80 percent of our land mass would not have access to high-speed links" (Richardson 2001).

The Swedish government has set aside $470 million to subsidize broadband to rural areas while the Dutch government is providing $39 million to help private industry figure out a viable business model for fiber to the home. Among the ideas being explored is open-access fiber, as discussed in Chapter 7, *Fiber to the Home*. Other governments, including the United Kingdom, are taking a more laissez-faire attitude, expecting that the private sector will bring broadband to its citizens.

The Role Cities Can Play in Developing Optical Networks

As seen in Chapter 5, *Optical Networking and Urban Planning*, cities can play a powerful role in encouraging municipal fiber builds that provide a leading-edge infrastructure not only to cities themselves but also to citizens and businesses. They can encourage the economic development of their areas and provide themselves with a competitive advantage by creating a high-speed networking infrastructure that is open to competition. With an optical network, the city can ensure that it will be served by that network both now and in the future.

Corporations and Optical Networking

Although fiber optic LANs are still the exception rather than the rule, there is a trend to use fiber when installing a new cabling infrastructure. Because fiber is needed between buildings due to distance limitations on copper wiring, it makes sense to consider fiber for the entire enterprise whenever a new facility is being wired. For now, copper has the lion's share of the market; Category 5 copper wire makes up about 80 percent of the installed base.

However, as we saw in Chapter 6, *Optical Networking and the Corporate Network*, deploying fiber is no more expensive than copper when cabling a new facility and allows for both greater longevity and greater administrative efficiency. Teré Bracco, director of e-business infrastructure for competitive intelligence firm Current Analysis, thinks that "the most important thing happening in the near future is the emergence of the all-optical enterprise" (Hochmuth 2001). Bracco states that fiber "will become the Category 5 cabling of the future" and predicts that it will change how IT departments provide services and the nature of those services.

As these fat pipes become ubiquitous, applications like videoconferencing will become far more common. Unlimited bandwidth will also change the nature of applications in general in ways that are still difficult to foresee. One thing is certain: Corporations that adopt an optical infrastructure will find they have made an investment that will serve them for many years.

The Future of FTTH

When one hears statements about the adequacy of today's broadband options to the home, it is reminiscent of early evaluations of computers. Thomas Watson, then chairman of IBM, said in 1947 that there was a world market for perhaps five computers. In 1977, Ken Olson, president of Digital Equipment Corporation, said that there was no reason anyone would want a computer in their home. In 1981, Bill Gates opined that 640k should be enough memory for anyone (Janger 2001).

Of course, such statements sound ludicrous to us today, but there are similar voices in the FTTH debate. Often enough, these voices come from companies deploying pseudo-broadband solutions that will not be useful in the long term.

Fiber to the home is increasingly economically feasible. The most successful business model for organizations deploying FTTH, whether utility companies, municipalities or others, separates access from service, allowing for competition among service providers and a choice for homeowners.

Conclusion

The importance of competition in optical networking cannot be overstated. Fiber is capable of carrying a wide variety of services. Monopolies on cable television service and telephone service have not been easily abated. In many areas of the United States and in many nations around the world, there is no choice about these services: The service provider owns the infrastructure. The same thing cannot be allowed to happen with fiber, which can carry all of these services, high-speed data transport, and future services yet to be imagined. If access is not carefully separated from service, this concentration of power in a single company would create an unprecedented monopoly.

Governments can own the access portion themselves or regulate it to help ensure equal access to organizations that want to provide services over that infrastructure. This will ensure competition and thus the lowest prices possible for end customers, as well as a greater variety of available services. Rather than one video offering, there could literally be hundreds; a variety of data services could be offered, including those aimed at a particular function or market, such as disaster recovery.

Could these services be provided just as well by the private sector? In some cases, forward-thinking companies are designing infrastructures that provide open access to fiber, allowing for competition. Even in these cases, only certain areas are likely to attract investment, such as the urban centers, the profitable suburbs. To encourage economic development in other areas, infrastructure may need to be developed by a party more interested in the success of the area than in its immediate profitability.

To see problems with the current infrastructure, simply look at the RBOCs and their current situation in the United States. The Telecommunications Act of 1996 served to deregulate the infrastructure and allow access to other providers. The problem is that the RBOCs still own the infrastructure and can charge high prices to provide access to others. Further, they argue that any infrastructure installed since 1996 does not fall under the Act. Because they have, in most cases, a near-monopoly on the local loop, they are in a regulatory Catch-22. If RBOCs invest in the local infrastructure, they will likely be asked to allow others to use it, so they have a disincentive to provide leading-edge services.

Further, telcos have historically been successful at offering telephone service, but little else: They move exceedingly slowly in offering other services. Meanwhile, their stranglehold on the market provides upstart carriers with a disincentive to invest. According to Dave Shaeffer, CEO of Cogent, 5 percent of buildings have fiber connections. He believes three times that many could be served economically. Part of the problem is that new providers, like Cogent, may build infrastructure that passes 25 buildings, but get only one customer to sign up. Incumbents have the remaining customers, and they have a disincentive to build out their infrastructure, resulting in gridlock.

Clearly, a fiber infrastructure that separates access from service and offers true competition is a far better arrangement. If organizations wonder about the business model for putting in such access, they might consider listening to David Isenberg, one of the many voices advocating this approach:

> Is our sewer a viable business? Are our roads a viable business? Who's your water pipe provider? What's the business model for city streets? It could be that other entities that aren't purely private businesses, that are more public sector, wind up handling this, or wind up handling at least the dark fiber infrastructure aspect of this. That's a successful model that's been used in Stockholm, Sweden, and in numerous places in Canada and in several places in the U.S. And, it seems to work. In fact, there's an argument to be made that it actually allows more service providers to offer a more widely competitive marketplace for communications services . . . bandwidth is as important or more important than electricity, good roads, clean water, modern sewers. It's a fundamental piece of the infrastructure (Moritz 2000a).

When it comes to creating a comprehensive infrastructure that can serve all citizens, the public sector has compelling interests, as does the private sector. A public-private partnership, such as that seen in many places around the world and in the United States (including Chicago; Grant County, Washington; and Alberta, Canada) is the most logical solution to providing a fiber infrastructure.

Private sector efforts to date have brought us to the place where there is a so-called fiber glut in some areas and a dearth of fiber where businesses and residents seem to need it most. This selective investment wouldn't work for building a system of roads and it hasn't worked for creating a high-speed, long-term solution to network infrastructure. A new approach is needed that fosters competition and assures services to the vast majority—if not all—of the businesses and citizens who want such access. Such an approach can impact the economy of cities, the profitability of businesses, and provide true telecommuting capabilities for residential users. In fact, without such an infrastructure, the United States will likely be left in the dark while fiber transforms economies around the world, enabling new applications that will change computing both in the short term and in the long term.

Optical networking is a long-term investment. These networks can be depreciated over 20 years as assets, offering a future-proof infrastructure that can grow and change by swapping out the components that light the fiber as innovations occur. Optical networks are not subject to interference or interception, as copper and wireless are. Their incredible capacity means that as data traffic continues to grow, optical networks can meet the challenge, providing the bandwidth we need for today and tomorrow.

Recommended Resources

General Resources

Periodicals

Billing World and OSS Today:
    online magazine covering OSS issues

www.billingworld.com/

BroadBandWeek (online only;
    email newsletter available)

www.broadbandweek.com

Business Communications Review;
    the search by topic section is
    especially helpful

www.bcr.com/bcrmag/
default.asp

Cabling Systems, an online and print
    magazine covering deployment issues

www.cablingsystems.com

Cook Report (a subscription online
    newsletter; some free content available)

www.cookreport.com

Fibre Systems, an online and print
    magazine with both European and
    global versions available

www.fibre-systems.com/

InteractiveWeek, especially the
    Infrastructure section (available
    both online and in print)

www.interactiveweek.com

ISPworld (print version called BoardWatch): aimed at ISP owners; in-depth feature articles; ISP directory

www.ispworld.com

Light Reading, a market-focused online publication

www.lightreading.com

Lightwave, a print and online publication; email newsletter available

www.light-wave.com

Network Computing: aimed at network administrators; print version available

www.networkcomputing.com

Network World: in-depth coverage of a wide range of networking applications; topical email newsletters; print version available

www.nwfusion.com

Optical NetBiz.com: headline news, to-the-point feature stories, and email newsletter

www.opticalnetbiz.com

Optically Networked.com: headline news and features about optical networking industry trends

www.opticallynetworked.com

Mailing lists and newsgroups

CA*net 3 News mailing list—an excellent resource for keeping up with optical networking developments at all levels; mailing lists specifically about applications and videoconferencing are also available

www.canet3.net/news/news.html

North American Network Operators' Group (NANOG) mailing list, primarily used by ISPs

www.nanog.org/mailinglist.html

sci.optics.fiber, a Usenet newsgroup for optical networking issues

www.sci.optics.fiber.com

Web sites

OpticsNotes.Com: Optics & Photonics Resources, References & Tutorials	www.OpticsNotes.Com/
StrandX: A site that integrates current headlines with network project information and some of the best resources highlighted in this appendix	www.strandx.com/

Optical Networking Glossaries

American National Standard for Telecommunications' Glossary of Telecommunications Terms	www.its.bldrdoc.gov/ projects/t1glossary2000/
The Photonics Dictionary	www.photonicsdictionary.com
Telium's Glossary	www.tellium.com/optical/ glossary.html
NYSERNET Glossary	nysernet.org/glossary.html

Recommended Online Resources by Chapter

Chapter 1: *The Optical Networking Revolution*

P2P Tracker: a news and information site about peer-to-peer applications	www.p2ptracker.com
Internet2 Advanced Applications	apps.internet2.edu
Starlight, international optical next-generation research network	www.startap.net/starlight
"Challenging the Bandwidth Glut Theory," white paper by The Phillips Group	www.colosource.com/ whitepaper/glut.pdf
"Let There Be Light: The Optical Networking Revolution," white paper by Keith Bough, Bob Day, Southard Jones, James Kim, and Yun Kyeoung Lee, Northwestern University; includes both market and technology analysis	www7.kellogg.nwu.edu/ techventure/website2001/ pages/white_paper/ documents/Sample_ Anthology_Papers_2000/ OPTICAL.pdf

Analysts with particular expertise in the optical networking market

RHK, Inc.	www.rhk.com
Communications Industry Researchers, Inc.	www.cir-inc.com

Chapter 2: *Optical Networking Basics*

A Fiber Optic Primer and Tutorial: Designing Networks for Optimum Performance, Joe St. Sauver	cc.uoregon.edu/cnews/ summer2000/fiber.html
Fiber Optic Cable Tutorial	www.arcelect.com/ fibercable.htm
Fiber Optic Chronology, Jeff Hecht	www.sff.net/people/Jeff.Hecht/ chron.html
Fiber-Optic Magic: Light Technology is Critical to the ëNet, *Smart Computing in Plain English*	www.smartcomputing.com/ editorial/article.asp?article= articles%2Farchive% 2Fr0501%2F04r01% 2F04r01%2Easp
International Engineering Consortium; online tutorials on networking topics	www.iec.org
Optical Networking Beginners' Guides from *Light Reading*	www.lightreading.com/ section.asp?section_id=29
Physics and the Communications Industry, Bill Brinkman and Dave Lang, Lucent Technologies, 1999	www.bell-labs.com/history/ physicscomm/

Chapter 3, *Optical Networking and Telcos*

America's Network: carries in-depth feature articles; email newsletter available	www.americasnetwork.com
CLEC Planet, an online news site with information pertinent to CLECs	www.clec-planet.com
FCC Reports on Local Telephone Competition and Broadband Deployment	www.fcc.gov/Bureaus/ Common_Carrier/Reports/ FCC-State_Link/comp.html

New Networks Institute   www.newnetworks.com/

Total Telecom, a print and online   www.totaltele.com/
   publication covering the telecom world
   from a market perspective; email
   newsletter available

Chapter 4, *Optical Internets*

Professor Raj Jain's home page (extensive   www.cis.ohio-state.edu/
   research on IP over DWDM)   ~jain/index.html

CA*net4 Request for Information   www.canet3.net/library/
                                             papers/CAnet4_RFI.pdf

CA*net4 design document   www.canet3.net/library/
                                             papers/CAnet4_Design_
                                             Document.pdf

Optical Internets and their Role in Future   www.canet3.net/library/
   Telecommunications Systems   papers/opticalnetworks.html

Overview of the Latest Developments in   www.canet3.net/library/
   Optical Internets   papers/latestdevelopments
                                             .html

Architectural and Engineering Issues for   www.canet3.net/library/
   an Optical Internet   papers/ArcEngIssues.pdf

"IP on Glass: Goodbye ATM & SONET,"   www.telecoms-mag.com/
   Stan Hanks   issues/199906/tcs/ipglass.html.

Chapter 5, *Optical Networking and Urban Planning*

Alberta SUPERNET   www.innovation.gov.ab.ca/
                                             supernet/index2.html

Blacksburg Electronic Village Digital   www.bev.net/project/
   Library: numerous papers and   digital_library/
   presentations about community
   networks

Brossard (Quebec) Request for   www.canarie.ca/MLISTS/
   Expression of Interest   news2000/0099.html

California statewide optical networking   www.cenic.org/NAD_
   initiative (CENIC ONI) design   July16.pdf
   document

Canadian School Board Investment in Private Fiber Optic Networks	www.canarie.ca/advnet/ workshop_2000/ presentations/waldron.pdf
Chicago CivicNet (register to gain access to RFI)	www.chicagocivicnet.org
Community and Municipal Fiber Networks (PowerPoint presentation)	www.canet3.net/library/ papers/ccfn.ppt
Community and Municipal Fiber Networks Presentation	www.canet3.net/library/ papers.html
Connectivity in Manitoba and The Role of Municipalities	www.smartwinnipeg.mb.ca/ connectivity_manitoba.htm
Customer-Owned IP Networks: Completing the IP Revolution through Customer-Owned Networks, T.M. Denton Consultants; many related resources also available at this site	www.tmdenton.com/
Do-it-yourself fibre optic networks: Canadian research groups find new ways to cut costs, *Communications Engineering and Design*, March 2001	www.cedmagazine.com/ced/ 2001/0301/03f.htm
Dublin, Ohio, network (Dublink)	www.dublink-duct.com/
FAQ about Community Dark Fiber Networks	www.canet3.net/library/ papers.html
Frederickton (New Brunswick) Community Network Project Report	www.canarie.ca/MLISTS/ news2001/0028.html
General Guide for a Future-Proof IT Infrastructure, The Swedish ICT Commission, 2001; a guide for developing a fiber infrastructure, focused on Sweden, but many general principles apply to developing municipal fiber networks	www.itkommissionen.se/extra/ document/?id=347
Glasgow, Kentucky's network	www.glasgow-ky.com/
Ottawa Dark Fiber Request for Information	www.canet3.net/library/ papers/OttawaDarkFiber-RFI.html
San Diego's Fiber Map	www.sangis.org/sangis/ intmaps/FiberMap.htm

Stokab's Fiber Optic Network in Stockholm, Sweden	www.stokab.se/english/ index.html
Telecommunications and Municipal Utilities: Cooperation and Competition in the New Economy	www.smartcommunities.org/ APPA_special_report.pdf
William Ray's writings about utilities and networks	www.glasgow-ky.com/papers/
Winnipeg's excellent white paper, The Case for Municipal Fibre	www.smartwinnipeg.mb.ca/ Municipal_Fibre.htm

Chapter 6, *Optical Networking and the Corporate Network*

Network World's Gigabit Ethernet research page	www.nwfusion.com/research/ ge.html
Optical Ethernet Resource Center: clearinghouse for news, white papers, standards information, and forums	www.optical-ethernet.com
Metro Ethernet Forum	www.metroethernetforum.org
10 Gigabit Ethernet Alliance Technology Overview white paper	www.10gea.org/10GEA_ Whitepaper_0901.pdf
Fiber Optics LAN Section of the Telecommunications Industry Association: articles, white papers, and case studies on fiber optic LANs	www.fols.org/pubs/index.html
GiantLoop white paper, Enterprise Optical Networking: The Infrastructure for the New Economy	www.giantloop.com/ newsandevents_publications .shtml

Chapter 7, *Fiber to the Home*

CA*net 3 and Gigabit Internet to the Home	www.canet3.net/library/papers/ GigabittoHome.html
Content-Neutral Video-Speed Ubiquitous Residential Gigabit Ethernet (CONVURGE): The True Next-Generation Broadband Last-mile Network, David Cheriton and Andreas Bechtolsheim	www4.nationalacademies.org/ cpsma/cstb.nsf/files/ wp-bb-bechtolsheim-cheriton. pdf/$file/wp-bb-bechtolsheim-cheriton.pdf

Ethernet in the First Mile Task Force	www.ieee802.org/3/efm/ public/index.html
Ethernet PON Security Considerations, Onn Haran, Passive Networks	www.ieee802.org/3/efm/ public/may01/haran_1_ 0501.pdf
Full Service Access Network (FSAN) standards group	www.fsanet.net/
Gigabit Internet to every Canadian Home by 2005	www.canet3.net/library/ papers/GigabittoHomeby2005. html
Måttgränd FTTH project in Umeå, Sweden	www.acc.umu.se/~tfytbk/ mattgrand/
Matti Rantanen's paper on FTTH	www.tml.hut.fi/Studies/ Tik-110.300/1998/Newtech/ ftth.html
Palo Alto FTTH site	www.city.palo-alto.ca.us/ utilities/fth/
Palo Alto: Bennett Smith's site on FTTH trial	www.wbsmith.com/fiber.html
Sky's the Limit with Ethernet over Fiber, Octavio Morales and Chris Setty	www.worldwidepackets.com/ news/articles/news_ lightwave_nov2000.jsp
Technical Feasibility of Gigabit Ethernet PONs, Brian Unitt, Nortel Networks	www.ieee802.org/3/efm/ public/may01/unitt_1_0501.pdf

Chapter 8, *The Outlook for Optical Networking*

Colocation Directory	www.colosource.com
Cost Sharing, Peering and Transit on the Internet	www.canet3.net/library/ papers/CostSharing.html
FAQ about Community Dark Fiber Networks	www.canet3.net/library/ papers.html
Internet Service Providers and Peering, William Norton	www-cse.ucsd.edu/classes/ wi01/cse222/papers/ norton-isp-draft00.pdf
Light Brigade, optical network training and certification	www.lightbrigade.com

Right of Way.com	www.rightofway.com
Short-sighted historical quotations about science and technology	www.engineering.csupomona. edu/civil/faculty/janger/ somefun/quotes.htm
Tek-Tips Forum (consult with others about cabling and other deployment issues; Wiring Closet/Cabling forum is particularly helpful)	www.tek-tips.com
Web100 Project, studying end-to-end throughput on the Internet	www.web100.org/
Workinoptics.com	www.workinoptics.com

Bibliography

● ●

Aberdeen Group. 2001. The Optical Opportunity: A Refractive View of the Present Market—and Its Future. *Emerging Technologies Intelligence Newsletter*, 29 August. www.aberdeen.com/eti/CurrentIssue/aug29/ioninsight.htm.

Agrawal, G. 1997. *Fiber-Optic Communication Systems*. New York: John Wiley & Sons, Inc.

Aragon, L. 2000. Yipes lights up dark fiber. *Red Herring*, 14 March. www.redherring .com/index.asp?layout=story& channel=10000001&doc_id=490012049.

Bannan, K. 2001. Continental Drift. *Internet World.* 1 March, 64.

Bradner, S. 2001. The view depends on where you stand. *Network World*, 2 July, 26.

Branson, K. 2001. Is There a Bandwidth Glut? *Broadband Week*, 4 June, 48.

Brown, B. 2000. Sprint Banking on Converged Services. *Network World*, 27 November. www.nwfusion.com/news/2000/1127carrier.html.

Brown, K. 2001. Knowing the Network. *Broadband Week*, 23 July, 12.

Bryce, R. 2001. Bandwidth Traders Gleeful Amid Gloom. *Interactive Week*, 16 April, 23.

Cahners In-Stat Group. 2000. SONET/SDH Markets to Remain Strong Despite Competition. Press release, 17 October. www.instat.com/pr/2000/wn0007ms_pr.htm.

Cameron, D. 1999. *Internet2 : The Future of the Internet and Next-Generation Initiatives.* Charleston, SC: Computer Technology Research, 116.

Caruso, J. 2001. Big bandwidth vs. QoS. *The Power Issue: Network World Signature Series*, 25 December–1 January, 73.

City of Chicago. 2000. Sections 1.1.3, 1.2.2.0, 1.2.5, 2.0.1.1, and 3.2.1 in *Request for Information: Chicago CivicNet*. Chicago: Bureau of Telecommunications and Information Technology and Department of General Services. www.chicagocivicnet.net.

Cook, R. 2001. SUPERNET to Bring Fiber to Entire Province. *Cook Report*, June. www.cookreport.com/10.03.shtml.

Cope, J. 2000a. Chicago Plans Citywide Net. *Computerworld*, 4 December, 14.

Cope, J. 2000b. Users: Optical Fiber Gives Copper a Run for the Money. *Computerworld*, 25 September, 14.

Cope, J. 2001. AT&T Lights Up High-Speed Backbone. *Computerworld*, 15 January, 30.

Cringley, R. 2001. Sorry, Wrong Number: Why Your Phone Company Hates DSL. The Pulpit. *I, Cringely*, 22 February. www.pbs.org/cringely/pulpit/pulpit20010222.html.

Cruz, G. 2000. Provo, Utah to Build Citywide Fiber Optic Network. *Government Technology News*, 13 October. www.govtech.net/news/news.phtml?docid=2000 .10.13-2030000000000513.

Dobrowski, G. and D. Grise. 2001. *ATM and SONET Basics*. Fuquay-Varina, NC: APDG Publishing.

FCC. 1998. *The FCC, Internet Service Providers, and Access Charges*. Federal Communications Commission. www.fcc.gov/Bureaus/Common_Carrier/Factsheets/ ispfact.html.

FCC. 2001. *Local Telephone Competition: Status as of December 31, 2000*. Federal Communications Commission. www.fcc.gov/Bureaus/Common_Carrier/ Reports/FCC-State_Link/IAD/lcom0501.pdf.

Federal Standard 1037C. 1996. *Glossary of Telecommunications Terms*. www.tiab2b .com/glossary/.

Fisher, C. 1994. *America Calling : A Social History of the Telephone to 1940*. Berkeley, CA: University of California Press.

Flamig, B. 2001. Fiber-Optic Magic: Light Technology Is Critical To The 'Net. *Smart Computing* 5, no. 1 (February): 24–29. www.smartcomputing.com/editorial/ article.asp?article= articles%2Farchive%2Fr0501%2F04r01%2F04r01%2Easp.

FOLDOC. 2001. Free Online Dictionary of Computing. www.foldoc.org.

Gall, D. and M. Shapiro. 2001. Shifting gears in the race. *Lightwave*, March, 34.

Gartner Dataquest. 2001. Gartner Dataquest Says Governments Should Appoint Public Agencies to Oversee Access for Fiber-to-the-Home. Press Release, 19 March. www.gartner.com/5_about/press_room/pr20010319a.html.

Gaudin, S. Spending on the Rise. *Network World*, 29 January. www.nwfusion.com/ research/2001/0129feat.html.

Gerwig, K. 2001. Can They Dig It? *Teledotcom,* 19 March. www.teledotcom.com/article/TEL20010319S0026.

GiantLoop. 2000. Enterprise Optical Networking: The Infrastructure for the New Economy, October, 1. www.giantloop.com/pdf/news_white_EnterpriseOpticalNetworking.pdf.

Goralski, W. 2000. *SONET.* New York: McGraw-Hill.

Government of Alberta. 2000. *Alberta sets direction for high-tech strategy.* December 1 press release. www.innovation.gov.ab.ca/release/ictimp.

Greim Everitt, L. 2001. Pumping Data. *Interactive Week,* 29 January, I-1.

Guerra, J. 2001. Regulatory Watch: FCC Finds CLEC Penetration Nearly Doubled. *Billing World,* August. www.billingworld.com/full.asp?id=2383&action=article.

Hailu, Saba. 2001. *The Fiber Optic Cable Global Market Forecast.* San Mateo, CA: Electronicast.

Hanks, S. 1999. IP on Glass: Goodbye ATM & SONET. *Telecommunications Magazine Online,* June. www.telecoms-mag.com/issues/199906/tcs/ipglass.html.

Hecht, J. 1988. *Understanding Fiber Optics.* Indianapolis, Indiana: Howard W. Sams & Company.

Hecht, J. 1999a. Wavelength Division Multiplexing. *Technology Review,* March/April. www.techreview.com/magazine/mar99/print_version/hecht.html.

Hecht, J. 1999b. *City of Light: The Story of Fiber Optics.* New York: Oxford University Press.

Hecht, J. 2000. New pipelines promise unprecedented speed. *Upside,* 25 August. www.upside.com/texis/mvm/ebiz/story?id=3999b24a0.

Held, G. 2001. *Deploying Optical Networking Components.* New York: McGraw-Hill.

Hobby, R. 2001. *Internet2 End-to-End Performance Initiative White Paper (or Fat Pipes Are Not Enough),* 28 February. www.internet2.edu/e2eperf/end-to-end-design-paper.shtml.

Hochmuth, P. 2000. Early copper Gigabit users rave on the technology. *Network World,* 13 November, 167.

Hochmuth, P. 2001a. Is 10G Ethernet for you? *Network World,* 30 April, 75.

Hochmuth, P. 2001b. The WAN: the all-optical company. *Network World Anniversary Issue,* 26 March, 104.

Hochmuth, P. 2001c. 10 Gigabit Ethernet to Step into the N+I Spotlight. *Network World,* 7 May, 146.

Hughes, T. 2000. Optical Nerve. *Global Technology Business,* June, 39.

Hunt, C. 1998. *TCP/IP Network Administration*. Sebastopol, California: O'Reilly & Associates.

Igor F., L. Gabuzda, and H. Lu. 2000. *Converged Networks and Services: Internetworking IP and the PSTN*. New York: John Wiley & Sons.

Intel. 2001. Gigabit Ethernet over Copper. *Intel Internet Data Center White Papers*. www.intel.com/network/idc/doc_library/white_papers/copper_guide/gigabit_lan.htm.

Isenberg, D. 2001. The Era of Customer-Owned Networks. *SMART Letter*, no. 56 (7 June).

Jander, M. 2001. So Long SONET. *Network World Optical Networking Newsletter*, 1 August. www.nwfusion.com/newsletters/optical/2001/00927085.html.

Janger, F. 2001. Insightful Quotes. www.csupomona.edu/~fjjanger/somefun/quotes.htm

Jones, S. 2001. *Gigabit to the home in the UK with customer owned networks*. CAnet-3-NEWS mailing list, 24 January. www.canarie.ca/MLISTS/news2001/0021.html.

Krause, J. K. 1999. How AT&T Got the Internet. *The Industry Standard*, 16–23 August, 100.

Light Reading. 2000. *Metro Optical Ethernet*. Special Report, November. www.lightreading.com/document.asp?doc_id=2472.

Lindstrom, A. 2000. The Blair Ditch Project. *America's Network*, 1 January. www.americasnetwork.com/issues/2000issues/20000101/20000101_blair.htm.

Luzadder, D. 2001. Talking Points. *Interactive Week*, 2 April, 52.

Mambretti, J. and S. Schmidt. 1999. *Next Generation Internet: Creating Advanced Networks and Services*. New York: John Wiley & Sons.

Mambretti, J. 2001. E-mail to author, 30 April.

Marsan, C. 2001. Faster 'Net growth rate raises fears about routers. *NetworkWorld*. 4 April. www.nwfusion.com/news/2001/0402routing.html.

Martin, D. 2001. Letter to the editor. *Network World*, 19 March, 52.

Martin, M. 2000. Flexibility sets Yipes apart, CEO says. *Network World*, 4 December, 33.

Martin, M. 2001. Shedding New Light on Dark Fiber. *Network World*, 5 March, 29.

Matsumoto, C. 2000. Optical Networking Booms, but Issues Persist. *PlanetIT*, 1 March. www.PlanetIT.com/docs/PIT20000301S0039.

Mercury Interactive. 2001. *Common Web Site Problems Identified by ActiveTest*. White paper. www-svca.mercuryinteractive.com/products/activetest/whitepapers/

Metannikov, M. 2001. Plumbing for Profit, *Interactive Week*, 2 January, 62.

Micek, J. 2001. Internet Blamed For California Power Emergency. *NewsFactor Network*, 18 January. www.newsfactor.com/perl/story/6817.html.

Moore, C. 2001. Optical Ethernet rewrites the rules of bandwidth. *Infoworld*, 25 December–1 January, 25.

Moritz, S. 2000a. The TSC Streetside Chat: Telecom Guru David Isenberg. *TheStreet .com*, 27 October. www.thestreet.com/comment/streetsidechat/1146285.html.

Moritz, S. 2000b. The TSC Streetside Chat: Telecom Guru David Isenberg. *TheStreet .com*, 28 October. www.thestreet.com/comment/streetsidechat/1138237.html.

Neel, D. and C. Moore. 2000. EMC extends storage through fiber. *InfoWorld*, 25 September, 16.

Newman, D. 2001. The All-Optical Myth. *Network World*, 30 April, 50.

Newton, H. 2001. *Newton's Telecom Dictionary*. 17th ed. Gilroy, CA: CMP Books.

Odlyzko, A. 2000. Internet Growth: Myth and Reality, Use and Abuse. *Information Impacts*, November. www.cisp.org/imp/november_2000/odlyzko/11_00odlyzko.htm.

Oram, A. 2001. The Hard Questions in Broadband Policy. *Web Review*, 23. www.webreview.com/pi/2001/03_23_01.shtml.

Pilieci, V. Small township, big-city infrastructure. *The Ottawa Citizen*, 21 October. www.ottawacitizen.com/business/001021/4726204.html.

Ploskina, B. and R. Williamson. 2001. Home Spun. *Interactive Week*, 2 April, 27.

Prior, D. 2001. Opening the Doors of the Possibility Factory. *Cabling Systems Magazine Online*, March/April, 22, Figure 1. www.cablingsystems.com/issues/2001/MarApr/page22.asp. David Prior can be reached at PBI Media (formerly The Philips Group), dprior@consultant.com

Ray, W. 2001. Glasgow Electric Plant Board. *The White Papers, Senate Testimony, Epistles and Manifestos*. Accessed July 2001. www.glasgow-ky.com/papers.

Richardson, Tim. 2001. France to spend FF30bn on broadband for all push. *The Register*, 7 July. www.theregister.co.uk/content/6/20254.html.

Rose, F. 2001. Telechasm. *Wired*, May, 128–135.

Rosenbush, S. 2001. Armstrong on the Record. *BusinessWeek*, 5 February. www.businessweek.com/2001/01_06/b3718157.htm.

Rugaber, C. 2001. Telecom Carrier Companies. *The Motley Fool*. www.fool.com/news/indepth/telecom/content/carriers01.htm.

Saunders, S. and P. Heywood. 2000. IT At The Speed Of Light. *InformationWeek*, 7 February. www.informationweek.com/772/optical.htm.

Scanlon, B. 2001. Next Star. *Interactive Week*, 7 May56.

Schwartz, S. 2001. Bandwidth on Demand: Build It, and They Will Come. *Billing World*, June. www.billingworld.com/full.asp?id=2350&action=article.

Shaff, W. 2000. Voice Puts Damper On WorldCom. *InformationWeek*, 27 November. www.informationweek.com/814/iufin.htm.

Shephard, S. 2001. *Optical Networking Crash Course*. New York: McGraw-Hill.

Silver, D. 2001. Power users drive fiber deployment. *Lightwave*, June, 31.

Smart Winnipeg. 2000. The Case for Municipal Fibre White Paper. 15 August. www.smartwinnipeg.mb.ca/Municipal_Fibre.htm.

Sorrento Networks 2001. *Point-to-Point or Mesh Topologies in the Metro Optical Network*. International Engineering Consortium. www.iec.org/online/tutorials/point_mesh/.

St. Arnaud, B. 1999. *Optical networks for the rest of us*. CANARIE, Inc. www.canet3.net/library/papers/opticalnetworks.html.

St. Arnaud, B. 2000. *Draft CA*net4 Design Document*. Unpublished PowerPoint presentation. www.canet3.net/library/presentations/CAnet4DesignDocument-Sept00.ppt.

St. Arnaud, B. 2001b. , *Frequently Asked Questions about Customer Owned Dark Fiber, Condominium Fiber, Community and Municipal Fiber Networks*. CANARIE, Inc., 1 May. www.canet3.net/library/papers/FAQdarkfiber.htm.

St. Arnaud, B. 2001c. *Gigabit Internet to every Canadian Home by 2005*. CANARIE, Inc. www.canet3.net/library/papers.html.

St. Sauver, J. 2000. A Fiber Optic Primer and Tutorial: Designing Networks for Optimum Performance. *Computing News* (Summer). cc.uoregon.edu/cnews/summer2000/fiber.html.

Stokes, J. World Stage. *BroadbandWeek*, 23 July. www.broadbandweek.com/news/010723/010723_news_fix.htm

Sullivan, J. 2001. *Examining Broadband's History, Its Successes and Failures: Lessons for the Next Generation of Broadband*. Kite Networks. www.ispworld.com/src/WP_Kite_041701.htm.

Telechoice. TeleChoice Launches First Strategic Network Capital Planning Model. Press release, 26 July. www.telechoice.com/newsdetail.asp?news_id=156

Terplan, K. 2001. *OSS Essentials*. New York: John Wiley & Sons.

T.M. Denton Consultants. 1999. Netheads versus Bellheads: Research into Emerging Policy Issues in the Development and Deployment of Internet Protocols. *Final Report for the Canadian Federal Department of Industry*. Contract Number U4525-9-0038. www.tmdenton.com/netheads3.htm.

Wages, J. 2001. Data-storage company selects fiber for its network. *Lightwave*, March, 37.

Wallin, J. 2001. Telephone interview with author, 30 August.

Weinberg, N. 2001. Here's a quiz: Can you name the top five ISPs? *Network World*, 16 April, 48.

Wetzel, R. 2001. Stoking the Content Fire: Breaking New Ground in Metro Interconnection. *Interactive Week*, 30 April, 53.

Whatis 2001. ILEC definition. *Whatis Dictionary Online.* whatis.techtarget.com/

Williamson, R. 2001. Who's Minding the Store? *InteractiveWeek* 12 March, 15.

Wolinsky, H. 2000. Optical boom spurs visions of grandeur. *UpsideToday*, 26 August. www.upside.com/texis/mvm/ebiz/story?id=3999bd380.

Glossary

● ●

10-Gigabit Ethernet   Ethernet reaching speeds of 10 Gbps. 10-Gigabit Ethernet runs only over fiber.

Acceptance testing   Testing of a communications network, component, or subsystem to ensure it meets industry standards.

ADM (add/drop multiplexer)   A component in SONET-based networks that multiplexes (adds) or demultiplexes (drops) traffic as needed.

All-optical   Optical components or networks that eliminate the need for converting signals from optical signals to electronic signals and back again. Applications for all-optical networks are very limited today; most so-called all-optical components reduce the need for regeneration of signals rather than eliminating it.

Amplifier   A device that strengthens an optical signal. Common amplifiers include EDFAs and Raman amplifiers.

Anchor tenant   A tenant in a condominium fiber network that has the primary investment in the network both in terms of dollar investment and in terms of network topology.

APON (ATM passive optical network)   A PON based on ATM standards and carrying ATM traffic.

ATM (asynchronous transfer mode)   A switching technology for carrying multimedia traffic of various types over an optical network. ATM uses fixed cell lengths.

Backbone   A high-speed portion of a network that links subnetworks.

Bandwidth   The carrying capacity of a communications line.

Bandwidth on demand   An arrangement in which a customer can request an adjustment to their network speed on short notice. Gigabit Ethernet providers offer bandwidth on demand.

Bit (binary digit)   One binary digit, that is, a zero or a one. In an optical network, a flash of a laser indicates a one while the lack of a flash equals zero.

Bit rate   The transmission rate of a network, typically expressed in bits per second (bps).

Bps (bits per second)   The number of bits per second transmitted.

Carrier-neutral facility   A facility in which telecommunications carriers interconnect their networks and exchange traffic.

Cladding   The portion of an optical fiber that surrounds the core. Cladding has a lower refractive index than the pure silica or plastic core of the fiber, which serves to guide the light along the core and prevent dispersion.

CLEC (competitive local exchange carrier)   In the U.S., a company authorized by the Telecommunications Act of 1996 to provide local telephone service in competition with the local telephone company that controls the infrastructure, referred to as an incumbent local exchange carrier.

CO (central office)   A building containing equipment needed for voice and data telecommunications networks. Prospective DSL customers must be within a given distance of the CO in order to be eligible for the service. ILECs control the COs, but CLECs are authorized by federal statute to be able to collocate equipment at the CO as well.

Condominium fiber   An arrangement by which a group of organizations band together to create a fiber-optic network that serves all of their needs. Each organization may own one or more strands of fiber. Like condominium owners, these organizations share maintenance costs in proportion to their ownership of the network.

Core   The center part of a strand of fiber, usually containing pure silica and surrounded by cladding.

Crosstalk   A situation in which two electrical signals interfere with one another.

Customer-empowered networking   A scenario in which customers own the portion of the network that connects them to a carrier-neutral facility or other open-access fiber, allowing them a choice of service providers.

CWDM (coarse wavelength division multiplexing)   A version of WDM that is less expensive than DWDM because it accommodates fewer wavelengths and uses a wider spectrum (from 1260 to 1620 nanometers).

Demultiplexing   Separating two or more channels that have been previously combined over a communications channel using multiplexing.

Dispersion   The tendency of optical signals to spread over distance, weakening them.

DNS (Domain Name System)   A core Internet service that translates domain names into numeric IP addresses.

Doping   The addition of an impurity to a material.

DSL (digital subscriber line)   A method of providing high-speed data services over copper telephone lines. There are varieties of DSL, including asymmetric DSL (ADSL), high-speed DSL (HDSL), and so on.

DWDM (dense wavelength-division multiplexing)   A version of WDM that carries many wavelengths over a single strand of fiber, multiplying its capacity. DWDM uses multiple wavelengths in the 1550-nanometer region of the infrared spectrum. Coarse wavelength-division multiplexing, by contrast, uses wavelengths that are not so tightly spaced.

EDFA (erbium doped fiber amplifier)   Treated fiber-optic cable that amplifies light waves at their original frequencies. Erbium doped fiber amplifiers strengthen the signals, reducing the need for signal regeneration.

EPON (Ethernet passive optical network)   A PON based on Ethernet standards and carrying Ethernet traffic.

Erbium   A rare earth element that can be added to fiber in order to amplify signals at their original frequencies.

Ethernet   A widely used LAN protocol defined as a standard (IEEE 802.3). Ethernet runs at 10 Mbps.

Fiber/optical fiber   A filament of glass (or in some cases plastic) that acts as a wave guide for light. A fiber consists of a pure core surrounded by cladding.

Free space optics   A method of optical networking in which lasers carry data across air rather than via fiber optic cable.

Gbps (gigabits per second)   A transmission rate measured in billions of bits per second.

Gigabit Ethernet   A version of Ethernet that runs at a billion bits per second. Gigabit Ethernet can run over fiber and some copper interfaces.

IEEE (Institute of Electrical and Electronics Engineers)   A standards body that defines electrical and information technology standards. Among others, the IEEE defines Ethernet standards.

IETF (Internet Engineering Task Force) A group responsible for developing Internet standards. Internet Engineering Task Force membership is open to all interested parties. The IETF is divided into working groups that focus on particular areas of standards development.

ILEC (incumbent local exchange carrier)   The local telephone company that serves an area of the U.S. In many cases, ILECs are also RBOCs.

IP (Internet protocol)   A protocol that defines how data moves across the Internet. IP is connectionless, meaning that data is broken into packets that may travel across the network by different routes. Connection-oriented or switched protocols, such as ATM, send data sequentially along a preset pathway.

ISP (Internet service provider)   A company that provides Internet service to its customers. An ISP may provide connectivity to individual users, to corporate users, or to other ISPs.

ITU (International Telecommunications Union)   An international organization headquartered in Geneva, Switzerland, that defines telecommunications standards.

IXC (interexchange carrier)   A company that provides long-distance telephone service, among other telecommunications services. Also known as a common carrier. A term used primarily in the U.S., where IXCs include AT&T, Sprint, and WorldCom.

Mbps (megabits per second)   A transmission rate of a million bits per second.

Meet-me room   A room in a carrier-neutral facility where networks are physically interconnected.

MEMS (micro-electro-mechanical systems)   Arrays of tiny mirrors that allow light to be redirected without converting the signal into electronic format and back to optical. One possible technology for creating all-optical components.

Mesh topology   A network topology in which all nodes are connected to all other nodes.

Mode   A light ray.

MPLS (Multiprotocol Label Switching)   An IP-based traffic engineering protocol that allows a connectionless protocol like IP to effectively behave like a connection-oriented protocol by defining a path across the network over which a given data stream must travel.

Multimode fiber   A type of fiber optic cable in which multiple light waves travel at the same time. Less expensive than single-mode fiber, which restricts itself to the transmission of one light wave at a time.

Multiplexing   Combining two or more channels over a communications medium.

MTU (multi-tenant unit) A building with areas for multiple occupants, such as an office building or an apartment building.

OC-1   An optical network connection with a line rate of 51.84 Mbps.

OC-3   An optical network connection with a line rate of 155.52 Mbps.

OC-12   An optical network connection with a line rate of 622.08 Mbps.

OC-24   An optical network connection with a line rate of 1.244 Gbps.

OC-48   An optical network connection with a line rate of 2.488 Gbps.

OC-192   An optical network connection with a line rate of 10 Gbps.

OC-768   An optical network connection with a line rate of 40 Gbps.

OEO (optical-electronic-optical)   The conversion of signals from optical to electronic and back again. Also called regeneration.

OLT (optical line terminal)   A device used in PONs that sits in the central office and controls data transmission to up to 32 optical network terminals.

Peering   A mutual agreement between two networks to carry one another's traffic at no charge. The exchange of traffic between networks.

Photon   A quantum of electromagnetic energy.

PON (passive optical network)   An optical network that splits bandwidth among a number of end users (typically 32). Active electronics are powered at the customer premises rather than by the carrier.

Protocol stack   A set of protocol layers that work together. Also used to refer to the software that implements the protocol stack.

Pump laser   A laser designed to excite ions, often used in amplification.

QoS (quality of service)   Technologies aimed at providing different service levels to different types of traffic.

RBOC (regional Bell operating company)   A regional telecommunications provider resulting from the breakup of AT&T's monopoly on local telephone service.

Regeneration   The conversion of a signal from optical to electronic and back again. This both strengthens a signal and allows data to be routed through electronic means.

RFP (request for proposal)   An RFP is a document that outlines an organization's requirements for a project. Vendors interested in bidding on the project respond with a proposal. Related documents include a request for information (RFI), which is preliminary to an RFP, and request for quotation (RFQ), which specifically discusses the pricing of the work to be done.

Ring topology   A network topology in which each network node is connected to its neighbor. All network nodes are connected in a circle, or ring.

Router   A device that reads the header of a packet and sends it toward its destination.

SAN (storage area network)   A high-speed network that connects storage devices.

SDH (synchronous digital hierarchy)   The term used for SONET networks in Europe.

Single-mode fiber   A fiber through which a single light wave travels.

SONET (synchronous optical network)   An ANSI standard for transmitting data over fiber-optic lines. SONET networks feature a ring topology in which half the bandwidth is reserved as protection bandwidth. In the event of failure, SONET networks sense a problem and automatically switch to their protection bandwidth in approximately 50 milliseconds.

Star topology   A network topology in which all systems connect to a central node. Also known as a hub-and-spoke topology.

Switch   A device that establishes connections among circuits.

T-1   A network connection at a line rate of 1.544 Mbps.

T-3   A network connection at a line rate of 44.736 Mbps.

Tbps (terabits per second)   A transmission rate measured in trillions of bits per second.

TCP (Transmission Control Protocol)   A protocol designed to guarantee end-to-end transmission of data. Packets must be acknowledged by the receiving system in order for transmission to continue. If congestion occurs, TCP automatically slows transmission of packets until the congestion clears.

TCP/IP   A protocol suite used for sending traffic over the Internet.

TDM (time division multiplexing)   An interleaving of signals. SONET is an example of TDM.

Topology   The pattern in which network nodes are connected.

Transceiver   An optical device that can both transmit and receive optical signals.

Transponder   An optical device that can transmit, receive, multiplex, and demultiplex optical signals.

Tunable laser   In optical networks, individual lasers generate light of various wavelengths. A tunable laser can generate light of multiple wavelengths.

VoIP (Voice over IP)   A standard for transmitting voice traffic over the Internet.

VPN (virtual private network)   A method for sending traffic securely over a particular data link. VPNs encrypt all data between two end systems.

Wavelength   The distance between two wave forms. On optical networks, wavelengths can be thought of as colors of light, just as prisms separate light into its component colors. Each color represents a different wavelength. Sometimes also referred to as a lambda.

Wavelength division multiplexing (WDM)   A technology that makes it possible to send multiple data channels over a single strand of fiber, effectively multiplying the capacity of that fiber. Each wavelength (or color) can carry as much data as the fiber itself could. WDM is the term used to discuss (a) the technology in general and (b) the original form of the technology, which carried relatively few wavelengths over a fiber.

Index